ANY COLD JORDAN

A NOVEL

DAVID BOTTOMS

Peachtree Publishers, Ltd.

Published by
PEACHTREE PUBLISHERS, LTD.
494 Armour Circle, N.E.
Atlanta, Georgia 30324

Lines from "The Good Bait Wiggles" from *In All This Rain*, by John Stone (LSU Press, 1980)

Cover painting:
"St. John's River, Florida," 1890
Winslow Homer, 1836-1910
Watercolor on paper, 34.2 x 50.5 cm. (13½" x 19-7/8")
Signed and dated lower right: "Homer 1890"
The Hyde Collection, Glens Falls, NY

Manufactured in the United States of America

First printing

Library of Congress Catalog Number 86-63529

ISBN 0-934601-12-7

This book is for Joe Taylor, Rick Lott, Leon Stokesbury, and Lt. Colonel Rob Jones, Special Forces, U.S. Army.

Books by David Bottoms

Poetry

Under the Vulture-Tree
In a U-Haul North of Damascus
Shooting Rats at the Bibb County Dump
Jamming With the Band at the VFW (limited edition)

Fiction

Any Cold Jordan

Anthologies

The Morrow Anthology of Younger American Poets
(with Dave Smith)

ANY COLD JORDAN

The unborn children are rowing out to the far edge of the sky...
Charles Wright

Part One

1

The moon was in the sky and on the water at the same time, and the sky was full of stars. The dock jutted out into a small cove, and all the banks were heavily wooded and dark, the whole cove alive with small sounds. From out of the woods across the cove, an owl hooted twice, paused, then hooted again. Beyond the cove the lake widened quickly, and three or four hundred yards out, an island bristled with pines. A mile beyond that island, two small lights flickered on the surface of the water. Billy Parker took those to be the lights of the fishing camp. He laid his tackle box on the dock and opened his can of Coors. In the woods behind the house the whippoorwill kept calling, but he tried not to listen. He stood very still and listened instead for the owl. He watched the moon on the water, then the moon in the sky, and when enough silence had passed, the frogs opened up in great bellows that telegraphed up and down the edge of the water, and he listened for a long time to the frogs.

From the hill behind the dock a laugh rolled out of the house. A deeper laugh followed it, then a short, hoarse cough. Then the owl finally called, and as an exercise in futility Billy shined the beam of his flashlight across the water and watched it fade against the dark wall of pines. He switched it off and looked back through the brush at the faint glow of candlelight from the window. Only the faintest mumbling of voices carried down the hill, then a long silence and the only sounds were the frogs bellowing up and down the cove, the wind rustling the brush.

Billy sat the beer on the dock and opened his tackle box. It was in a shambles, something else to straighten out. He shined the flashlight into the tangle of lures and found the plastic syringe, pulled a nightcrawler out of the cup of dirt and shot a tiny bubble of air into his tail, another into his middle. From the tackle box he took a straight-shanked hook on a leader and ran the hook easy into the worm's head, and thought of an old biology teacher who had told him once that only the higher forms of life were afforded the luxury of pain. He snapped the line swivel onto the leader, stood up, and cast the worm easy off the edge of the dock. The lead shot made a plink on the surface and sank slowly to the bottom where it would stay while the nightcrawler floated above it like a little flag.

If Billy didn't feel like fishing, he felt less like watching Jean put herself through it all again. But there was no way of stopping her. He'd learned all the signals, what lay behind each one, and there was no way of stopping her. To try was only to make things worse, only to point a finger at it, to underline it. It was easier just to get away for a while, to let it run its course, then come back when all the luxury was gone.

The wind blew up strong off the lake and whipped the tip of the rod. He sat down on the dock and thought about Jean and about the man she was with in the house. How far would she push it? It didn't matter, anything would be too much. But how far? Not very with a stranger. Still, she took to this guy, though he was not the sort you'd think she might take to. Ex-military, twelve years in Special Forces, not the sort you'd expect her to take to at all. It was something about his voice, deep and gravelly, a quality about it that made you feel comfortable, made you feel absolutely at ease, even if he was a total stranger, even if you didn't know him from Judas and he'd phoned straight out of the blue. At first Jean resisted. So he was new in town. So he knew Charlie Waldrup. Then Billy handed her the phone.

After that, they followed his directions—fourteen miles down the Panama City Highway, then right onto Harvey Road. The only landmark he'd given was a black mailbox, but it wasn't hard to find, it was the only mailbox for miles. Behind it the pines opened around a narrow road. They turned and rode gravel for fifty yards, then the road broke sharply to the left and ran to dirt. When it narrowed again and dropped suddenly downhill, they saw through the tall trees the first patch of water, brown water around the bank and bright yellow where it held the sun in a circle at the end of the dock.

The house was a square green box made of concrete blocks, and it was hard to see among the pines and the shrubs. The road ended beside it in a small clearing where a Jeep with a canvas top sat beside a storage shed that leaned a little toward the water. On the edge of the clearing that brushed the house, Jack Giddens sat on the bench of a picnic table, in front of him a scattering of oily rags, a can of Outer's gun oil, and the disassembled parts of an automatic pistol.

Billy already liked the place, the way the light glanced off the trunks of the trees, the water and the island. He pulled the truck behind the Jeep, and Jack Giddens stood up and waved his hand.

He was a big man, over six feet and barrel chested, two hundred or two hundred and ten pounds. His beard was full and streaked with gray, and he had on a green T-shirt and a pair of double-kneed khaki pants, the cargo pockets bulging. Billy thought for a second of a huge kid coming home from school with his pockets stuffed with marbles, then of a picture he'd seen once of Ernest Hemingway on safari.

The shadows of the tall pines striped the clearing, and as Jack walked toward the truck it looked like he was walking under a strobe, his long strides breaking the bars of light. When he was almost on

5

the truck, Billy opened the door and shook his hand.

"Glad you talked us into it," he said.

Jack nodded and watched Jean climb out of the cab and walk around the bed of the truck. She held out her hand and he shook it.

"Always great to meet a beautiful lady," he said.

She looked a little puzzled, but returned the smile.

Billy took a twelve-pack of beer from the truck bed, and Jack pointed to a cooler behind the picnic table. "Power's been out for a couple of hours. I called Talquin Electric, transformer's down somewhere. Won't make any difference though, we're cooking on the grill, and the meat's on ice in the kitchen." He looked over into the truck bed. "So you brought some gear. Good. You'll catch some fish when the sun goes down."

While the coals heated they sat around the table and talked about Charlie Waldrup. Jack Giddens had known him since the war. He was stationed at Bragg when Charlie went through basic. Billy had known him for almost as long, close to eleven years. They'd gone to school together in Athens, had played a lot of music. Charlie Waldrup was a very talented guitar player in the Chicago-blues style who was making his living now by playing in a rock band. Jack had seen him a month or so ago at a club in D.C. The band was good, he said, but they were getting into theater rock. Billy remembered Charlie's music, the reserve, the taste, and it depressed him to think anybody that talented would have to resort to makeup and funny clothes in order to make a living. And Billy didn't want to talk about music anyway, because that meant talking about his own music, which he had begun to believe was hardly any music at all.

"So what can I catch in this lake?" he said.

"Bass, I suppose. I don't fish much, but this cove gets its share of bass boats. And they pull some good fish out of there. I drag out the glasses and watch them sometimes in the mornings. Harvey's Creek empties about three hundred yards down cove. That's supposed to be a hot spot."

"And you don't fish?" Billy kept staring at the pistol parts scattered over the oily rag.

Jean gave him a glance and raised her eyebrows.

"Never had the patience for it. Mostly I hunt. When I hunt I can move. And a lot of the sport for me is the moving, knowing where to go and how to get there. Not that I don't think fishing is good sport. But it takes a special sort of patience to be a good fisherman."

Jean sat up straight on the bench. "Sometimes I wonder about the so-called virtues of patience."

"Well, whatever they are," Jack said, "I've never had them. Maybe if I'd been raised to fish, but all my people were hunters. I love water, though. Always wanted to live on the water. Seems sort of strange."

"Not too strange," Billy said. "Jean's the same way about water."

Jack put his elbows on the table and leaned toward her. "You don't fish much either, I take it."

"Nothing that lives in the water interests me."

"She likes to sun-bathe nude," Billy said.

"That's not true, of course. He's joking." She gave Billy a glance, then looked away toward the house.

"No, it's true. She likes to sun-bathe nude. But only with her girlfriends." He took a swallow of his beer and looked down toward the water where the sun held a yellow patch off the end of the dock.

"Well, true or not," Jack said, "there's a very nice and private dock down there. No one around for miles. And any time you want it, or your girlfriends, it's all yours."

"Thank you," she said. "But it's not true. Billy's only pulling a tease, a little private joke. He isn't quite right, you know. It's his humor, it's quite sick. I think it has something to do with this Florida sun."

"It may not be just the sun," Billy said.

"No, it's the sun. It's frying his brain. It's already burned away all but the most primitive cells. That's why he has this tremendous affinity for fish. Christ, he dreams about them. He's getting back to his origins, you see. Any lake for him is a gigantic womb."

Billy frowned and shifted on the bench. "Not everything has to

7

do with wombs, you know."

"Yes, it does," she said. "Wombs and tombs. All the same thing."

Jack pushed back from the table and stretched his legs. He gazed over toward the grill. The flames had died down and the charcoal bricks were starting to burn white around the corners. "So you guys came down here from Athens?"

"Atlanta," Billy said. "We've been here two years. I was booking jobs out of an agency there. On my way to the top, next stop Nashville. Then Jean decides she wants to go back to college."

"Florida State?"

"It was the only theater department in the country that would give her any money."

"Not true again," Jean said. "They really have a very fine program."

"That's interesting," Jack said. "I've got a friend over there. He's one of the main reasons I'm down here. Name's Nolan Hughes. You know him?"

"Oh," Jean said. "He's our resident movie star, or as they say, our artist-in-residence. I've met him a few times, but he came down after I'd left the program."

"I don't know if you'd exactly call him a movie star." Jack took another beer from the cooler and sat back down at the table. "What did he make, three B movies? Two hot rod dramas and a surfing flick?"

"Anybody in Tallahassee who's been to Hollywood is a movie star."

"Who is this guy?" Billy said.

"You've seen him on TV," she said. "He's the guy on the motorcycle who does those commercials for Country's Barbecue."

"Barbecue?" Jack smiled over the top of his beer. "I haven't seen that one."

"It's amazing. But then he's done a lot of those things. Must pay well. Why else would anybody do them?"

Jack smiled again. "I think he has right expensive tastes. And everybody doesn't make a fortune in Hollywood."

"So how do you know this guy?" Billy said.

8

"We went to school together, that's all. A little private school in Macon. We were pretty good friends. Kept up over the years."

"Well, he's big time here," Jean said. "I hear he's practically that whole program now."

"Well, if he's not," Jack said, "I'm sure he thinks he is. So what kind of a degree is that? You get an MA, an MFA, or what?"

"She didn't get anything," Billy said. "She's a dropout."

"I am not." She gave him another glance. "I'm only on vacation. I ran into some trouble, weathered it, and now I'm taking a well-deserved vacation. I'll be back punching."

"I don't quarrel with taking leave," Jack said. "Good stuff. So what are you doing with it? You acting? Writing?"

"I work for world peace," she said.

Jack looked at her for a few seconds. He was puzzled.

"World peace," Billy said.

Jean took a swallow of her beer, then she laid her hands palms down on the table. "It's just something I say. It doesn't mean anything. It's just that I've been home for two years now, and I say that when people ask me what I do. It's entirely defensive."

"I see," Jack said. "Or I think I do."

"It's just that everybody expects you to do something. To have a job, a career, a family. Or at least a goddamned fascinating hobby. So it's just something I say, that's all."

Jack raised his eyebrows. "I can understand that."

"I don't mean to be rude, of course. I just get a little tired of that. Like you aren't really worth anything if you don't do something. Something valuable, I mean."

He put his elbow on the table and leaned slightly toward her. "Well, I'd think that just about anything you'd do would be something extremely valuable. And I'm delighted you don't really work for world peace. That's not the sort of work I approve of."

He dropped the questions and started reassembling the pistol. It was a Colt Government .45 with smooth walnut grips. With only slight alterations this was the pistol American troops had carried into battle since World War I. It was a single action automatic and had a trigger pull of seven pounds. It would shoot a 185-grain bullet at a thousand feet per second and consistently shoot two-inch groupings at fifteen yards. It was probably the most dependable handgun ever made, and it was moron proof, which was a major reason it continued to be standard issue in the United States Army.

Billy was only half listening to what Jack said about the Colt. His attention was focused on Jack's hands. Other than a few musicians, a Sonny Osborne or a Raymond Fairchild, he couldn't remember ever seeing a big man exhibit such agility with his hands. It was almost as though the fingers were operating of their own accord, picking up the slide, the spring guide, the recoil spring, in exactly the right way to facilitate the quickest possible assembly. In no time at all the Colt was in one piece and cradled in a rag on the corner of the table.

When they'd finished eating it was almost dark, the sun down low on the water, the light coming up in a deep orange rust under the canopy of trees. The mosquitoes had started to come out, and Jack wedged the pistol under his belt and went inside the house to light some candles. Jean and Billy raked the paper plates and napkins into a trash bag, screwed the tops on the mustard, ketchup, and pickles, and put the jars into the cooler. A dull light flickered through the window of the house, and Jack came back outside, told them to go on in and relax.

The door they walked through led into the corner of the house that served as the kitchen. Except for the bathroom, which separated the kitchen and the bedroom, the whole house was one large room. The front half of that room was Jack's living space, and in the center of the front wall a door led onto a screened porch.

Two candles on the kitchen table lit one side of the room, and another candle sat in a dish on a shelf beside the porch door, but it had blown out. Just beyond the table there was a fireplace, and on the mantlepiece sat an assortment of rifle cartridges, machine gun cartridges, and three hand grenades, which Billy took to be duds. The wall above the mantlepiece was covered with photos, mostly military, a composite of a Special Forces unit, a few jungle candids, a candid of three soldiers at a road block. In the corner of the room sat a desk, and the wall to the left of the desk was covered with stacks of books.

Billy sat down in a chair beside the kitchen table, and Jean crossed the room and sat on a sofa in the dim border of the candlelight. She leaned back on the big cushions and crossed her legs.

"Why the sun-bathing business?" she said.

"Don't be so touchy."

"You know I'm not much up for needles."

They sat for a minute and looked over the room. Billy glanced at the magazines lying on the desk, a *Gun Digest*, a few *National Geographics*, a *Time* with Yasir Arafat's turbaned profile on the cover.

"So what do you think?" Jean said.

"About what?"

Then the screen squeaked open and Jack came through the kitchen door. He had the cooler in his arms and sat it on the floor beside the stove. When he dropped into the chair across the table from Billy, he took a deep breath and let the air out in a long steady stream through his nostrils.

"Sorry about the dark," he said. "Still, it does make things a little more intimate, doesn't it."

"I really like your place," Billy said.

"It's all I need. Not much room, but it's really all I need. I'd get lost in anything bigger, by myself and all. And I like being hidden away out here. Never liked being around a lot of people. That was one thing I didn't much like about the army. Not a great deal of privacy."

He was gazing across the room toward the end of the sofa where Jean sat in almost total darkness. She had taken a cigarette from her purse and had wedged it into the corner of her mouth. He eased off the chair, crossed the room in two long paces, and held out a lighted

Zippo. The corner of the room looked suddenly like a jungle camp—cartridge belts, holsters, rucksacks, camouflage hanging from the ceiling, sleeping bags, canteens, mess gear edging from the shelves and walls into the small light cupped in Jack's hand. For a moment Jean's eyebrows dipped toward a question as she stared up into his face, then she leaned toward his hand and lit her cigarette. He snapped the Zippo shut, and the darkness closed in again.

"Thank you," she said. "That's very courteous."

"Listen, I don't get nearly enough chances to be courteous." He turned toward Billy. "Yes, this is a damn fine place. You can squeeze off a .45 in the front yard, and the only person in earshot is the drunk who runs the fishing camp across the lake. And he's half deaf."

He put the Zippo back into his pocket, stepped over to his desk and pulled out the bottom drawer. From each cargo pocket he pulled two handfuls of nickel cartridge hulls and dumped them in.

"Don't ever throw any center-fire hulls away," he said. "We can always use them." He held up a cartridge case. "When the army ships me my equipment, we can reload. Only way I can afford to shoot."

"You shoot all those today?" Billy asked.

"Not hardly. That's close to two hundred rounds. We could take that and bring down a banana republic. No, they've been rattling around for months in the back of my Jeep. I just got around to picking them up. One of my bad habits. I'm always putting things off."

"Who isn't?" Jean said. She gave Billy a look.

"Like this thing." He walked over to a curtained closet beside the bathroom and came out with an old guitar. He propped the body on the kitchen chair and tilted the face to catch the candlelight.

"This piece worth putting any money into? I've been meaning to fix it up, but I can't get around to it."

It was a Gibson B-25, a small-bodied guitar. Two of the tuning heads were missing and the nut was cracked. Billy picked it up and sighted down the neck. It had a good neck, and the body didn't seem to be hiding any cracks. He stuck his hand into the sound hole

12

and felt what braces he could find. They were a little thick, but they seemed to be in good shape. "It's a B-25. It just needs some keys and some polish and a new nut. The bridge is okay. The braces aren't cracked."

"A B-25?" Jack said. "Sounds more like a bomber."

"No, just a guitar."

"All right," he said. "But is it a good one? A guy at Bragg owed me fifty on a pistol I sold him. He didn't have the money, so I took this thing. I can't play it, but I thought I might get it fixed up and give it to my daughter."

"Sure, it's worth that." Billy handed the guitar back to him. "It cost three or four times that when it was new, and it ought to be a lot better guitar now."

Jack propped the Gibson against the wall and gave it a careful going over. "And it's a better guitar now?"

"Well, the wood's dried out. So it ought to have a better tone. Generally, the older the guitar the better. If it's been taken care of."

Jack sat back down in the chair and picked up the Gibson again. "And this one's been taken care of?"

"I didn't say that. I said it was a good guitar. It needs some work, but it can be put back into shape, and it'll be a good guitar for a girl. The neck's small and it shouldn't be any trouble for her to get her hand around it. When the action's set right, it ought to play real easy."

"The action?"

"The strings, how far they're set off the neck. When they're set up right—"

"How old is your daughter?" Jean said. She leaned forward from the sofa and into the light. She picked up the ashtray sitting on the coffee table, leaned back, and cradled it in her lap.

"Twelve," Jack said. He was still staring at the guitar. Then he looked through the candlelight and into the corner of the room. "She'll be thirteen on the third of September."

"Do you see her very often?"

"No, I don't. And that's another reason I'm at Florida State. She

13

lives in Gainesville with her mother."

"And you didn't want to go to school in Gainesville?"

"I'm afraid that might've been a little too close. I don't know if her mother and I could have worked that out. Tallahassee's probably close enough. Decent enough English Department, and I can get what I want in terms of a doctorate."

"Gainesville's not a very bad drive," Jean said. "What? Two hours? And interstate all the way."

"And I want to get over there soon. Or have her mother put her on the bus. She's old enough to make a trip like that now. I need to get on it before school cranks up, but this place is still a mess."

Billy pointed toward the neck of the guitar. "Listen—"

"What's her name?" Jean leaned up again toward the front of the sofa and set the ashtray back on the coffee table.

"Cathy. Catherine was her grandmother's name."

"Your mother?" She stood up then and walked over to the pictures hanging over the mantlepiece.

"No, my ex-wife's. I didn't have anything to do with naming her. In fact, when she was born I was with a II corps Mike Force out of Pleiku. We'd agreed that if it was a boy, we'd name him after my father. If it was a girl, well, Nancy could name her whatever she liked."

"How long have you been divorced?" Jean was studying the wall of pictures.

"About six years now."

"Oh, so you were married a long time."

"Long enough to figure out it wasn't a good marriage. It takes a whole lot of patience to be an army wife. Nancy didn't have it. A good woman, but it was one of those marriages that never should have happened."

"And this is her picture?" Jean pointed to a photograph of a little girl with straight blonde hair and bangs. She was wearing a red and white striped sweater and a pair of bluejeans, and she was sitting sidesaddle on a red Harley Sportster.

Jack leaned up in his chair and looked around Billy. "That was taken a few years ago. She's grown a lot since then."

"She doesn't look much like you," Jean said.

"Looks like her mother. Same eyes and mouth."

"Well, she's a very pretty little girl."

"Listen," Billy said, and pointed again toward the tuning heads. "I can fix those things for you."

"You work on guitars too?"

"It's not exactly what you call major work. Just a matter of taking those off and screwing on another set. The nut'll have to be replaced, though. That's a little trickier, but it's no real problem."

"I'd be glad to pay you whatever you think it's worth. I'd really like to get this thing in decent shape."

"It's not worth anything that money'll buy. I'll just take it with me and put it right. You can buy the heads."

Jean took a drag off her cigarette, walked over and crushed it into the ashtray. "She's quite a doll all right. Has she discovered boys yet?"

"I wouldn't know about that."

"What, no boyfriends?"

"I'm hoping that's still a few years off. But Nancy just sent me a picture of her dressed for her first dance. Can you believe that? They have dances in junior high."

"That's not unheard of," Jean said.

"Maybe not. But that's still pretty young. For me, anyway. Believe me, it can be a shock to see your twelve-year-old daughter in eye makeup. But I don't think she had a date or anything like that."

"Probably went with some of her girlfriends," Billy said. "They do that at her age."

Jean gave him a glance, then turned toward Jack. "Could I see that picture?"

"Listen," Billy said. He stood up from his chair. "I came over here to do some fishing. If you've got a flashlight, I'll put out a line."

Jack pointed to the floor under the desk where a black plastic lantern sat on a stack of magazines.

Billy walked over and picked it up. "Bang," he said, and shot a

15

beam of light onto Jean's stomach. "Works. I'll be back in a minute."

"Take your time," Jack said. "The lake's nice at night. I've got some Cutter's if you need it."

"Got some in my tackle box." He stopped at the cooler and took out a beer, then he pushed back the screen and walked out into the yard. The air had cooled and the wind carried the scent of honeysuckle and pine. The lightning bugs were still going off in the brush above the lake, and somewhere in the woods behind the house, a whippoorwill gave a faint call.

When the can was empty Billy took the flashlight and walked back up the steps and the hill. When he reached the truck he could hear them laughing in the house. Then there was a silence. He stood outside the door until the laughing started again, then he opened the screen and walked into the kitchen.

They were standing in the candlelight, looking at a field knife balanced on Jack's palm.

"No," Jack said. "That's standard issue."

"It's a menacing looking bastard." Then she turned to Billy, "Look at this. I'll bet you've never seen one of these."

He walked over to the candle and Jack tilted the knife blade toward the light. It was a stubby little knife with a saw-blade and a plastic handle. It was cheap and ugly.

"It's Russian," she said.

Jack turned the blade in the candlelight. "Twice as practical as U.S. issue. It's a survival knife, a bayonet, a decent enough fighting knife, a wire cutter. You'd think the Swiss had designed it. The steel's not worth a damn, but then I've never seen a standard issue military knife that was cut out of decent steel. Too expensive."

Jean took the knife out of his hand and wrapped her fist around the handle. "Where did you get it?"

"I got that one in Cambodia a few months before I shipped home."

She ran her finger down the back of the blade and felt the saw teeth. Then she handed the knife to Billy.

16

It was much lighter than he'd expected it to be. He ran his finger over the edge, flipped it over and felt the teeth. "Were they using a lot of Russian weapons over there?"

"Russian and Chinese, but I took that one off a Russian."

"You traded him for it?" Jean said.

"No, not exactly."

She gave Billy a look.

"He took it off a soldier." Billy handed the knife back to Jack.

"He gave it to you?" she said.

"Let's just say he had no further use for it." Jack slipped the knife into its sheath and laid it on the shelf with a dozen more.

Jean sat back down on the sofa then, and Billy stepped into the kitchen to get more beers from the cooler. "I didn't know there were any Russians in Cambodia," he said.

"There weren't supposed to be. But there weren't supposed to be any Americans there either." Jack pulled a kitchen chair into the corner, sat down, and took a pipe from the top drawer of his desk. "So what's happening on the water? Where's the catch of the day?"

"I'm giving them a chance." Billy handed him a can of Coor's. "The worm's out there on the end of the line." He handed a can to Jean, sat down in a rocker, and leaned back against a shelf of books.

"There's a great little poem called 'The Good Bait Wiggles.'" Jack took a tobacco pouch from the drawer. "You ever read it?"

"No, I don't think so."

"Nice little poem. I can't remember who wrote it, but one line goes like this, 'The good bait wiggles at the right time.'"

"I like that," Jean said. "I like that very much."

"Yes," Jack said. "Says quite a lot, doesn't it. 'The good bait wiggles at the right time.'"

When Billy walked back down to the dock, the moon was hanging directly over the fishing camp. The frogs were quiet and the whippoorwill was gone. The tip of the rod wasn't bent, but there was no slack in the line.

17

He picked up the rod and felt the weight. The fish had tired and came up easy. He let it down on the dock and shined the flashlight. It was a catfish, a young one, eight or nine inches long. Too small to keep. He laid the rod on the dock, opened his tackle box, and took out a pair of needle-nosed pliers. Then he opened the fish's mouth to see how far down the hook had gone. The catfish tried to gill air and made a small crying sound, something like a seabird. Billy couldn't find the hook, it was buried in the belly. He put the toe of his boot on the fish's head, took out his knife, and cut the line. Then he made a deep slash just behind the gill, flipped the catfish over and made the same slash under the other gill. He sawed through the spine, and the body of the catfish slid away from the head. He spooned out the entrails and retrieved the hook. Half of the worm had worked up the leader. Good bait, he thought, and stopped for a second and looked up the hill toward the house. A sudden uneasiness passed through him, and he raked the body, the entrails, and the head off the dock and into the water.

2

Billy started his morning with a Bass Ale. It was Friday but he wasn't celebrating the weekend. Just the opposite, because Friday was for Billy the worst of all days. It led to Friday night, which meant the bars would be crawling with drunks. And The Under Thing, the club he played three nights a week, sported a fairly obnoxious clientele — a few fraternity types and their loud dates, a trucker or two hung up on Kenny Rogers or Ronnie McDowell, but worst of all the young professionals who shucked their Austin Reeds for a pair of Levis and a Western shirt and became for the weekend good old boys. They were the customers lousy with requests, the "Rocky Tops," the "Foggy Mountain Breakdowns." And Billy swore this was what broke so many good musicians. Not the hours or the travel or the incredible difficulty of finding jobs to travel to, but the endless repetition of tasteless music they were forced to play, the endless string of country and western clichés.

Billy stood for a few seconds in the kitchen, drinking the Bass in long slow swallows. He was glad to be working alone again, no more banjos. In his immediate future lay an unknown number of "Rocky

Tops," but thank God the only breakdown he'd have to face today was the dishwasher. It had been on the blink for a day and a half, and the kitchen was already a wreck, the cabinet littered with dishes, cups, glasses, a cookie sheet, an opened jar of grape jelly, a cake of margarine, an empty orange juice carton. The sink powdered with a fine black dust where Jean had scrapped burnt toast.

He sat the Bass between the burners of the stove, the only decent surface, and put the margarine and the jelly back into the fridge. He ran some hot water into the left side of the sink and shot in two squirts of Ivory Liquid, rinsed off the dishes and slid them in. The garbage was pouring over the top of the can, so he crushed it back into the bag and tossed in the empty carton.

Jean was on the screened porch. He could hear her radio. It was playing the public station, harp music. Something Irish. It sounded like Carolan, and at first Billy thought it may have been the "Farewell to Music."

He picked up the Bass, walked through the den, and stopped in the doorway of the porch. She was sitting in her favorite chair, a wicker rocking chair with thick padded cushions on the back and seat. The print on the cushions was a bright green floral, and she had wedged the chair into a corner of the porch almost completely covered with hanging plants. When she sat there she was surrounded in her own private jungle of Swedish ivy, ferns, and wandering Jew. Billy leaned against the door frame and watched the curtain of leaves brush back and forth.

"What are you reading?" he asked.

She kept on rocking. She didn't look up from her book.

"So what are you reading?"

"Ngaio Marsh. *Death of a Peer.*"

He took a swallow of the Bass and watched the leaves sway back and forth with the chair. "So how can you rock and read at the same time?"

No answer.

"Good book?"

20

"Okay."

"What's it about?"

The rocking stopped, the leaves hung straight and still. "Someone gets murdered. They try to find out who did it."

"Really?"

"No, it's really about a bunch of unlucky fishermen who burn down a fishing peer on Lauderdale Beach."

He shoved off the door frame. "Mind if I sit down?"

"Help yourself."

He sat in the wicker chair behind the coffee table and propped his feet on the corner of the plexiglass. He'd always liked the porch. It was on the west side of the house and was screened on three sides and shaded in the front by pines. So it was usually cool in the summer, especially in the mornings. Behind the house there was a four-acre pond, and you could see about half of it from the porch. It had a good stock of fish, bream and crappie and some decent enough bass, and on good days someone was usually fishing from the bank. Today no one was on the pond, only the ducks in the shallows of the far cove where the posts of an old fence slipped out into the water. It was the tennis tournament. Everyone was at the tennis courts. Good. He hoped they would stay there all day. He liked the pond quiet, only the birds and the ducks and the white dog pacing in his yard across the pond.

Beyond the west cove stood the remains of the barn and outbuildings of the farm the subdivision had been cut from. They were left standing, of course, for their rustic value. But Billy liked them anyway. They always made him wonder what the place was like before some developer dreamed it into Colonial Farm Estates. This, he imagined, must have been very fine pasture, rolling green pasture spotted with watering ponds.

"I don't mean to be ill, you know." Jean closed her book on her finger and brushed aside the curtain of leaves.

"I know that."

"Hand me a cigarette."

21

He leaned forward from the chair, picked up her cigarette case and lighter from the coffee table, and tossed them into her lap.

"Is that the robe your mother sent you?"

Her mother was always sending her robes. For Christmas, for birthdays, for anniversaries, for anything, she always sent robes. Robes seemed like a very intimate gift, but with a robe you didn't really have to know anything about a person. You didn't have to know anything as personal as size, only small, medium, or large. Billy liked this one, though. It was a beige satin robe with padded shoulders.

"Yes, it is," she said. "You like it?"

"Very Lauren Bacall."

Jean lit a cigarette, dropped the case and lighter onto the floor beside her chair, and went back to her rocking and her book.

On the far side of the pond, a kid with a tackle box and a rod came out of the trees. Billy remembered that he had dreamed again of fishing. This time something about a river, but he couldn't bring it back. Usually they were about lakes or ponds, sometimes rivers, sometimes swamps. And they were generally about places he knew, like the Wakulla River where the water is almost crystal clear and you can see the huge uncatchable mullet swimming ten feet below the boat. But they were also about places from his past that had suddenly, of all things, flooded — his grandfather's store flooded to the top of the Coke box, his father's yard entirely under water, a baseball field, a pasture, a park split suddenly by a great river. And Billy always there with the rod and the lure, trying to dredge something up.

The kid had rigged a plastic worm and was flailing the water around the bank. He was snapping it out like a whip, and he wouldn't give the worm time enough to sink. Billy wanted to tell him that everything depends on patience, on the bait looking natural, acting real. The kid was retrieving too quickly. He wasn't putting any action on his lure, wasn't giving himself a chance.

"So what have you decided about Atlanta?" Jean asked.

"I don't know."

"You'd better make up your mind. If you're going to change your mind, you'd better let that guy know soon so he can find somebody else." She let the chair ease to a stop and closed the book on her finger.

"I already told Leon I was going so he could book that weekend. But I can always back out."

"Well?"

"I haven't decided."

She was talking about Grover's, an uptown saloon in Atlanta. A few days ago the manager had called to ask if Billy would be interested in coming up in two weeks to play some opening sets. The job was for a Thursday and a Friday night and the main act was Frank Wiley, a flatpicker and songwriter. Wiley was a comer who was about to release his third album.

Billy had played Grover's twice before. It was a good club and the money was more than he could make anywhere else, but it was depressing in the same way The Under Thing was depressing. And the weekend good old boys in Atlanta were twice as obnoxious as they were in Tallahassee. In Atlanta, the whole of Buckhead turned out in designer jeans and three-hundred-dollar boots. Billy had told him he'd play the job simply because he needed the money, but he'd begun to have second thoughts.

"You know," Jean said, "if you aren't careful, you'll get a reputation for that sort of thing."

"Not at this point. Everybody knows me."

"No, I'm serious. It doesn't take any time at all for people to change their opinion of you. And that guy really has been very nice to you. You owe it to him to play that job. Either that, or tell him now. You can't expect him to book a replacement a day ahead of time."

"I don't know," he said. "It's not just Grover's. Grover's is a good enough place." He took a swallow of the Bass and watched the kid cast out as far as he could toward the center of the pond. The worm struck little circles on the water, then cut a line of V's as he reeled it back toward the bank.

"I thought you were getting over all that. It's a phase. You go through

23

it every year. You get over it."

"I suppose."

"You'd better suppose. What else can you do?"

Something hit the kid's line and his rod bent toward the pond like it was divining water. He jerked up and the tip arched, then the line began moving away. The kid pulled up and started reeling, and the water broke twice about twenty yards down the bank.

"The kid's got a fish," Billy said.

"What?"

He leaned up in his chair and pointed to the edge of the pond where the kid was bringing out a little bass.

"I can't see that far," she said.

"The kid's got a fish. Looks like a small bass."

"Good for him. Who is he?"

Billy didn't know his name. He was one of the kids who lived in the subdivision. He was thirteen or fourteen, and he fished a lot in the pond. Sometimes when it was too hot to fish, he swam. Once Billy had watched him swim the whole length of the pond on his back.

"One of the kids across the way," he said. "The swimmer."

They'd been in that house two years and hardly knew anyone in the neighborhood. Billy rationalized that by saying it was the kind of neighborhood where people who didn't hang out at the swimming pool or the tennis courts never met anyone. It was a bridge club neighborhood, a garden club neighborhood. It was the kind of neighborhood where everyone wore tennis whites on the weekends, then once a month on Saturday night, for a kick, put on jeans, boots, and a Western shirt and went out to a bar like Grover's.

But Jean liked the house, a light blue saltbox with cream trim, and it had the screened porch on the west side and a deck that ran from the porch down the side of the house all the way around the back. And Billy liked it too, even if Jean's money had covered the down payment. Or her father's money, though it was hers now. Money from two Cadillac dealerships dropped into a trust fund, more tied up in stocks. Not a fortune, but solid money. But Billy couldn't help that, and he liked the house, and he kept up the payments, or his share of them, so he didn't feel too low about living there.

"His father teaches at Florida State," she said.

"How do you know that?"

"I saw the kid on campus once. I think his father's in history. His name's Sissman."

"You never told me that."

"You forgot."

The kid had the fish on a stringer and was letting it back down into the water. He bent over, stabbed the spike into the bank, and stepped on it with the heel of his shoe. Then he reset the hook in the head of the worm and started flailing the water to his left.

Jean turned back toward him. "I wish you'd make up your mind about Atlanta. You know I need to phone Marilyn."

"Oh."

"She needs to get away from that shop, and I don't want to stay here alone."

Billy stared into the curtain of leaves, then he looked again toward the lake and the kid flailing the water. "You could go with me."

"I don't think so."

The kid threw his lure close to the bank and it snagged on one of the bushes jutting out over the water. He jerked the line a few times, but it was wrapped in a tangle of limbs and wouldn't give. Billy thought then about rowing over in the jon boat. That was the only way the kid would ever get it loose, unless he wanted to wade down the bank.

"So I can't have friends over now?"

"I didn't say that."

She opened her book again and sat for a minute holding it in her lap, but she wasn't reading. She was staring out across the yard and the pond. "You didn't say anything, did you. I know what you're thinking, and I thought we settled that a long time ago. Let's not make things worse, all right?"

"Sure," he said. "Have her down." He was still thinking about crossing over in the jon boat. He wanted to get out on the water and feel the boat rocking under him. Being on the water was like being in a dream, where he didn't have to think about Marilyn or Grover's or the Friday-night rowdies at The Under Thing. He wanted to row across the water and help the kid retrieve his worm, then he just wanted to lie down in the boat and drift. But the kid was already sitting on the bank, rolling up his jeans, kicking off his tennis shoes. Billy thought then of his guitars, and he pushed himself out of the chair and walked upstairs to change his strings.

3

The Under Thing occupied the basement of The Thing, one of the dozen or more saloon-restaurant combos lining the strip of Tennessee Street bordering the Florida State campus. It was the brainchild of Leon Thibodeaux, a five-foot-eight, two-hundred-and-fifty pound Texan who had wandered into the South in the late sixties as the bass player for a hard rock band called The Aztex. After four or five years on the road and two albums, both bombs, the band burned out in Tallahassee. The singer and the drummer moved on to New Orleans, but Leon and the guitar player took what money they had saved, leased the basement of The Thing, did some minor remodeling, and opened The Under Thing. It went well from the start because it was one of the few bars in Tallahassee, and the only one on the strip that didn't cater to Florida State students. There were, for instance, no football jerseys tacked to the walls, no photos of players, no fraternity or sorority pennants, not one thing to suggest that anything like Florida State University was directly across the street. It was a place, as Leon liked to point out, for the regular folks.

But two years after it opened Leon found himself the sole owner.

His partner smashed a Triumph bike into the back of a Ryder truck and died on the highway a mile south of Thomasville, Georgia.

Leon paid homage to his partner by commissioning a local artist to paint his portrait from an old promotion photo of the band. The artist was one of their better customers, an MFA dropout from the art department at FSU, but the portrait was horrible. Billy thought it looked like a paint-by-number picture of Jesus, or the head of a stoned guru — red hair, yellow face, black eyes — and the first time he saw it he told Leon to hang it under a black light. But the portrait, ugly as it was, had hung behind the bar for almost eleven years, and this was one thing Billy liked very much about Leon Thibodeaux. He possessed a remarkable sense of loyalty, and for that loyalty he possessed a number of good friends.

When Billy walked from the bright parking lot into the near darkness of The Under Thing, he heard Leon before he saw him. The click of glass against glass, the tap of the bottle coming down on the bar. Just about every time Billy came into the place, whether he was playing music or killing time, Leon bought him a shot of Irish whiskey.

"You're early," Leon said.

Billy leaned his guitar cases against the bar, sat down on a stool and picked up the shot glass. "Had to get out of the house."

"Again?"

"Always." He propped the edge of the glass on his lower lip and let the whiskey spill onto his tongue.

"Same obsession?"

"One of them."

Leon reached under the bar and came up with a towel. "She still trying to get you under the knife?"

Billy gave him a look.

"You know," Leon said. "If I were you I'd go ahead and do it, or get the hell out."

"Maybe it's not quite that simple, Leon."

"Why not?"

"Because maybe it just ain't."

"Then I'd just tell her to knock it off, or get the hell out."

"Everything's pretty black and white for you, isn't it?"

"I try not to let it get complicated."

Billy took a sip of the Irish. "She's all right. She's just not happy, that's all."

"You want me to tell you about not happy? I was married for a year."

"I think we've been through that song." It was the last thing Billy wanted to talk about.

But Leon didn't follow it up, only started wiping off the top of the beer cooler. "I need to get a new one of these things." He rapped his knuckles on the lid. "You got any idea what one of these costs."

It didn't sound like a question, so Billy didn't answer.

"You'd have to take a pay cut."

"I sort of like that one. Gives the place a quaint charm." He took another sip of the whiskey, and his eyes began adjusting to the dark. If Leon was in the mood to spend some money, he could drop a few bucks on the decor. The Under Thing was a fairly big room and almost as fancy as a soda cracker. The floor was concrete and the walls were concrete blocks. And there wasn't much on those walls either—a Bud clock with six Clydesdales pulling a beer wagon, a three-by-three poster of Bob Wills and the Texas Playboys, a horseshoe somebody had given Leon for luck, and of course, the guru behind the bar.

The stage was in the corner of the room opposite the bar. It was a small plywood platform about a foot off the floor, and Leon had painted it red. There were two large Peavy columns on both sides of it, an amp head on a table behind the stools and mikes, and one monitor on the floor in front of the mike stands. Two of the Peavy columns belonged to Billy. He had them on sort of permanent loan to Leon. All of that concrete tended to echo, and four columns carried the room much easier than two.

Of the twenty-five or thirty tables, only two were occupied. A man and a woman were sipping tall drinks through straws at a table near the stage, and Sarah Libby Cook, one of the barmaids, was reading

29

a *Rolling Stone* at a table near the center of the room.

Billy finished his whiskey and sat the shot glass beside the bottle. He slid off the stool, picked up his guitar cases, and carried them to the stage. According to the Bud clock, it was a little after six-forty. He usually didn't start playing until eight-thirty or nine, so he had some time to kill. He'd go up to The Thing and have a pizza and a beer, and after that walk down to The Brew and Cue and shoot some pool.

"Leon," he said. "You had anything to eat?"

"Where you going?"

"Thought I'd walk upstairs and get a pizza."

"I better hang around."

"Want me to bring something back?"

"Not for me." Leon rapped the bottom of a glass on the bar. "Libby, you want anything from upstairs?"

She shook her head. "Certainly not a pizza."

The Thing was a fairly sharp contrast to The Under Thing. The floors were all natural and polished to a high shine. The bar was laminated oak and stretched the entire length of one wall. The lower half of that wall was covered with glasses and wine bottles. The upper half was one solid, immaculately clean mirror, and the ceiling and two other walls were painted sky blue with very white fluffy clouds drifting across on the steady breeze of ceiling fans. Against one of those walls a skinny oriental tree stretched from a white ceramic pot all the way to the ceiling where it blossomed suddenly into a ball of green leaves. The tables were heavy white plastic with white wrought iron legs, and the whole front wall was a huge glass window. The place had a very clean, airy look, and seemed a lot bigger than it actually was.

Dinner time, and the room was crowded with a flock of sorority angels in jerseys and satin shorts, pastel Izods and tennis skirts. Around them hovered an assortment of fraternity boys strutting back and forth to the bar. They were all having beer and wine and pizza, and to look at them you'd think nothing sour had ever happened in the world.

Billy ignored them, read the paper he'd picked up from the street box, and waited on his pizza.

He was halfway through his dinner when Jerry Lamberti came in. Jerry was a decent and kind guy and a good enough friend, but seeing him walk through the door of The Thing raised in Billy a slight sense of dread. Jerry was a perfect example of what could happen to a musician who had any integrity. He was a very fine blues guitar player in the style of Josh White or Big Bill Broonzy, and in the late sixties and early seventies, he had done fairly well for himself in the Southeast, playing clubs and folk festivals and colleges. But his audience faded away, and he thought that changing with the times would be compromising his music. Maybe so, but Jerry hadn't played on a stage in two or three years. He worked now as a carpenter and odd job man, and he lived in a rooming house on Call Street.

Jerry went to the bar, ordered a draft, then waded through the frat crowd and disappeared into the back of the room. He hadn't seen Billy, and Billy felt bad about not going back and speaking to him. But he didn't need that, not when he had to think about the Atlanta job.

The problem with opening a set for Frank Wiley was very simple. They played the same sort of material, and Frank Wiley played it a lot better than Billy Parker. Billy knew what his talents were and didn't see much point in kidding himself. He was a decent enough flatpicker, certainly the best in Tallahassee and probably the best in the area. He could pick a solid, no-frills version of just about any fiddle tune. But Frank Wiley was an exceptional guitarist who could play six or seven variations of every tune Billy knew, and when he had played those he could improvise a few more. He was an Arkansas boy who had grown up playing in the best bluegrass bands in the South. At seventeen he was playing professionally with The Blueridge Gentlemen, and at twenty-five he struck off on his own and started The Frank Wiley Group. They'd been together a year and a half and had already cut two albums.

But Billy knew what to do. Come up with some new material, something a little different, and he knew the easiest way to come up with new material was to find old material that folks had never heard, or at least had long forgotten. So he'd spent most of that afternoon going over old country and western albums, things recorded twenty and thirty years ago. He'd gone through everything he had by Ernest Tubb, Hawkshaw Hawkins, Jimmy Dickens, Johnny Horton, Lefty Frizzell, no small stack of records. And he'd picked out five or six songs he'd done in his dim past, all songs with a honky-tonk flavor. He'd try them out on the crowd at The Under Thing.

When he finished the pizza and beer, he thought again about Jerry Lamberti hidden in the crowd somewhere in the back of the room. Maybe he should just walk back and say hello. He stood up, wedged a dollar under his plate, and looked back across the sea of fraternity jerseys. He could just say hello, make some excuse, and leave. But he didn't. He only walked over to the cashier and paid his check.

At the Brew and Cue he shot five or six games of eight ball with Turner Kay, the baseball coach at Florida High. Billy beat him once, Turner Kay's notion of charity, and paid him a buck apiece for the games he lost.

When he got back down to The Under Thing, the hands on the Bud clock showed a quarter to nine. Something vaguely country was blaring off the jukebox and the place was packed, the smoke already thick enough to choke the devil. Billy walked down to the end of the bar and slid onto a stool. Sarah Libby Cook was drawing a draft from the Miller tap, and he motioned for her to draw one for him.

"A guy called for you a few minutes ago," she said.

"Who was it?"

She took a slip of paper out of her apron pocket. "A guy named Reed. He left a number." She dropped the paper on the bar and sat his beer on top of it, then she put three glasses of draft on a tray and headed for her table.

Billy picked up the paper and read it. He wadded it into a ball and tossed it into the trash can behind the bar. It was from Russell Reed and Billy knew already what he wanted, he wanted to sit in on a set. It wasn't that Russell Reed was such a bad banjo player, he was actually a pretty good chromatic picker. His problem was taste, and he didn't understand that a banjo player with no taste can bring out the worst in a crowd. He was what Billy liked to call an undergrad picker, the usual campus variety, all of the talent and the drive, especially the drive, but none of the taste and maturity. None of the professionalism. They were stage struck, all of them, and they'd play a job for nothing or next to it, which made it very hard for professional musicians to make a living. No, Billy didn't want to talk to Russell Reed. About the best thing a picker could bring to his music, aside from raw talent, was taste and experience. And Russell Reed didn't have enough of the first quality to make up for his lack of the other two.

Billy finished his beer and walked to the stage and tuned his guitars. He flipped the switch on the P.A. head, let it warm for a second, and sat down on the stool to test the mikes.

When Leon signaled from the bar that the P.A. was all right, he picked a fairly quick medley of "Whistling Rufus" and "Billy in the Low Ground." Most of the crowd tuned it, so he went into a regular set.

Half an hour later, he looked across the room and saw Jack Giddens sitting at the bar. Jack raised a brandy snifter in a silent toast. He was all smiles, and loose, and looked as though he'd had a few already.

When Billy finished the set he walked over to the bar and sat down on a stool beside him. Leon eased over with a snifter and a bottle of Martel. He sat the glass on the bar in front of Billy and poured a drink. "On your buddy."

It was too hot to drink cognac, but Billy nodded to Jack and drank it anyway. By that time Jack was working on his third or fourth, and sweat was starting to bead on his forehead.

He leaned a little in Billy's direction. "You play here every weekend?"

"Thursday through Saturday."

Jack finished his drink and sat the empty snifter on the bar. "If this was my place, you'd be in here every night."

"And folks would get tired of me and you'd close down. No, sometimes Leon'll have other acts in here during the week. And sometimes I play the Ramada on Mondays and Tuesdays. But I've about stopped that."

Sarah Libby Cook came up behind the bar and asked Jack if he wanted another drink. He sat up straight on the stool. "Yes, ma'am. Martel, and a beautiful smile to go with it."

She poured the drink.

"So," Jack said. "How's my guitar?"

"I'm cleaning it up."

"That thing you're playing is a little bigger than mine, isn't it?"

"A little bit. I play a couple of Martins, a D-18 and a D-28."

"One's not enough?"

"I suppose it is. I just like both of these. I use the 28 for backup, it's mellow. The 18's a little brighter, better for flatpicking."

"Different wood, right?"

"One's rosewood, the other mahogany." Billy took a swallow of the Martel. "Listen, Jean and I had a fine time last night."

"Well, I was glad for the company. It's not easy being new anywhere and only knowing a couple of people. It was a nice gesture. Hell, it's a long way out there, I know that."

"But worth it."

"Oh," Jack said. "I saw Nolan this afternoon and he gave me four good tickets to the play Thursday night. They do a late summer stock, and it's opening night. *Cat On a Hot Tin Roof.* How about it?"

"I'd like to, but I got to work. Bills to pay and all. Give Jean a call, though."

"They don't ever give you a night off?"

"They already have. I've got to play an out-of-town job. You ought to call Jean, though. She'd enjoy it."

"If you don't mind me asking her, I will."

"Why should I? She might have a house guest, though, a girlfriend

34

from Atlanta."

"This girlfriend married?"

"Far from it."

"Even better," Jack said. "Like I say, I've got four tickets and I'd hate to waste them. I think it might be a decent show."

Billy finished the Martel and sat the glass on the bar. Sarah Libby Cook picked it up and gave him a look, but he shook his head no.

"So what's happening on Thursday?" Jack said.

"A job at a saloon in Atlanta. I'm supposed to be opening for Frank Wiley on Thursday and Friday."

"I'm sorry, I'm not much up on music."

"Frank Wiley's a flatpicker. Young guy, but he's been around for years with one group or another. On his way up."

"Sounds like a good job."

"Maybe."

"Why not? Sounds like it might be a break."

Billy smiled at that. "I don't know. I may be just a little past the good break stage."

"I don't believe that."

"Let's just say that it never pays to fool yourself. And in a business like this, that's an easy thing to do." But Billy didn't want to talk good breaks, bad breaks, or music. "So tell me about Nolan Hughes," he said. "You never really said how you got to know him."

"We went to school together, that's all. And then I shot him."

Billy didn't say anything. He thought he'd misunderstood.

"No, I did," Jack said.

Billy took a guess. "Hunting trip?"

"Of course not." Jack gave him a fairly serious look. "I never shoot anybody accidentally. This was the summer we graduated, sixty-seven, the war going full blast, guys getting drafted right and left. I was ROTC, so I was on my way, but Nolan was riding a deferment, academic. Then like everybody else, he got reclassified 1-A and called down for his physical, which he passed with flying colors. Anyway, he was terrified about going into the army. Just about lost his ability

35

to function."

"It was a scary time."

"Well, that's not the sort of behavior I normally sympathize with. But we were good friends. Besides, this didn't have much to do with the war. Nolan was never a coward. We talked about it, or tried to. He told me finally it had to do with, get this, free will. Crazy, huh? But he was a very independent guy. Still is."

Jack took a sip of Martel and looked at Billy as though he thought he had something to say. Billy only raised an eyebrow.

"Anyway," Jack said, "his daddy had a farm in Bibb County, and I went out there a lot with Nolan and his brother to shoot skeet. They were both real fine shots. In fact, his brother won five or six trophies in state competitions, junior division."

"Younger brother?"

"Fifteen, sixteen. And a fine shot. So we were out there one day about two weeks or so after Nolan had taken his physical. And Nolan couldn't hit a thing. He was on the verge of going to pieces. You could literally see it in his face, and he'd miss a pigeon and start to shake. He'd call for another one, miss that one, and shake a little more. I thought if he missed one more bird, he might just break down right on the spot.

"So I had this little .22 Beretta model 70S I carried to plink around with. Nolan's brother was in the trap house, and Nolan was standing on the line waiting for another pigeon. He was already shaking, every muscle shaking. So I took the Beretta out of my pocket, walked over to him, and shot him in the foot. It was actually sort of funny. He relaxed almost immediately. Then he just stood there for ten or fifteen seconds watching this stream of blood ooze out of the hole in his boot. Then he said, 'I guess you know you shot me.' I said, 'I guess so.' Then we put a tourniquet on his leg, put his foot in a bucket, and drove him to the hospital."

Billy had to smile a little. "And when it healed? They didn't draft him then?"

"No, they had to take his toe off. He was wearing these canvas jungle boots, just tight enough to make out the outline of his little toe, just this little green ridge on the edge of his boot. Anyway, I was shooting hollow points and the muzzle wasn't half a meter from his foot, so I chopped most of it off. The doctor got the rest."

Billy raised his eyebrows.

Jack leaned up. "Ever see any of those surfing movies he made?"

"I don't think so."

"Well, if you do, watch close. They never show a shot of his feet." He smiled and took a swallow of the Martel.

"And that didn't look a little strange to his draft board?"

"I had to testify that it was an accident. But in Macon, Georgia, the sworn word of an officer of the United States Army carries a lot of weight." He was looking across the room at a woman sitting alone at a table near the stage. She was a redhead, an attractive woman, and was giving them an occasional glance. "And it was sort of an accident."

"How you figure that?"

"Well, in the way a lot of things are accidents. None of us were responsible for any of the things that led up to it. As far as I'm concerned the war, the draft, and the army were all accidents. At least for Nolan. So was his shot foot."

"I'm not sure that makes any sense."

"The sense is this," Jack said. "Nolan Hughes never served a single day in the army."

Billy couldn't argue with that. "Well, you're lucky you both didn't work yourself into a jam."

"Sometimes you have to work yourself into a little bit of a jam to work yourself out of a bigger one. And if I had a dollar for every jam I've bailed Nolan Hughes out of, we'd drink free all night."

Jack drank the last of his Martel and sat the snifter on the bar. He flipped his check over, took a bill from his pocket, folded it, and laid it on top of the check. "Listen, I've got a date. Come out next week and we'll do some fishing."

"Maybe, but probably not till I get back from Atlanta. I need to spend some time with the guitar."

"When you get back then. We'll take Nolan's canoe around the island and run back into those coves."

"I'll do that, and you call Jean tomorrow."

Jack nodded, turned on the stool, slid off, and walked toward the door. Billy sat there for a minute and thought about a .22 hollow point chopping off Nolan Hughes' little toe, then he glanced back over at the red-head. She was still there, still smiling.

On Friday and Saturday nights Billy played until twelve-thirty or one, which meant three solid sets. The first one was always easy, but halfway through the second the beer and the wine and the whiskey started to set in, and with that the requests. And Billy hated requests. The problem was that if you played one, they started coming in from all over. And if you didn't feel like singing "Coward of the County" or "Rocky Top" all night, you were in trouble. That night they started coming in early and hard, and Billy wound up playing requests for most of the second set.

Two songs into the third set Jerry Lamberti came in with a woman Billy had never seen. Jerry was very much a loner, and it was strange enough to see him with anyone, much less a woman. They stood for a minute in the back of the room and looked around for a place to sit. There were a few stools at the corner of the bar, but all of the tables were taken. Billy looked around for Leon but couldn't find him, so when he finished the tune he was picking, he called for him over the mike. A second later Leon came out of the office behind the bar. Billy nodded toward the door, and when Leon saw Jerry and his girl, he rushed around the bar and cleared a table stacked with candles and napkins. Sarah Libby Cook was right behind him with two chairs.

Someone at the bar yelled out "Tennessee Waltz." Not a bad song. He was a joker, though, and he didn't expect Billy to know it. So Billy went into "The Tennessee Waltz," and Jerry and his girlfriend sat down at the table.

There was something slightly familiar about Jerry's girl. She had an odd, striking look, almost oriental, with long straight hair, jet black and cut in bangs across her forehead. Billy had seen her somewhere before, and it bothered him that he couldn't put his finger on the place.

When he wrapped up "The Tennessee Waltz," somebody in the back of the room yelled out "London Homesick Blues," everybody's favorite TV theme. Then a guy near the stage yelled "Black Mountain Rag," and the woman next to him shouted "For the Good Times."

Billy's voice was a little tired, so he picked the fiddle tune. After that he played another twenty minutes of requests, the crowd working itself into the usual Friday night whoop, then he simply ignored them and went into one of the old tunes he'd dug up that afternoon. It was a song called "There's No Fool Like A Young Fool," a thing Ernest Tubb recorded in the fifties about a young girl who throws her life away in a honky-tonk. He'd worked out a nice intro on guitar and a turn-around after the first verse. There's no fool like a young fool with wild and careless ways, who forgets about tomorrow and lives just for today. The drunks loved it, whistles and whoops. But that's the way they loved everything, and he couldn't tell anything from that. Billy looked over at Jerry Lamberti. Jerry took a sip of his beer and sat the glass on the table, then he winked and nodded twice. Suddenly Billy felt nothing short of good. When a guy like Jerry Lamberti noded his head in approval, he knew he'd played something right.

The requests came again hard and fast. Billy ignored them for two more songs, things from a regular set, then he finally had to play "London Homesick Blues." Half a dozen drunks felt the need to sing along, and halfway through it Jerry and the girl stood up from their table. Billy knew they'd sensed it was all downhill from there.

Jerry pointed toward his watch and gave a quick wave. Billy nodded and watched them turn and walk toward the door. He felt pretty sorry that he hadn't spoken to Jerry at The Thing, and he made a note to buy him a beer the next time he saw him.

4

Billy spent most of Saturday afternoon going through his Lester Flatt albums. He was looking for another song or two to take with him to Atlanta, something with a mountain flavor that might also appeal to a country and western crowd, some sort of ballad, maybe one of the those murdered lover songs like "Poor Ellen Smith" or "Omie Wise." He put on the first record just after lunch. Poor Ellen Smith, how she was found shot through the heart, lying cold on the ground. And by late afternoon he had decided that Lester Flatt was without question one of the greatest folk, country, or bluegrass singers who had ever lived. Of course, he had known that already, but that afternoon he learned it all over again and rededicated himself to the music of Lester Flatt the way certain Baptists over the years rededicate their lives time and again to Jesus.

First Billy listened to Lester's early recordings with Bill Monroe, when he and Earl Scruggs were part of the Bluegrass Boys. Then he listened to just about everything he owned by Lester, Earl and the Foggy Mountain Boys, then to the three albums he had of the Nashville Grass, the band Lester formed when he and Earl parted ways.

And what struck him again and again was not just the quality of Lester's voice, always rich and pure, but what he could describe only as taste. Lester, surely you must have been tempted to chunk it all, surely when times were lean you must have been tempted to go country, to go commercial.

Even when Lester and Earl were breaking into a few commercial markets, when they were appearing on *The Beverly Hillbillies* and other network TV shows, when they were playing colleges and reaching city audiences other bluegrass musicians couldn't reach, Lester Flatt sang every song he recorded with an incredible amount of restraint and good taste. Never any of the vocal high jinks you hear so often from most country singers. Billy loved that uncompromising purity, the faith the man had in his voice and the respect he had for the music.

And Billy could listen to Lester sing anything, truck songs, heart songs, ballads. But what he loved most was listening to Lester Flatt sing gospel. Lester sang gospel songs with so much ease and honesty it made you want to go out and join a country church. Billy remembered the year at Horsepen's Forty when he'd heard the Nashville Grass do a whole set of gospel music. Not that that was so unusual, most festivals set Sunday mornings aside for gospel. What was unusual was everything else. First of all the heat, it was July and a blistering sun was rising straight over the back of the stage, and the stage was in an open field, not a square foot of shade. Most of the women sat under umbrellas, and the men pulled their hats down low over their eyes. A lot of the folks, Billy included, had gotten there at nine for the first band. The sun was fierce even then, and after a couple of hours Billy's forearms felt like they were deep frying in their own sweat. Then the Sullivan Family finished their set, and it was time for the last group of the morning. The M.C. came onto the stage and stood in front of the microphone. Billy remembered exactly what he said. "Ladies and Gentlemen, please make welcome Mr. Lester Flatt and the Nashville Grass." Every hat came off every head. Billy's included.

They started with "The Sweet Bye and Bye," and from the very first note Lester sang, arms started going up all through the crowd. At first up front, one lady's arms waving aimlessly in circles, then a few rows back another lady's arm, then on the far side of the crowd a man's arm, and more and more arms waving in the air as though they were literally catching the Spirit and passing it around.

Between songs the band hardly stopped for a breath, straight from "Where the Soul of Man Never Dies" into "Mansion on the Hill" into "The Great Beyond," then halfway through "Pass Me Not, O Gentle Savior" an old man on the front row stood up, turned toward the crowd and started preaching. For a second the music and the preaching went on together, neither one winning out, then Lester saw what was happening and stopped singing and held up his hand. The band died away with him, and there was only the preacher, his right hand drawing halos in the air, his white hair falling into his eyes, the crowd's whole attention focused on his voice, his hand, and the little red Testament he waved above his head. He was cranking up on the Word, hands waving all through the crowd, an Amen from the back, and another Amen. Then just as suddenly as it all began, the preacher, a little groggy, a little stunned with the Spirit, stopped mid-sentence and sat down. The Nashville Grass started up exactly where they'd left off, and Lester sang on.

That was Billy's only memory of Lester Flatt, but it was a solid one. And it was one of the reasons that all afternoon, between records, he kept coming back to the one gospel album he had by Flatt and Scruggs, an album called "When the Saints Go Marching In." After a while he gave up on the other records altogether and listened to that album two or three times straight, then found himself coming back to one song, the last cut on the second side, a song called "Who Will Sing For Me?" It was an old song about a man who sings at the funerals of his family and friends. Then one day all those relatives and friends are gone, and he wonders about being left all by himself in the world. When I'm called to cross that silent sea, who will sing one song for me?

Billy listened to that song over and over, the stereo turned up as loud as he could stand it. Oft I sing for my friends when death's cold hand I see, but when I'm called who will sing one song for me? He listened to that song eight or nine times, trying to catch what it was in Lester's voice that made every word so real. He listened to it until Jean finally walked upstairs and, without a word, switched off the turntable. That was the moment Billy first understood the incredible sadness of those lyrics.

Halfway through a typical Saturday night: "Billy in the Low Ground," "The Wild Side of Life," "Swinging Doors," "Blue Eyes Crying in the Rain," "Alabama Jubilee," "Moving On," "Tonight the Bottle Let Me Down," "Whiskey River," "Sing Me Back Home," "Together Again," "For the Good Times," "Rag Time Annie" . . . .

The room is more than packed. Billy has a headache. The beer, the smoke, the red lights coming off the floor, the white lights coming off the ceiling. In the back of the room a waitress drops a glass. Somebody is shouting. Nobody pays much attention. It feels like ninety-five, sweat from Billy's forearm rolling down the face of his Martin. Another glass breaks behind the bar, the office door slams, Sarah Libby Cook slides a pitcher of beer onto a table. The office door slams again, Billy starts "Bully of the Town" too fast but grits his teeth and goes on, a guy whistles in the dark, he thinks it's good. The door opens and a couple walks in, they stand by the door and wait. Somebody in the far dark is slapping his hand on a table, other hands are clapping, glasses sliding up and down the bar. All the beer taps are open, trays hitting the tables, glasses scooping through crushed ice. Billy's head throbs, his shoulder catching fire, a cramp working into his hand, the song not wanting to end, the crowd not wanting it to end, and then it does anyway. A whistle, another whistle, a couple of whoops, some applause, a shuffling of chairs. A guy at the bar shouts, "If I don't hear some Kenny Rogers, I'm going home." Billy scoots up on the stool and points the way to the door.

Late Sunday morning Billy woke up to a ringing telephone. Jean answered it in the kitchen. Yes, we had a fine time. No, I've been up for hours. That sounds truly inviting. No, not at all. I'm sure she'd love it. A chance to dress, look smart in the provinces. Just about anytime would be fine. What night is that again? No, sometime in the early afternoon might be better. Let me write that down. Not yet, but he should be soon. Sure, I'll be glad to. And you.

When she hung up the phone, a cabinet door closed. Then the door of the fridge opened and closed, and her footsteps clicked across the kitchen floor and faded into the dining room carpet. Billy sat up in bed and waited for his head to clear, then he swung out and slipped into some jeans.

A few people were already on the pond, four or five kids fishing from the bank at the end of the west cove and a guy anchored in a canoe about midway between the center and the far bank. Billy stood for a minute by the window and slipped on the shirt he found hanging across the back of the rocker. Clear sky, bright sun, it looked like a nice day to fish. Not a good day to catch fish, too hot for that. But a good day to sit around the bank or in the jon boat, nurse a beer, hang out a line. He thought about that possibility, then he raised the window. It was was already too hot to catch anything but a sunstroke.

When he found Jean in the living room, she was down on her hands and knees, dusting the legs of an end table. He stood in the doorway until she noticed him.

"Top of a very fine morning," she said.

"You're certainly cheery."

"The world isn't always a funeral procession, you know."

"It is when you have a headache. Was that Jack on the phone?"

"We're going out Thursday night. You don't mind, do you?"

"Why should I?"

"There's a Tennessee Williams play at school. It ought to be fairly interesting. I can't believe they'll pull it off."

"Why not?"

"*Cat on a Hot Tin Roof?* Give me a break. I think there's some Bufferin in the upstairs bathroom. Want me to have a look?"

"It'll pass."

"Why didn't you say something about the play?"

"Like what?"

"Like Jack planning to call. He said he'd mentioned it to you."

"Why spoil a surprise?"

"I thought about going but couldn't get up for it. But now that I've got somebody to go with. And Marilyn's coming down too, so it should be fun."

"So you called her?"

"This morning. You don't mind, of course."

He felt something sink inside him, it felt like five requests coming from the back of The Under Thing. He didn't say anything, only watched her dust the shelf under the table, then up one of the legs and around the edges of the top. She sat a coaster and an ashtray on the carpet, dusted the front of the table top, slid the lamp forward and dusted the other half. "Listen," she said. "I have some little things for you to do today if you feel like it."

"For instance?"

"For instance, the yard." She sat the coaster and the ashtray on the table, pushed back the lamp, and gave him a look. "You know, I'm having a pretty decent day. You aren't going to spoil it, are you?"

"All I said was 'for instance'."

"So, for instance the yard. It hasn't been mowed in two weeks. It's going back to the wilderness. And I'd like you to edge it this time too. And trim the tops of the redbuds, especially in front of the porch. They look awful."

"Is all of this terrifically urgent, or can it wait till this afternoon when the heat lifts?"

"Yes, I suppose it can wait. But let's not keep putting it off, okay?"

He pointed to the glass sitting on the mantle. "Is that Coke?" She nodded that it was, and he walked over, picked it up, and took a swallow. It was a little warm. "So when is Marilyn coming?"

"She's driving down Thursday morning. So sometime tomorrow or the day after I'd like you to help me shampoo the carpets. I thought we could rent one of those steam cleaners from Eckerd's."

"You think that's really necessary?"

She gave him a quick glance. "I think it is. The carpets are due for a good cleaning."

"Those things are such a pain. You know that."

"I know I'd like to have the house looking nice. Is that all right? How many people are ever over here to see it?"

"Sure," he said. "It's all right. It's fine."

She sat the Pledge and the dust cloth on the table, stood up, and brushed her hands on her jeans. "And I want to clean both bathrooms and polish the bed. And your tub is a disaster. It looks more like a toilet."

He finished the last of the Coke and sat the glass back on the mantle. "Sure."

"And I thought you might take down the curtains in the guest room. I'd like to air it out and have them cleaned."

"The guest room? Isn't that overplaying it just a little?"

She reached over to the mantle and picked up the empty glass. "I didn't hear that." She walked halfway across the room, stopped and turned around. "Jack wanted you to phone him this afternoon. Something about shooting guns or some other macho business."

Billy shrugged, walked into the kitchen and poured himself a bowl of Cheerios. He sat down at the kitchen table and watched the action on the pond. The kids on the bank were huddled under the shade of the pines, but the guy in the canoe was out there for the sun. He had taken off his shirt and stretched out across the bottom of the canoe, his legs drapped over one of the benches and his head propped up on a flotation cushion. He didn't care whether he caught any fish or not. Billy envied that, the shift of body weight and the easy rocking, the careless drift.

When he finished the cereal, he rinsed the bowl in the sink and stacked it in the dishwasher. Then he gave Jack a call, no answer.

The grass was dry and the front yard went easily enough, and Billy felt good too. He'd gotten some work done in the afternoon, had spent some good time upstairs with the stereo and on the porch with the guitar. All of that netted him maybe a half a dozen new tunes. He'd play a new song through and imagine Jerry Lamberti sitting at his table at The Under Thing. If Jerry nodded, the song stayed in the set. If not, it went. Billy had gone through ten or twelve songs, and in his head five or six had passed the Lamberti test. Good songs, the old country and western, the pure stuff, not the watered-down commercial stuff on the radio. Tunes by Hank Snow and Ernest Tubb, and one great old song by Jimmy Martin. There's no such thing as sleep for a jealous fool, and being jealous about someone like you is sort of foolish too. Heartfelt, Billy thought.

The back yard took longer because he had to mow the bank beside the pond, which meant he had to stop every ten or fifteen feet to pick up rocks and chunk them into the shallows. He finished that around seven-thirty, swapped the lawn mower for the step ladder and clippers and trimmed the shrubs beside the porch. By that time he was tired enough to think twice about the edging. Besides, the sun was almost down, and the house lights across the pond were cutting through the pines and floating off the surface of the water. Billy thought the water was always a little eerie then, as though something were buried down there and glowing up from the bottom, and the pond seemed almost beautiful, all the banks being smudged away in the dark until there was only a patch of water speckled with vague elongated lights quivering under the wind. In the summer this wasn't the best time to fish because the water hadn't had time enough to cool. The best time was very late at night, or early in the morning, but this was the time when Billy most liked to be on the water, when the stars began to snap on one at a time over the roof tops and the pines. He took his rod and tackle box from the corner, lifted a paddle from the rack on the wall, and walked down to the boat.

5

Two hundred yards off the gravel he began to hear it. First a crisp hammer rap twisting up through the trees, then a sharper whack, whack, whack, like the sound of a whip. He edged the truck down the hill and into the clearing, and the firing stopped. The Jeep was parked beside the shed and a canoe was tied to the end of the dock, but there was no sign of Jack.

Billy parked the truck behind the Jeep and blew the horn. After a few seconds he blew it again, this time heavy and long. Still no sign of Jack, only the wind coming up off the lake and blowing a few sheets of newspaper off the picnic table. Billy hit the horn again, and this time Jack came out of the trees below the house. He didn't say anything, only waved Billy over with the target he held in his hand.

Billy got out of the truck and followed him around the house and into a small clearing that bordered the lake. Here Jack had sunk two creosote poles into the ground, the distance between them about the width of a crosstie, then another pair six or seven feet away. He'd dropped nine or ten crossties between them and bolted each pair together at the top to keep them from separating. Billy thought the backstop looked something like the wall of a small fort, some remarkably preserved ruin of the Civil War or some obscure Indian conflict. Against this wall Jack had hung two clean white targets, each with a black bull's eye in the center.

"Looks like you already got it finished," Billy said.

"Well, we got a little eager, but this is only half of it. We hauled this thing over three and four at a time last night in the Jeep. Got a little dangerous going down the highway with five feet of crosstie hanging out the back, so we decided we'd better wait on the truck."

"And the rest are still over at Nolan's?"

"Down by his fence. He's had these things for nearly a year. Bought them at some nursery to use in his yard, then never got around to it."

They walked over to the metal table Jack had set up in front of the targets. On the table lay a towel, a pair of hearing protectors, three or four riddled targets, two automatic pistols, and a revolver. On one target Jack had taken a pencil and drawn circles around groups of bullet holes, then marked the distance they were shot from.

"They make a great wall," he said. "You can fire just about anything you want into it. Anything from a handgun, anyway." He picked up the revolver, checked the cylinder, and eased it back into place. "Here," he said. "You want to squeeze off a few rounds before I clean these things?"

It was a heavy pistol with a six-inch ribbed barrel, and oddly enough Billy did want to shoot it. Something about the gun fascinated him. He'd grown up with rifles and shotguns, but a pistol was a novelty. He couldn't remember ever having shot one.

"Makes you sort of feel like holding up a gas station, doesn't it?"

Jack turned and gave him a long look. "Not with that, no. But if you're interested I could show you something else."

"No, I'll let it pass."

"That's a Colt Diamondback. In a .22 long rifle it's a good all-around plinker and a decent enough target gun. It'll shoot into an inch at twenty-five yards. A good squirrel hunter, but you wouldn't want to use it for anything else."

"I'm really not much with handguns."

"I thought you were a country boy."

"We didn't hunt much with pistols. It's a little easier to hit a rabbit with a shotgun."

"Everybody ought to learn how to shoot a pistol. Basic self-defense."

"Jean wanted to take a course once, but she got distracted."

"Well, I don't imagine she'd have much trouble learning. Seems like she can handle herself."

Billy looked at the gun. "Jean? No, that's the actress in her. She's about the most insecure person I know." He held the pistol at arm's length and tried to steady the barrel. "So, how far is that?"

"Twenty yards, maybe. A good pistol shot."

Billy dropped his arm, leaned against the edge of the table to steady his stance, then raised the pistol again.

"Okay," Jack said. "Take your finger completely off the trigger."

Billy lifted his finger and held it against the trigger guard.

"All right, now take your left hand and cock the hammer."

He cocked it.

"Good," Jack said. "Now get a solid grip with your right hand. Not so that it's uncomfortable, but a good firm grip. Then wrap your left hand around your right and let your left thumb rest on top of your right thumb. Okay, can you line up the sights?"

He could see the target wobbling off the end of the barrel. "How much of the front sight do I need to see?"

"The top of the back sight and the top of the front sight should make an even plane. Line it up like that and let the center of the bull's eye sit right on top of it."

"Okay," he said.

"Take a deep breath, let it out very slowly, and squeeze the —"

Whack! The pistol jumped, Billy's ears rang like a church bell on a clear morning. He let the gun hang at his side and tried to see where he'd hit the target. He couldn't see the hole.

"That's damn good," Jack said. "You're about five o'clock in the black. See if you can do that again."

"For a .22 that thing makes some noise."

"Here." Jack picked up the hearing protectors and cupped them over Billy's ears. Then he pointed toward the target.

Billy raised the pistol and went through all the steps again. This time he saw his shot immediately. It was nearly a foot to the right of the first hole.

"You rushed it a little," Jack said. "And you tensed up trying to keep the barrel steady."

Billy eased off the hearing protectors and let them hang around his neck. "I what?"

"You tensed up trying to steady the barrel."

"It's a little hard to hold it still."

"Well, forget that. You'll never be able to hold it still. Your job is to control the movement, then squeeze the shot off at the right time. Try it again, and this time let your sights rock just a little under the target. And when you feel like you're controlling the barrel swing, start squeezing it off."

Billy cupped the hearing protectors back over his ears, raised the pistol and aimed at the bull's eye. He took a deep breath, let it out slowly, and started to squeeze, the barrel rocking just a little under the black circle. Whack! It went off before he was ready, but it was a better shot. About an inch or so below the first one. He sat the pistol back down on the table and pulled off the protectors.

"Not bad," Jack said. "You might get the hang of it. We may even make you a charter member of The Greater Talquin Target and Hunt Club. And that's a very exclusive membership."

"Is that right?" Billy said. "Who belongs to it?"

"So far, you and me and Nolan."

Nolan Hughes. Not what you might expect if you'd seen any of his movies. A little shorter than you might have imagined. Five-nine or -ten, but well built. Very bright blue eyes, almost cold. Dark hair, disheveled in an arty sort of way, and graying around the temples. A sort of kid's face that had recently started to weather. A dimple in his chin. Great teeth.

Actually, Billy hadn't known what to expect. He'd seen Nolan Hughes only on television, the commercials for Country's Barbecue and Pharr Toyota. Nolan kicking off a black Harley Sportster, a barbecued rib between his teeth. Nolan slapping the hood of a red Toyota wagon. Don't talk car till you see Pharr. 2121 Tennessee Street.

The house was a huge brick ranch house that sat on a corner lot in the middle of Weston Fields, the yard as green as a dollar bill, a solid acre sprinkled with pink dogwoods, a split rail fence crawling with rosebuds separating Nolan from his neighbors.

Billy stopped in the street in front of the house, backed the truck up the driveway, and parked it in front of the garage.

"Blow the horn," Jack said.

He hit it once, and almost immediately the door of the garage went up. The first thing Billy noticed was the Porsche, jet black and polished like a trooper's boot. Then the black Harley parked next to it.

"The barbecue bike," he said.

Jack winked. "He fancies himself something of an outlaw. The local bikers let him ride around with them on Sundays. Good for his image. Theirs too."

"The Generals?"

"Might be. Some car club, bike club."

Nolan Hughes stepped into the driveway and pointed toward the side of the house. "Pull up," he said, "and back it through the yard."

Billy pulled up a little in the driveway, then eased back onto the grass. A huge patio opened up right behind the garage and ran almost the entire length of the house, and at the far end of the patio was an oval-shaped pool. He backed through a stand of dogwoods, across the back yard, and stopped beside the fence where the crossties lay piled against two of the fence posts. Then he cut the engine and they got out.

Nolan came out a back door and onto the patio. He took a box from the table beside the pool and headed across the yard. Billy watched close for a limp, but Nolan looked like he could march all day in any man's army. When he reached the truck he shifted the box to his left hand and held out his right. Billy shook it.

"Nolan," Jack said. "Billy Parker. Billy, Nolan Hughes."

"You a shooter?" Nolan said.

"Not much of one."

"He's a better guitar player," Jack said. "But he shows some promise, already talking about holding up gas stations."

"Is that right?"

"Not really," Billy said. "I think I'll just stick to the music."

"Right, Jack told me you were playing around here."

"At The Under Thing."

"Sure, I know where it is. Just a couple of blocks from the theater." He handed the box to Jack. "Here's that Walther. I haven't even put a fingerprint on it."

"The P-5?"

"What do you think?"

Jack opened the box, pulled back the rag the pistol was wrapped in. It was a black automatic with dark wooden grips. "I think you may have bought yourself a fine piece. What'd you give for it?"

"Two-fifty. Not bad, huh?"

Jack raised his eyebrows and gave him a look. "I wouldn't be planning on registering it anywhere, you wouldn't look good in stripes."

Nolan shook his head. "No way, there's nothing funny about that gun. I bought it from a guy who picked it up at a trade show."

"One of your biker buddies?"

Nolan looked at him and smiled. "Absolutely not."

Jack only stared at him for a few seconds. He looked like he might say something, but he let it slide.

"Shoot it a few times," Nolan said. "I'm anxious to see how it handles that flat nose."

Jack took a deep breath and looked back down at the pistol. "So you're not coming out today?"

"Like I said, I'd like to but I've got dress rehearsal tonight. And I've got to get over there right now and check on the set."

Jack gave him another look. "Otherwise the whole show'll fall apart, the theater department collapse, and the School of Fine Arts crumble like a squashed cracker."

Nolan smiled. "You guys are coming to the opening, aren't you?"

"I'll be in Atlanta," Billy said. "But Jack'll be there with a woman on each arm."

"At least that, and I may try to pick up another one somewhere. Hate to waste that fourth ticket." He pressed the top back onto the box and wedged it under his arm.

Nolan turned to Billy. "Maybe you can catch the show next week, we'll run through the first. Shows every night. Anyhow, we'll for sure do some shooting, and I'll straighten out all the misconceptions this guy's given you about pistols."

"He thinks he knows something about handguns," Jack said.

Nolan pointed his finger like a barrel and cocked his thumb. "True enough," he said. "Pistols, handguns, pieces, rods, heaters, those beautiful instruments of power and destruction, the artifice and the physics of death, the embodiment in cold steel of the power of God, the Grim Reaper forged into a barrel and a cylinder, the only absolute a man can wrap his fist around. Yeah, I know something about handguns."

Jack reached through the window of the truck and tossed the pistol onto the seat. Then he turned back to Nolan. "You think you could neglect your career long enough to help us load a few of these crossties?"

"I'd like to," he said. "But I'm running way late."

The moon, almost full, hung just over the tops of the pines on the south end of the island. It threw a sheet of light over the trees and onto the water, and in that light Billy could see near the bank the brown shells of turtles riding the tops of stumps. Jack hit easy strokes from the stern and pushed the canoe toward them at a quiet, steady speed. After a twenty minute crossing from Jack's dock, they were almost there, and Billy didn't see anything promising.

"Watch the top of the water," Jack said.

"For what?"

"The eyes. All you'll see is the eyes. Bright red balls riding the top of the water."

Twenty yards from the turtles, Jack stopped paddling and let the canoe drift. It cut a smooth course through the water and drifted to a stop just beyond the point of the island. Jack took his binoculars from the case and scanned the water around the bank.

"What do you see?" Billy said.

"Turtles. A few ducks bedded down on the bank. We'll slide on around to the other side."

Jack slid the glasses into the case and began to stroke the canoe easy around the edge of the island.

It was a beautiful island filled with hardwoods and pines, and just around the first bend, a stand of cypresses waded out into the water. Jack steered toward them, hitting his easy J-strokes, moving the canoe quietly over the lake.

"I don't know," Billy whispered. "I never heard of any gators around here. Maybe back up in one of these creeks."

"This is what the guy told me."

Jack stopped paddling and took the binoculars out of the case. The canoe drifted slowly toward the cypresses, and Billy watched the shallows and the bank. They moved into the narrow shadows of the trunks, then into the deeper shadows nearer the island, and the canoe bumped gently into one of the trees. Billy put his hand on the trunk and pushed them past.

"See anything?" he said.

"No. Maybe we should paddle down to Harvey's Creek."

"You sure nobody'll hear that pistol? This ain't real legal."

"You worry too much. It's only a .22." He hit a hard stroke with the paddle and the canoe moved off toward the open lake, the water growing darker with distance until it blended far off with the bank and the sky.

"Will that thing kill a gator?"

"Sure, we don't want a monster, just a small one with a fat tail."

Billy sat in the bow and enjoyed the ride. He'd offered twice to help paddle, but Jack protested. If Billy had no experience with a paddle, Jack said he could do it easier himself. That was fine. Billy sat in the bow and enjoyed the lake. And Jack didn't seem to need any help. He was good. By the time they broke around the north end of the island, he'd already worked up some speed.

"When I come back from Atlanta," Billy said, "we'll bring the jon boat out here and motor up to Fisher's Creek. People tell great bass stories about that place."

"Sounds good." Jack took a deep breath and let the canoe drift. "So how's it going, the Atlanta thing? You getting your act together?"

Billy sat quiet for a second and stared out over the water. "I don't know," he said. "It just gets harder and harder to get into it."

"I know what you mean," Jack said. "I felt the same way about the army."

6

He was in a jon boat on a river. It was a narrow river, and the sun shot down like rain through the trees and trapped itself between the fog and the water so that he and his father were trolling their lines through a tunnel of orange light. The Johnson motor gave off a quiet electric hum and rippled the water behind the boat. Billy watched his father hold the tiller under his elbow and guide his line around the snags and underbrush. The air had a dark moist smell that reminded him of the black dirt worms were boxed in, or the damp walls of a dirt cellar. It chilled his nostrils and the back of his throat. He looked down at his fingers, the tips were purple under the nails. He wedged the rod between his knees and slipped his hands under his legs.

The boat cruised down the tunnel of light, the trees on the banks leaned out over the water. The fog hung like a gold roof between the trees, and suddenly his father cut the engine. The boat slowed, caught the current and drifted on toward the sun coming up behind the trees at the end of the river. The only sound was the rustle of slow water grabbing at the bottom of the aluminum boat. Then there were the voices rising out of the light, muffled, and coming in waves through the thick orange light trapped above the river. And being on the river was like being in church, the waves of sound becoming a song caught in phrases as the boat came around sideways and his father caught an oak branch reaching out like an arm, and they hunched quietly under the wet trees as bodies sloshed down into the water where the river bent sharply and the fog opened in a great burst of yellow light that made their clothes look like gold leaf. A head went under the water and came back up. Then more of them began wading into the shallows, waving arms like wings, until they became a great bathing flock of mysterious golden birds, and the yellow light sang hallelujahs at the end of the river.

Billy has had that dream so many times he can't decide anymore whether it's based on anything real or whether it's only a fantasy he's built about his father. And he knows the dream so well that occasionally he catches himself anticipating the end and trying to extend it, as though it were a scene from some movie and he's trying to pull a few more feet of film through a jammed projector. But it always ends on the same frame, his father's arm anchoring the boat to the oak branch and the faces indistinct and the bodies all gleaming like gold and the voices ringing out through the yellow light.

The sun cut through a gap in the curtain and threw a thin screen of light across the room. Billy watched the particles of dust swimming like worms in that light, like larva skimming the surface of water. The travel clock whined from the table, and he propped up on his elbow and saw the blue ducks circling like buzzards. He swung his feet to the floor, reached for the clock, and punched the alarm. It was six-thirty.

Usually when Billy played a job out of town, he tried to catch a nap in the afternoon. A sort of boning up for the night, a way of building the resistance, of charging up enough energy to face a strange crowd. He'd done that for years, but still there was that brief sense of confusion, that moment of waking up lost. He sat for a minute on the edge of the bed and tried not to look at the walls, then he closed his eyes for a second and opened them for a long stare at the floor. But he knew where he was. He was staring at the carpet of room 205 of the Pine Top Motor Lodge on Howell Mill Road, the best cheap motel in north Atlanta. It was a red carpet, dark red, like dried blood. But it was clean, and so was the room, and the air conditioner worked, and so did the TV.

Billy had stayed at the Pine Top once before, and it wasn't bad. A little small, but comfortable enough. So he'd phoned ahead for reservations. This time the desk clerk, Arab maybe, thanked him for calling the New Pine Top Motor Lodge, which meant they'd recently done some remodeling, and the rooms were now twenty-two dollars for a single and twenty-eight for a double.

The only remodeling Billy could see was the new wallpaper, and he wasn't at all sure it justified the two dollar hike. The background was a bright sky blue, the kind of blue you might imagine the sky to be on a perfect, cloudless day in the middle of summer. But the pattern was something hard to look at, widely spaced lines of green and purple ducks, probably meant to be mallards, flying one behind another around the room, so that if you looked at one of them your eyes wanted to jump ahead to the next and then to the next, and of course if you did that, you found that the ducks were spinning you around in circles.

Billy stood up and shook the fog out of his head. He looked again at the clock, then he remembered that he'd promised to check in with Jean before the show. The phone was behind the lamp on the night table. He picked up the receiver, dialed a nine to get a long distance line, and the desk clerk came on and asked for his room number.

It rang once, twice, then a third time. On the seventh ring Billy was ready to hang up.

"Hello. Parker residence." Her voice was full and throaty.

"So you got there all right," he said.

"Bill? Certainly, no problems at all. I pulled in around one-thirty. The Benz just hummed on down, and how have things been with you?"

"Good enough," he said. "Can I talk with Jean?"

"Jean is looking simply luscious, isn't she? I'm delighted to see she's doing so well. Tallahassee has been a real tonic for her."

Was that sarcasm? Marilyn was always so matter-of-fact, everything so understated, that he sometimes had trouble telling when her tongue had an edge. After a day or so he'd remember something she'd said and how she'd said it, and suddenly he'd notice his ego bleeding puddles on the carpet.

He wondered what sort of expression she was wearing. And whether or not she had her hand propped on her hip the way she sometimes posed. Or, if she was sitting down, did she have her legs crossed? Was she bending her ankle and admiring her arch?

"Yes," he said. "Jean does seem to be doing very well. Could I speak to her?"

"Listen, Bill. Don't you think Jean should do something with her hair? Wouldn't that be nice for her? It's so un-with-it, you know. I think she'd look very sophisticated in a frizz. And so does she, but she's very much afraid you might not approve."

Nothing was wrong with Jean's hair. Jean had beautiful hair, dark auburn, long and straight. And Billy liked it that way, the way it had always been. She'd never said a word about changing it.

"Listen, Marilyn—"

"I told her she was silly to think you'd mind. And her heart's just set on it now. You don't mind, of course."

"Of course not," he said. Already he was determined not to let Marilyn make him play the villain, any degree of villain. "Anything Jean wants to do with her hair or anything else is fine with me. She knows that."

"Good," she said. "Of course, you know she'll have to come to Atlanta. No one in Tallahassee could possibly work on her hair. But I have a boy at Lenox who's absolutely—"

"What?" He felt like he'd just lost some kind of kids' game, but he dropped it. "Sure," he said. "That goes without saying, doesn't it.

That's fine. Could I speak with Jean now?"

"I'm sorry, Bill, but she's just stepped into the shower. We're going out tonight, you know. Some theater thing with a friend of yours. Can I have her phone you?"

He tried not to look at the ducks. They were circling faster, trying to catch his eye, trying to get him to follow them around the room, trying to grab everything in his head that was spinning and spin it faster. But he wouldn't look, he only watched the sunlight melting through the yellow curtains, the little screen of bright light slicing across the bed.

"Yes," he said. "Have her call me when she gets out. I'm at the Pine Top Motor Lodge. Room 205. I'll be here for another hour or so." He gave her the phone number. "Did you write that down?"

"Bill," she said. "I have a wonderful memory."

When he hung up the phone he remembered another reason why he disliked Marilyn McKinley. Most things about her were a little too wonderful. Her perfection bordered on the intolerable. She was bright enough to be most anything she wanted, or so she'd lead you to believe. She was attractive enough to be a model, even at thirty-two, and she was wealthy enough to be a bitch. She was also arrogant, determined, and cagey. The cagey part bothered Billy the most. She was always careful never to upset the balance of things as long as she suspected those things might not fall her way. But it was clear to Billy that she believed he was the primary reason for Jean's self-proclaimed depressions, her boredom, her lack of self-worth, and her dreary prospects. In short, her total misery. Billy had whisked her away from Atlanta, the one haven of culture in the South, and was now holding her captive in Tallahassee, a backwash of civilization where there was no art, no music, no fashion, and most of all no night life. Little did it matter that it was Jean's notion to move there. He sensed that in an odd way Marilyn even held him responsible for that.

He slipped off his undershorts and walked into the bathroom for a shower. The Benz, that was really funny. The Benz had belonged to her ex-husband, a very rich Buckhead attorney who had bought himself a seat on the Atlanta City Council.

The Benz, that was as funny as their whole story, which was short and sour and extremely funny. Marilyn and Jean three years out of Agnes Scott and sharing an apartment in Buckhead, busting their tails at Rich's to make the rent, when Marilyn meets Roy Saunders, Attorney at Law, and wildest dream becomes reality. They romance, they marry. Four years later, Roy Saunders decides to run for city council and discovers that Marilyn's long string of indiscretions, which haven't bothered him very much before, could be, as he phrased it, a liability. Being white and rich are all the liabilities he can handle, so they divorce as suddenly as they married, and Marilyn somehow walks off with a new Mercedes diesel and a very chic dress shop in the heart of Buckhead.

He wondered what she had brought down for Jean this time. He could see the boxes piled all over the bed, Marilyn tugging at Jean's hem or fastening her necklace. Then they would both stand for fifteen minutes in front of the full-length mirror.

After Billy dried his hair and dressed, he stretched out on the bed to watch some TV and listen for Jean's call. The world beamed in on the evening news, and Dan Rather testified to the fact that the Parkers were not alone in their misery. The globe was swarming with misfortune — strikes in Poland, assassinations in Italy, war in El Salvador, Iraq, Afganistan. Billy took no comfort in the company. His misery most often loved nothing. At a quarter till eight he thought about calling home again, but he didn't. He only picked up his guitars and left for Grover's.

7

Billy has considered the tragedy of his circumstance: A truly sad thing when a man dislikes what he does to earn his living, and an even sadder thing when he is very good at what he does, even though he hates it, and continues to do it because he is good. But the saddest thing of all must be when a man is only competent at what he does, hates it, and continues to do it simply because he can't do anything else. This was the feeling that hit Billy occasionally. And this was the grief that clubbed him squarely across the shoulders when he walked into Grover's with his guitars in his hands and saw the Buckhead crowd hunkering over their mixed drinks at the tiny round tables covered with white tablecloths.

Billy felt a kind of fear and dread in this particular brand of sadness because in a very real way he sensed his own mortality. Despite anything he could do the stage became a gallows, the mikes standing right on top of the trap door. Billy, something said to him, you are not a good enough musician to live through this. And even if you slide by this time, things will never get any better. This is it for you — warm-up gigs for the big acts at the local clubs. The Gong Shows of real life, night after night of expecting the stage to drop right out from under you.

He crossed the room, walked up on the stage, and propped his guitars against the back wall. Then he went to the bar and ordered a Jameson. While the bartender poured the whiskey, Billy sat down on a stool and gave the room a good look. Frank Wiley was nowhere to be seen. Either he hadn't arrived or he was backstage in one of the dressing rooms. Or Billy didn't recognize him. That was a possibility. He'd seen him only a few times at the festivals, and that was years ago.

Billy noticed that several people were staring at him. One was a woman in a red satin jumpsuit and a black beaded belt. She was sitting at a table with three models from Jean's Bloomingdale catalog. She had short blonde hair cut above her ears and brushed straight back off her forehead, and she wore black beaded earrings that hung down almost to her shoulders. They swung back and forth as she turned her head slightly away and looked past him, as though she weren't really staring, then turned back casually for another glance.

The guy two tables over was less subtle. He stared straight at Billy, and when he saw that Billy had noticed, it didn't seem to bother him. He just kept on staring. Finally he lifted his mug of beer, took a swallow, and turned back to his girlfriend. But other people were staring too. They were giving Billy the look, what Billy called the "Is this the music?" look, the look he got a lot on the road, the look he got when people weren't quite sure what to expect and then they saw that what they were getting was only him. But Billy had gotten used to the look. He took a swallow of his Jameson.

A hand came down on his shoulder, and he turned around and saw Joe Harvey. "I was beginning to worry," Joe said. "Thought you were going to call when you hit town."

"I was beat. I took a nap and woke up late. Just got a hamburger and came on over."

"No matter. You're here. You met Frank yet?"

"No. Is he around?"

"Backstage. Get yourself another drink and come on back. I'll introduce you, and we'll go over the game plan." He rapped his knuckles on the bar, "Give this guy another drink," then walked off toward the stage.

Not a bad sort, even if he did try too hard to be with-it — designer jeans, sports jacket, yellow Grover T-shirt, what Billy liked to call contrived casual. But he could forgive that. When you manage a music club in the middle of Buckhead, you're either with-it or out quick. Imagine Leon trying to manage a place like this. Ridiculous, which was no slight at all toward Leon.

The room was filling up quickly, people coming in two and three couples at a time, standing at the door and looking around for a place to sit. Most of the tables were already taken, and it looked like it was going to be a very full house. Billy finished his Jameson and picked up the shot the bartender had left on the bar, then he slid off the stool and headed for the stage.

When he got there he could hear music coming from one of the dressing rooms. Someone was picking a fairly outstanding version of "Are You From Dixie?" Billy walked behind the speaker columns, through a beaded curtain, and into a narrow hall. The music was coming from the first door on the left. He didn't knock, only turned the knob easy and pushed back the door. The room was small and full of people, four women on a sofa against the wall, a fiddler and a bass player standing in a corner. Frank Wiley was leaning back in a beat-up easy chair, the arms ragged and the stuffing worn all the way through to the wood. And he sat like it was made for him, his body slouched down into the lumpy cushion, his hands behind his head, his legs stretched out in front of him. The guy playing guitar was sitting in a straight chair next to Wiley. He was just a kid, eighteen or nineteen years old, and he was playing a brand-new Gallagher guitar. Joe Harvey was sitting on the arm of the sofa. He motioned for Billy to come in, so Billy closed the door behind him and stood there listening to the kid wear out the Gallagher.

When the kid wrapped it up, nobody said anything. Then Wiley leaned over and slapped him on the knee.

"Frank," Joe said, pointing toward Billy. "This is Billy Parker. He's playing the opening shows tonight and tomorrow."

Wiley stood up, and Billy stepped across the room and shook his hand. He was a short guy, five-six or so, but stocky. And he had fairly large hands, a good stout grip.

"Okay," he said. He pointed to the fiddler, "Ed Pierce." Then to the bass player, "Barry Thompson."

Billy stepped up and shook hands with both of them, and Wiley pointed to the kid holding the Gallagher. "This is Barry's brother, Mike. He lives over here in Decatur. These are the girls — Sally, June, Punky, Lynn."

Joe stood up from the sofa and checked his watch. "What we need to do is come up with a game plan. Frank's going to play two sets. About what? Say fifty minutes or so?"

"Something like that," Wiley said, then sat back down in the easy chair. "Five or ten minutes of it, anyway. Depending on how it goes. But we won't cut you short."

"Well, we need to run till twelve-thirty. So if Frank takes fifteen or twenty minutes between sets that means he'll need to start around ten. We need for the music to crank up at nine sharp, so Billy'll have to carry around fifty minutes or so."

"Fine," Billy said. "No problem for me."

"Just not too long between shows," Wiley said. "Like I said, I usually like to come out right on top of somebody. Folks don't like to wait much between acts. They won't mind it too much between sets, but when they have to wait on the main act, they'll get restless."

"Ten minutes is okay, isn't it?" Joe checked his watch again. "People need a chance to make a pit stop and order a drink."

"Ten is great, fifteen might be too long."

"Good enough. We'll run a tight show. It's about eight-thirty now." He looked over at Billy. "You need anything?"

"Nothing I can think of."

"Good enough. How about that P.A.? Any help with that?"

"I think I can handle it."

"Okay. At nine sharp I'll do a quick intro and we'll go from there. Break a leg."

But what he broke was a string. Joe Harvey walked across the stage and stood in front of the microphone. "Ladies and gentlemen," he said. "Please give a big Grover's welcome to Mr. Billy Parker." Then a round of applause as Billy crossed the stage, strummed a C chord into the mike, and started picking "Billy in the Lowground." All the way through the first part clean as a bell, and halfway through the bridge the B string popped. Not such a tragedy if you're singing something, but you don't flatpick a fiddle tune with five strings, so Billy had to stop cold, put down the guitar, and finish the tune on the D-28. That was a sign. He'd seen a hundred nights begin with something like that and just get worse, and there was nothing to do but tighten his neck against the noose and go right on. So he did, and he played a very uneventful fifty minutes of music, including five or six of the old country and western tunes he'd worked up. Polite applause.

When he got to the bar, he sat on the only empty stool and ordered a Jameson. He felt low, only an inch or two from walking right back up on stage, getting his guitars, and going back to the motel. But he wanted to leave the place just a little less than he wanted to go back up on that stage. And he couldn't leave the Martins, so he just sat on the bar stool and sipped the whiskey.

When Wiley's bass player and fiddler came out for a mike check, the room fell as quiet as a grave. Billy remembered what it was like to walk out on the stage at a festival and watch the whole crowd come to attention. It was something that could send a chill through you, an expectation so intense it could freeze you solid, and you'd stand there like a block of ice, waiting for the first note to thaw you out. It was the best kind of fright he knew.

Joe Harvey walked out again and stood in front of the center mike. All he said was "The Frank Wiley Group," and there was a roar of applause, the real stuff, and out came Wiley with a Martin as dark as a Hershey bar. The fiddler went right into a tune called "Cattle in the Cane," a nice old up-tempo piece that swings into a minor on the bridge. He played it through twice, then Wiley cut into it on the Martin. His playing was flawless, every note crisp and clean, perfectly timed. Billy sat up on the bar stool and gave it some attention. It was the kind of playing he called human, an effortless and natural quality about it. None of the mechanical sound you hear in most flatpickers, pickers who are just playing the notes and trying to get them fast and right. It didn't take long to hear that Wiley was playing the music, and he was enjoying it. He wasn't trying to impress anybody by sticking in every hot lick he knew. He was just playing it the way he wanted to hear it, the way it made him happy to hear it. And he was making everybody in the room happy to hear it that way too.

Wiley wrapped it up, and before the applause had died out the fiddler went into something else, a slower tune Billy had never heard, a waltz. He wanted to move up closer to take a look at Wiley's guitar, but he resisted. He thought it was a D18, but it was hard to tell.

They played a few more tunes before Wiley sang one, an old Gid Smith song called "Otto Wood, the Bandit." It was clear from the first note why Wiley never sang much. He had one of those voices that folk music people call "authentic." But what did impress Billy was his restraint, he never tried to do more with it than he could.

After another fiddle tune, Wiley called out the kid. He came onto the stage with the Gallagher in one hand and a Gibson A-style mandolin in the other. Wiley took the mandolin from him, then laid his Martin down on the stage. He bent the goose-neck on his voice mike and slid it over in front of the kid's guitar. The kid tapped the mike once to see how hot it was, then he went straight into "Blackberry Blossom," a little too fast, but clean enough. He played it through once, then the fiddler played it. Then Wiley played it on the mandolin with all the ease and taste he had shown on guitar. This was supposed to be the kid's spot, his time to shine for a few minutes with the big boys, but Wiley couldn't help stealing the show. Not that he was trying to. He was laying back, just playing the music, but he was too good, even when he wasn't trying to be. If there ever was such a thing as a natural, he was it.

They played another tune, then the kid went off to a round of applause, the real stuff. Wiley and the fiddler played two more, a polka and a waltz, and that was the set. People were standing at the tables around the stage, drunks were hooting and whistling. It was the genuine stuff and it went on for a while.

Billy decided not to order another Jameson and ordered the first of several beers. He was halfway through it when he felt the hand on his shoulder again.

"Good set," Joe said. "I heard most of it from the wings."

"Thanks." Billy felt the hand fall away and he turned on the stool.

"How about that Frank? Is he something?"

"Amazing, all right."

"I've got to get him down here for a whole week. And do some radio spots. I didn't do one radio spot for this gig, just the papers. And, hell, look at the place. Maybe around November. You too. You come up and do the opening sets. How about that?"

"I don't know," Billy said. "That's a while off. Let me know if it all works out."

"What's to know? You come back up and do the first set. You make some money. What's to know?"

"Sure," he said. "What's to know?"

"Listen." Joe slapped him again on the shoulder. "After we close tonight there's a little party. A few of us, a few of the girls. Hang around."

"Maybe. I'm kind of beat."

"No, you hang around. You look like you could use a good time." He pointed his finger at Billy and started to walk off. "You hang around."

But Billy didn't feel like hanging around. And as the next set went

71

by, he felt like it even less. He kept thinking to himself, Billy, you need to get with a group again. Get yourself a mandolin player or a fiddler. Some variety, a fuller sound. At least, find yourself a bass player. No, that's not what you need to do. He knew what he needed to do. He just didn't know what he'd do after that.

After Wiley closed out the second set, Billy waited at the bar for things to die down. A few people left right away, others sat finishing their drinks. But before long, the place started to clear, and Billy walked up on the stage to pick up his Martins. A lot of noise was coming from the rooms backstage, some laughter, a half scream, a terrible screeching fiddle. He didn't even go back to see what was happening. His head was spinning a little from the Jameson and the beer, and he just wanted to lie down in a friendly place and close his eyes.

Half an hour later Billy opened the door of the motel room and sat the guitars on the floor. When he switched on the light, the ducks went crazy, flocks of them flying around and around on the blue walls. He steadied himself against the dresser, closed the door, and looked down at the carpet. His head was wobbling, so he sat down on the edge of the bed and propped his elbows on his knees and sat there for five or six minutes just staring at the toes of his boots, the only things in the room that would keep still. Then he shifted from his boots back to the carpet, then to the leg of the chair, and the shock of it all began to pass, and he learned how to look around the room without seeing the ducks.

Twenty minutes on the bed made him feel better, then something like loneliness struck. He switched on the TV to hear somebody talk and found an old western, Walter Brennan and Gary Cooper. He lay back on the bed, closed his eyes, and fell into a half-dream of gunshots and hoof beats, the creak of wagons. In one of the wagons a baby cried. Billy's heart sank. The baby wailed, and he remembered something Jean said once and the way she said it, so matter-of-fact, so much like Marilyn, standing at the bottom of the stairs, her hands in her back pockets, her lips cocked in a half-smile. Billy, she's smiling at you. Yes, she meant what she said, even if she said it like a tease. You're not holding a monopoly on what it takes. But God, Billy, you did it once, didn't you?

He woke up like you wake up from a nightmare. The clock said one-thirty. Odds were good they'd still be up. He sat up on the bed and reached for the phone, then he thought better of it. What if he woke them up? He thought for another second. So what if he did? He dialed for an outside line, then dialed his number. When it started to ring, he stretched the phone cord across the room and turned down the TV.

"Hello," Jean said. She was laughing and trying to choke back the laugh. "Hello?" she said again.

"Jean."

"Hi," she said.

"Didn't Marilyn tell you I called?"

"Yes, she did. Of course, she did. I meant to get back but we were so pressed. We were really running very late. Didn't think you'd mind." The noise in the background sounded like the laugh track for a television sitcom.

"So what's going on?" he said. "What are you up to?"

"I'm not up to anything. Why do you assume I'm up to something?"

"I wasn't assuming anything. I was just wondering what you're doing. Is that all right?"

"Then why do you say it that way?"

"What way?" he said. "I was just wondering what you're doing?"

"Oh," she said. There was a pause on the line, then her voice went cheery again. "Well, right now I'm smoking something very dark and Cuban."

"You're what?"

"I think it's called a panatela. And I'm drinking a glass of very dry champagne. I can't remember the name. You want me to look at the bottle?"

"So where did you get Cuban cigars?"

"Your friend Jack, of course. Where else does one get such

73

delicacies?" The noise in the background swelled again. "We're having a little party. Can you hear?"

"Sounds more like a riot."

"No, Baby. Just a little get-together. People gather in one place, you know. They have drinks. They talk. They laugh."

"Who's over there? Is Jack over there?"

"Let me see," she said. "I'm looking around. Okay, there's Jack. Yes, he's here. And there's Brick. And there's Marilyn. God, you should see Marilyn. She's wearing the most delicious black dress. And there's Big Daddy. And there's Nolan. And—"

"Who the hell is Brick?" he said. "Are you sure you aren't smoking something else?"

"No, Baby, just the cigar. Brick's in the cast. So's Big Daddy. The cast party split about three ways. We ended up over here. God, the play. The play was wonderful. You missed the very best play in the world. I'm so sorry you missed the best play in the world."

"Listen, don't make yourself sick. You know what'll happen if you drink too much of that carbonated booze."

"Don't be such a straight arrow, Billy. I'm having a good time. It that all right?"

"That's great. Have a good time. I want you to have a good time. But don't make yourself sick."

"Enough of the lecture," she said. "How was the club? Did everything go all right?"

"I wasn't lecturing."

"So you weren't," she said. "How was the club?"

"It went fine. Things couldn't have been better."

"Good. Now don't you feel a little better about it all?"

"Sure," he said. "He wants me to come back sometime in November and open for a week."

"Wonderful. That'll be a nice check. And how was the other guy? Was he all right?"

"He was fine," he said. "Just about what I expected."

"What about the crowd?"

"Full house. Standing room only."

"Any beautiful women cruising around?"

"A few, I guess."

"And you didn't pick up any lookers?"

"Only two," he said. "A couple of Japanese girls, twins. One of them's massaging my feet right now."

"Sounds yummy. Look, Baby, I'm being awfully bad. I've got to get off the phone."

"Don't be too bad."

"Of course not."

"Listen," he said. "I think I miss you."

"Me too."

"Tell Jack I said hello."

"Truly," she said. "See you Saturday. No need to phone again. Everything here is fine."

Light streaked into the room through the gap in the curtain, a bright light full of dust. Billy had a slight headache and his stomach felt hollow as a cave. He remembered the rows of circling ducks and dreaded sitting up. But he took the room slow and when things seemed stable enough—the back of a chair, the clock, the phone, the corner of the night stand—he tried the walls and found the ducks lying still against the blue wallpaper, a good sign. He looked again at the clock, it said eleven-thirty. He supposed he had a right to be hungry.

He walked over to the window and opened the curtain. The sky was a bright blue, the same blue as the walls of the room, and what he could see of it between the roof of the motel and the pines across the parking lot was perfectly clear. That was something else to be glad for, and it made him feel a little better about the day.

He thought he'd like to spend the afternoon outside. Maybe drive around Atlanta for a while, see if anything had changed, and he could look for something to take home to Jean. That was an old habit. Whenever he'd go out of town, even for a day, he'd try to bring back something for Jean. Never anything large or expensive, just something, a gesture. It was sort of a game he played with himself, a game with only one rule. He had to buy something meaningful, whatever that might be. For instance, once he was playing a weekend in Charleston, and he came across an old bookstore. He bought Jean a book called *Maida's Little House*. There was a old series of Maida books, something like Nancy Drew or the Hardy Boys, and when she was a kid Jean had read just about every one of them. But they had all been lost somehow, or given away, or thrown away, and Billy found one in the bookstore in Charleston. He thought he'd walked into the house with a box full of gold.

Today he'd drive down to the tenth street area and check out the Old New York Bookstore, one of Jean and Marilyn's old haunts, a storehouse of used and out-of-print books. Over the last couple of years, Jean had gotten heavily into mystery novels and had read everything she could find by women writers. At the Old New York he might run across something strange and out of the way. If he didn't, he'd prowl north up Peachtree until another idea struck. That wouldn't be too painful.

He'd been inside only a couple of times, and always with Jean, but it was still the way Billy remembered it, an old white frame house with a rotten front porch. The parking lot in front of the store would hold only five or six cars, but it was empty, so Billy whipped in under one of the big oaks that stretched out over Juniper Street. He locked the truck, walked up the brick steps, and crossed the porch.

Other than the guy at the desk, a red-headed guy with glasses, the front room was empty. He looked up from the paper he was reading and pushed back his chair. "Anything special?"

"Mysteries," Billy said.

"Straight back, all the way to the end."

Billy walked down the hall past an office, a bathroom, three rooms full of books, and into the room marked science fiction and mystery. There were literally three walls of mystery titles, and for a second he was truly excited. Here was a room full of treasure. Then all the books became overwhelming and he began to see that he really didn't know what to buy. There were simply too many of them for anything to seem special, and he realized too that if he recognized a writer's name, odds were good that Jean had already read it. He spent a solid half hour fretting through the stacks before he finally decided to take a chance. He bought two books by writers he recognized. Better that than going home with something totally bizarre, so he left with *The Singing Sands* by Josephine Tey and *More Work for the Undertaker* by Margery Allingham. Both copies were a little battered and looked like they might have been book club editions, but if Jean hadn't read them, she wouldn't mind.

By the time he got to the truck, he was worried again. And when he refigured the odds, they seemed incredibly against him. Okay, maybe he'd stumble across something at Lenox Square. He wanted to drive up there anyway to check out a couple of record stores, see if he could pick up a copy of one of Wiley's albums.

He headed south down Juniper, a one way street, took a right on Eleventh, then turned north onto Peachtree. When he rolled down the window, the cab of the truck filled up with restaurant smells. Someone was cooking Italian and baking bread. Two or three blocks of those good smells, then a traffic light caught him, and the air turned to gasoline fumes and carbon monoxide.

He kept thinking about the mysteries and what else he might find for Jean. A scarf? Earrings? But that was Marilyn's territory, and he never intruded there. It was too well covered and his taste was no match for Marilyn's, so he never bought her clothes or jewelry. In fact, Jean hardly ever bought any clothes herself, maybe a pair of shoes or a dress to wear around the house, but never anything she would go out in. Marilyn was the picture of fashion, so Jean let her do most of that buying for her.

The cars ahead pulled off slowly and Billy cruised under the light. On his left he passed the High Museum, another spot Jean and Marilyn used to frequent from time to time. A huge new billboard on the corner of the grounds said:

Pepe Romero, guitar, with Atlanta Symphony,
Robert Shaw conducting
8:30, Symphony Hall
Tickets all Seats Locations

Pepe Romero? Billy wondered what he was going to play. What if it was the Concerto de Aranjuez? The Christmas after they were married, Jean had given Billy a recording of Pepe Romero playing the Concerto de Aranjuez with The London Symphony. It was the first time he'd ever really listened to classical guitar, and the music and the playing were so beautiful they actually disturbed him. It was an incredibly dangerous and thrilling kind of beauty, something brand-new and strangely different from any feeling he'd ever experienced. But it was a beauty he couldn't resist, and since then he'd bought every Romero recording he could put his hands on—the brothers Pepe, Celin, Angel, and their father Celedonio, all incredible musicians. Now the strangest irony. He was playing in the same city at the same time as Pepe Romero.

Billy wondered if Frank Wiley had ever heard anyone like Pepe Romero. How many country or folk guitar players had ever really listened to a guitarist of that caliber? Maybe more than he thought. Didn't Doc Watson say he had learned a lot from the records of Django Reinhardt? But that's different, much different. Maybe a few have, but not many. How could you hear something as beautiful as Rodrigo's Concerto de Aranjuez and ever be satisfied playing "Black Mountain Rag?" Except that you had to keep playing "Black Mountain Rag" because a very good version of that or "Ragtime Annie" or some other fiddle tune or folk song was all you would ever be able to accomplish. And you knew that, of course. But if you ever heard Pepe Romero, any of his brothers or his father, or Christopher Parkening or Julian Bream, or the great Segovia, guitar music was changed for you. From that moment on, your whole notion of the guitar, its limits and its possibilities, had to be reconsidered. And what you had to do to go on playing was admit the difference between art and entertainment. Of course, you could try to convince yourself that the two kinds of music were really altogether different things. But the fact remained that the instruments were essentially the same. The same fret board and the same tuning. And someone was taking this instrument called the guitar, the instrument you professed to play, and was doing things infinitely beyond your ability and understanding. Someone was redefining your notion of art on the guitar, and in doing that he was excluding your own music.

And admitting, finally, that you are no real artist can be a shattering thing. Billy knew a hundred pickers who clung to this illusion like the gospel. It's the illusion that allowed them to go on playing through years of moderate or little success. For a long time he counted himself among that flock, but no more. All of this was hard knowledge, but Billy thought the toughest part must be giving up that illusion and discovering that you still wanted to play music. Because in order to do that you had to put some stock in the value of popular entertainment, which meant putting some stock in the popular taste. And if you did that and you weren't making it big, you had to admit, finally, that you were a failure.

He rounded the curve in front of Saint Philip's Cathedral and came into Buckhead. On his right was the Fine Arts Theater, "Hitchcock" in red letters across the marquee. He passed a string of small sandwich shops, a bicycle shop, a BMW dealership, an antique shop, an art gallery. He cruised through two traffic lights, passed Grover's and a few bars and shops beyond it, then stopped at the light in the center of Buckhead.

On his right sat Aunt Charlie's. It hadn't changed much over the years either. He remembered the last time he was there and how drunk he'd gotten. That was only the second or third time he and Jean had gone out. They'd spent the evening at his apartment, Jean playing harp music on the stereo, trying to educate him in one night to the wonders of Irish music, making love to him on the fold-out sofa, telling

79

him how wonderful it was to find a man she could feel alive with, all the soap opera clichés. But this time it was real, all the words in terrible earnest. And then to Aunt Charlie's for a late sandwich and a beer before he took her home. Only they both had more than one beer, and when they pulled into the parking lot outside Jean's apartment, she discovered that she had left her keys at Billy's. But that was all right because the light was on in the living room, which meant Marilyn was home to let her in. The keys were an excuse to come by tomorrow.

Billy remembered the light behind the living room curtains as he watched her close the door, and the hazy yellow light from the street lamp. He remembered the bar lights at Aunt Charlie's where he went for a nightcap because he felt so good he knew he wouldn't be able to sleep, the bar lights growing more and more hazy as he chased Irish whiskies with Pabst Blue Ribbon and studied his situation with increasing fret. Billy, he remembered asking himself, what is it about this woman that makes going home to an empty apartment seem absolutely unbearable? Billy, you think you might actually be falling in love, the real kind? And why ought anybody in love have to spend the night alone? So he wouldn't, he'd go back. He'd drive home, pick up her keys, and take them to her, and he'd stay with her or she'd come back with him. It wasn't that late. She'd still be up.

He lived then in an apartment off Piedmont, across from the Clairmont Hotel, and by the time he drove home, found the keys where she'd left them on the end table, and drove back to Buckhead, it was late. All the lights were off in her apartment, and he stood on the front stoop wondering what to do. He could ring the bell. No, he couldn't do that. He'd wake up both of them. He'd just let himself in, stroll into Jean's bedroom, and crawl into bed like the sweetest gift from Cupid. Then he thought about it again. No, that was crazy, drunk crazy, totally crazy. Yes.

He slid the key into the lock, turned the bolt, and eased the door open. A light from the mantle bubbled off the aquarium and faded quickly in front of the fireplace. He stepped into the room and closed the door behind him. Two goldfish eyed him from the quivering light, and he watched them while his eyes adjusted to the dark. He crossed the carpet, quiet as a criminal, and stood at the top of the hall. Jean's door was on the left, he remembered that. It stood slightly ajar, and he stepped down the hall and eased it open. In the light from the street lamp sifting through the curtain, he could see her under the white sheet. Then something cold swept through him. Billy, not one figure lying under the icy sheet, but two. He stood there until he believed it, two heads throwing a tangle of hair across the pillows.

A horn blew behind him and Billy saw that the light had changed. He eased on through the intersection past the Buckhead Cinema and Coles Antiques, and there on his right was Lookin' Snooty, Marilyn's dress shop. He thought again about the tangle of hair on the pillow and the weeks of coming to terms with that. What was it Jean had called it, an experiment? Billy, she'd said, be an adult. Then his eye caught the mannequins in the window, they all looked like the women at Grover's. He gunned the pickup, beat the next light, and made it all the way to Lenox without thinking again of Grover's or Marilyn.

Billy's first stop on the mall was The Record Bar. He went straight to the bluegrass section, one rack of forty-five or fifty albums tacked on at the end of the country section. There were three Norman Blake records, a Doc Watson record, and a Dan Crary, but no Frank Wiley. He tried the country section. But no luck there either, so he asked the two sales clerks. No one in the store had ever heard of Frank Wiley.

"You might try Lenox Vintage," the register girl said. She was sort of a mild new waver in black nylon. "Second level at the other end of the mall."

Billy was doubtful. Vintage was Buckhead talk for used, and Lenox Vintage was a shop that dealt exclusively in old sheet music and used albums. But he had nothing else to do, so he walked down there anyway.

Lenox Vintage looked a lot like The Record Bar, long and narrow, but instead of rock posters, the walls were decorated with album covers and photos of jazz greats from the thirties and forties — Harry James, Benny Goodman, Louis Armstrong, Glenn Miller, Ella Fitzgerald. The racks running down the left side of the store were filled with sheet music, neatly wrapped in clear cellophane, and the racks running the entire length of the right wall were stacked tight with vintage jazz recordings.

Of course, they had no country or bluegrass records at all, but the racks against the back wall were filled with old rock albums. Billy drifted back and discovered hundreds of albums from the sixties and seventies, recordings by Gary and the Pacemakers, The Kinks, Cream, Jimi Hendrix, The Moody Blues, Sam the Sham and the Pharoahs. He thought he might find something for Jean there, something from her dim adolescence. The problem was that the albums were arranged in no particular order. All the jazz recordings were alphabetized meticulously according to the artist, but the rock records had just been dropped at random into the bins. He had to start with the first album in the first rack and flip every record.

Billy worked at that for ten minutes with very little luck, then he came across something interesting. It was an album called "Cloud 9" by a group called The Aztex. The cover was a surrealist painting of a sky full of white clouds, all of the clouds elongated and with red numbers painted on their sides. On cloud 9 sat a blue space ship with four faces staring out of four windows. One of those faces looked something like Leon. He flipped the album over and saw a full-figure shot of the band standing in a desert with the space ship in the background. In blue jeans, leather vests, and mocassin boots, they made a fairly unlikely crew of space travelers. A remarkably slimmer Leon Thibodeaux stood on the far right, a Fender bass slung like a rifle over his shoulder.

Billy laid the album on top of the stack and started to look for another copy. He went all the way through the five or six racks without any more luck at all. Still, he'd found one little piece of gold, so he took the record out of the cover and checked it for scratches. The only thing to do now was to take it home, put it on tape, and give it to

Leon. He'd appreciate it.

The guy at the register looked like he might have been a golf pro, blue Izod, white slacks. He pushed his glasses up on the bridge of his nose and took a close look at the album cover. "I don't believe I recall this group."

"Probably not," Billy said. "Listen, you wouldn't happen to have another copy of this tucked away somewhere, would you?"

"Not unless it's in the stacks." He punched the code into the register and $15.95 came up in green numbers in the window. "But I could give you the names of a few collectors."

"No," Billy said. "That's all right. It's not that important." And he remembered that vintage in Buckhead also means expensive.

For the next hour or so he wandered around the mall, mostly in and out of department stores and jewelry stores. Twice he went back to a pet shop and almost bought a black kitten, but he remembered that Jean had always had a thing against pet shops. Too many animals in pounds, too many strays, to ever justify buying a dog or a cat at a pet shop. Of course, he could have lied to her, told her he'd found it in the parking lot or on the side of the road, but he couldn't really decide if he wanted another cat around the house. He'd closed the garage door on the last one they'd had, and for a week Jean had made him feel like a murderer.

At this point he started to feel fairly low about not finding anything, and on top of that his legs felt like pure grief. There was a newspaper lying on a bench outside the pet shop. He thought he'd rest his legs for a minute and check out the entertainment page, see if Joe Harvey had really run any ads for Wiley. Maybe Joe had given him a mention.

The ad was there all right. A small ad at the top of the page, and all it said was "Grover's. The Ray Wiley Group. Thurs. & Fri." Not very imaginative, or complete. But what was it supposed to say? Warm up act, Billy Parker?

At the bottom of the page there was a much more interesting ad.

It began "Robert Shaw conducts The Atlanta Symphony Orchestra with Pepe Romero, guitar." He wasn't playing the Rodrigo, he was playing Giuliani. The Concerto No. 2 in A. The Giuliani concerto was a good piece of music. Billy had a recording of it by Alirio Diaz, or maybe it was Pepe Romero. He couldn't remember. But it was a great piece of music. He tore out the ad, folded it, and tucked it into his shirt pocket.

He found a pay phone near the mall entrance, flipped through the book, and dialed. As it rang he kept thinking about his clothes. He'd brought an old sport coat, a light gray linen, a little worn, but clean. And he had a solid blue shirt.

"Grover's," the voice said. "Jim speaking."

"Is Joe Harvey around?"

"Joe was in here a few minutes ago, but I don't see him around right now. Want me to have him call you?"

"How about digging him up. This is important."

"Mind if I ask who's calling?"

"Sure. This is Billy Parker."

"Okay," he said. "Hold on. I'll see if he's in the back."

But the only pants he had were blue jeans, though he thought he'd packed a pair that wasn't too faded. Still, he'd look pretty funny.

"Billy," Joe Harvey said. "What's up?"

"I got a little problem."

"What's up, buddy?"

"Listen, I'm just about to fall over. I don't think I can make it tonight."

"What?" he said. "What are you talking about?"

"I don't think I can make it tonight. I'm sick. I got an awful sore throat and a fever."

Joe Harvey didn't say anything, and Billy just stood there listening to the line crackle. Then Joe said, "You're kidding, of course."

"Sorry," Billy said. "But I don't kid about things like that. It's bad for business. I've got an awful sore throat and I'm running a fever. I think it started coming on yesterday. I woke up this morning about half dead."

"We wondered what happened to you last night. You must have been pretty sick to miss that party."

"Listen, I know this leaves you in a mess."

"Something like that."

"Like I said —"

"These things happen. I'll find somebody to cover the show. If I don't, then Frank'll have to play another set. It won't kill him."

"I appreciate it," Billy said. "And how about just mailing me the check for last night. I don't think I can get over there to pick it up."

"No problem. I'll get it in the mail on Monday. You take care of yourself, and I'll work on this thing in November. How does that sound?"

"Sounds good."

Billy hung up the phone and took the ad out of his pocket. As he turned around to read it in the light, he caught the window display at Muse's, two mannikins in summer suits and one that looked like the salesman at Lenox Vintage. He could go over there and buy a tie. That would help some. Yes, he'd look a lot better with a tie.

8

Billy remembers the salad bowl shattering across the edge of the sink, the slivers of glass peppering the cream linoleum, the blood trailing off the bottom of his heel, and he wonders whatever made him believe Jean would swallow the business about being sick.

Sick my ass, she said. Sick of what?

Sick of you.

Sick my ass, couldn't you come up with something better than that?

Yes, if he'd given it some thought. But lying is such a hassle. A good lie, anyway. And he is so bad at it. But yes, maybe he could have, if he'd had a place to come to, a place like the jon boat, a place to drift and think.

Jack shifts his weight and the boat rocks. He turns on the seat and takes a beer from the cooler between Billy's legs, and the boat rocks again as he turns back toward the bow. It's an easy rock and Billy stares straight up into the blue sky and goes with it.

He remembers what Jean said about the pond being a womb. He smiles at that, and he thinks of the jon boat as a cradle he likes to feel rocking in the easy breeze. Billy, that metaphor isn't quite consistent. But that's all right. Don't think the feeling away. Don't think away that long drift and easy rocking. Don't think away the one place you've got to come to. The little lifeboat, the boat of refuge. How does that song go? Take me in your lifeboat, take me in your lifeboat, it will stand the raging storm.

Truer words, Billy. The life boat, the jon boat, the little boat of refuge, and he remembers the first time it became that for him. Remembers the three stars cradling the full moon, and below them the barn and the two outbuildings, the way the moonlight glanced off the roofs into the little strip of pasture, into the pond where it snagged on the rusty strands of barbwire running halfway into the cove.

He remembers rocking back like he's rocking back now, his legs stretched over the center seat, a towel under his back, a flotation cushion under his head. He remembers some man's black cows rolling full-bellied on the ground around the barn, salt blocks growing like new teeth around the lip of the pond, wind combing the ragged Johnson grass, wrinkling the skin of the water. His line was out there somewhere, drifting, far out somewhere in the middle of the cove. It had been out and drifting for an hour or more, as though the pond were absolutely empty, nothing in it alive except the one nightcrawler shot full of air and floating a foot above the bottom, anchored by a lead weight. And he thought about emptiness as though it were a pond he might fall into and never get out of. Billy, how long did you float there in the empty pond under the full sky, the jon boat wedged on a strand of buried wire, the wind crackling in the high branches, the wind raining dry leaves into the cove and into the pasture? How long did you drift there, thinking of Jean in the house at the edge of the pond, the ferns nodding from her dresser, the wandering Jew quivering from the window basket to the floor? A long time, Billy. You loved the drift.

Something thrashes deep in the cove where a cluster of willows leans out over the shallows. A frog or a salamander. It thrashes again, but a thrash too large to be either. Jack reels in his line and casts out toward it, and Billy listens to the slap of the water and remembers another pond, a fish pond built in the center of a bricked, kidney-shaped plaza, a plaza covered with islands of shade trees and shrubs. And all around it the the squat, modern office buildings of urologists, opthalmologists, gynecologists, pediatricians. But Billy is homing in on that pond, that little concrete fish pond where he stood time and again on the brick bank, where he stared into the green quivering water and watched the goldfish large as his arm thrash in circles under the lily pads.

That first time, Billy, the first time you stood on that brick bank and looked down into those pads, remember how hot it was? You sat down on a wooden bench in the shade of an oak, sat there for almost an hour in the awful heat and watched the huge goldfish swimming among all those exotic tropical fish, the sort you see in dime store aquariums, fan tails striped and wider than their bodies, fish you'd never believe might grow larger than your hand, darting over the rock bottom and making the water seem suddenly all colors at once. Billy, whoever built that complex knew something about people. Remember the way you sat there absolutely still, absorbed by the goldfish gliding under the pads, the way the light bounced off the stones on the bottom of the pond, the reds, the golds, the greens, the way the scales of the goldfish picked up the colors and made them shiver? And how you forgot the heat entirely, and for a few minutes even forgot why you were there?

Billy closes his eyes and feels the slap of the wind against the side of the jon boat. He is thinking of Jean. He remembers her walking out the door of one of those buildings, her arms full of papers and plastic bottles. And how he stood up then off the bench and walked around the edge of the pond to meet her near the path that ran between the buildings and into the parking lot.

"What's all that business?"

"Vitamins," she said. "And literature of several sorts. You need to read all of this too."

And very surprised, he looked at her for a moment, and she looked back at him with the same expression. And everything changed. How do you describe it, Billy? Something like discovering a whole new dimension, like suddenly discovering you have a future.

All the way home they hardly spoke. He drove in a half stupor and focused what attention he could on the road and the traffic and the lights. Jean skimmed the directions on the labels of the bottles, then flipped back and forth through the pamphlets. Out of the corner of his eye, Billy could see the diagrams, the way the future was laid out in penciled lines. He felt like they'd just joined some secret society and were on their way home with the book of mysteries. When he pulled into the garage, they sat for a few minutes.

"Listen," she said, laying the pamphlets in his lap. "Let's not tell anyone just yet. Let's let it slide for a while."

"You've got to tell people."

"But not right now. Let's give it a little time. I think we may need to adjust to this."

"Are you thinking about your mother?"

"And other people."

"You can't wait too long. You'll hurt feelings."

"I know. Just a while."

And he nodded. He had nobody special to tell.

He remembers that he spent most of that afternoon in his room. But it was something like the daze after a dream that won't come back. Not much to recall really, only a few stray things—Jean moving under him from room to the room, the vacuum cleaner humming in the living room, the needle of the stereo lifting off one record and onto another. For a while he thumbed through the pamphlets without reading very much or even studying the diagrams. They all seemed too much like junior high biology texts, and he couldn't muster enough interest to focus his attention.

Instead, he kept going back to the pictures on the walls of his room, mostly photographs of Jean when she was a child. But also some wedding pictures, Jean and Billy standing on the lawn at her parents' house in St. Petersburg. Then a shot of the whole family, the newly-weds and Jean's folks, her mother smiling and holding her hand, her father staring off in a daze, looking out into the future toward his third heart attack.

And of course there were several pictures of Billy and of his parents, though the only one he had of them all together was a snapshot taken on his first birthday. They were all sitting on a blanket behind a huge birthday cake, Billy a puffy kid with one blond curl in the middle of his forehead. Then there was a photo of his parents' wedding, his father in his dress blues, his mother in a white dress and a wide-brimmed white hat that sat on her head like a straw halo.

Billy thought these pictures were better texts, and he kept moving from one to another, trying to fathom the connections between them. What sort of accident brought these people together? What sort of equation of history or love or whatever? To think about that was astounding. And he felt a little foolish for it, but also uncontrollably happy. As happy as he had ever been in his life.

But wasn't that also the first night he started questioning the music? That night or the night after. He was sitting behind the microphone at The Under Thing, looking down at the faces, the smoke boiling up from the tables. The room was packed, but the lights were down and he could see only a few people and none of them very clearly. But he remembers a blonde at a table near the stage, a blonde in tight designer jeans tucked into a pair of red, high-topped cowboy boots, toes tapping to the music.

And at the table behind her two guys in baseball caps and jerseys. They might have been students, but they looked a little old for that. Billy remembers the guy with the beard, how he kept watching the woman in the red boots, how every time her toe went up, his fingers rapped down on the table.

And he remembers asking himself, Who are these people? And why am I up here singing songs for them? Here was Billy Parker, nearly thirty-three years old and making his living, what there was of it, by singing songs to these people, these people and a hundred more like them. And suddenly it all seemed to him very peculiar, very insubstantial and tentative, almost foolish and adolescent.

During the break he walked over to the bar for a shot of Irish. The feeling he'd had on stage had turned into a vague uneasiness. He remembers trying to drown it in the Jameson, then the hard look on Leon's face. And he turned on the stool to see what Leon was watching. Some joker at a table near the door was trying to wedge a tip into the front of Sarah Libby Cook's blouse. Who are these people, Billy? Take a look around. Who the hell are they? She finally let him tuck the dollar into the cup of her bra, and when she picked up the tray of empties and walked off smiling, Leon relaxed.

"Leon, how long since you did any playing?"

"What you call playing?" he said.

"On stage. How long?"

And Leon didn't even have to think. He threw his right thumb over his shoulder toward the portrait hanging behind the bar. "Spring 1970. That was the year The Aztex broke up."

"How hard was it to get out?"

"Of the band?"

"Of music. You quit, didn't you?"

"We all quit," he said. "And it was hard enough. But I'd saved up some money. Larry'd saved some money too. But nobody else had a dime. If it hadn't of been for what I put back, I couldn't have done it."

"But you wanted to quit, right?"

"Everybody wanted to quit. We'd had enough. It happens."

"The Aztex did all right for a while, didn't they?"

"We made some money. And spent most of it."

"Who doesn't?"

92

"Some don't. Some got sense enough to save it. But things dropped off too. Hell, it's hard to stay on top playing rock music. Too many bands now, too many fad bands. Some clown comes up with a new way to comb his hair and suddenly you can't draw a crowd."

"But you liked the music you were playing?"

"Most of it."

Billy, remember when you turned around and saw the woman in the red boots staring straight at you? Remember how she wouldn't look away, how she waved at you with the toe of that boot?

"Leon, I hate country music."

"It the worst. But it draws a crowd."

"It's still the worst."

"You do all right. You do what you can with it."

"I don't mean the fiddle tunes or the bluegrass. I mean the country, the commercial stuff, the radio music. It's the worst."

"People like it."

"People don't have much taste, do they?"

"Who said they did. I tried to have some blues in here a few times. Nobody'd listen to it. They think it's nigger music. You take Jerry Lamberti. I went over to Goodtime Charlie's the other night to catch a set. Jerry's so fine I wanted to cry, but he couldn't draw a crowd at a fire. Maybe four or five people in the place."

Billy, remember the way she pushed herself out of that chair and crossed the room? The red lipstick, the red earrings, the red boots? Remember the red fingernails coming down on your knee? Billy, who the hell are these people? Where do they all come from?

"Listen," she said, tilting her head a little toward the bar. "When are you going to play me that song about taking the ribbon out of my hair? I've been waiting on it all night."

"I don't see any ribbons in your hair. Leon, you see any ribbons in this lady's hair?"

"No ribbons," he said. "Maybe a little dandruff."

The wind shifts and the boat spins slowly like the needle of a compass. Jack leans back a little in the bow. "Hey, are you fishing or sleeping?"

"Drifting."

"Drift fishing or just drifting?"

Billy catches a whiff of something burning, somewhere beyond the pines and the highway, a construction site, somebody clearing a field. It occurs to him now that Jean never liked country music. In fact, she may have never even liked bluegrass. An irony of sorts, since they met in Lavonia at the Georgia State Bluegrass Festival. Billy was playing guitar with a group called High Grass, a traditional band that specialized in gospel. Jean was there with Marilyn and her boyfriend, a tall guy in a sport jacket who roamed the fields all night with a Sony cassette deck. But they didn't know anything about the music, they were only there for the fad.

He can't remember now who spoke the first words or what they were. But he does remember the first time he saw Jean. He was on stage with High Grass, and she was sitting with her friends in lawn chairs they had pulled down close. She had on a wide-brimmed red straw hat, not the sort you buy in a feed store, and she looked very much like the big-city girl at the county fair.

Later on that afternoon they bumped into each other at one of the concession stands, and she stopped him to ask a question. Something about a song he'd sung, "Knoxville Girl" or "Omie Wise." So he told her what he knew about it and they started to talk, then he offered to walk her around the fields so she could hear the jams.

It was her first festival and, fad or not, she was taken back by it. And Billy remembers the fields at Lavonia, the green shallow lap of valley, forty-five or fifty acres sloping down from a ridge of scrub pine backing into thick woods. And the sun edging down into the pinetops, and the long gray shadows streaking the tops of the tents scattered all along the side of the slope. Pup tents and cabin tents and tarps stretched into lean-to shelters, and people buzzing around them, kindling fires in the last good light sifting down through the pine needles, lighting and globing lanterns, putting everything just right before the sun dropped all the way over the hill.

And farther down the slope, acres of pickup trucks and campers and Winnebagoes and trailers and Chevy vans and every other kind of motor home imaginable strewn all over the field. Everywhere the smell of charcoal and steak and gasoline and whiskey. Everywhere a confusion of sounds. Car doors slamming, people shouting, the rustle of ice in coolers, beer cans popping, dogs barking, the snatch of a three-part harmony way off in a cluster of trailers, a bass voice frogging up from a river of pickups winding down the center of the field, a banjo riff, a mandolin run, the train-brake scratch of someone tuning a fiddle, but most of all the urgent cricket-like crack and twang of hundreds of miscellaneous banjo notes and dobro notes and mandolin notes and guitar chords and bass thumps singing out all over the valley, the urgent and haywired telegraphing of bluegrass for as far as you could hear, like the static of insects warming up for a big night. And she fell into that the way you fall out of a boat and into a pond.

They spent most of the night walking from one jam session to another, and that night was only the beginning. They went to two more festivals that month. Then Jean started catching Billy's club dates in Atlanta, and there were the fiddler's conventions and the cookouts and the parties.

But Billy, in a year she had soured on bluegrass entirely, and you were out of the group and working as a single, playing mostly country. It wasn't any change you'd planned, but you were married then, and you don't make very much money playing bluegrass music, and what you do make you have to split with three or four other pickers.

Jack jerks back hard on his rod and the boat rocks. Billy opens his eyes and watches him shake his head as the line goes slack. He reels it into the boat and studies the naked hook.

"Hand me those crickets," he says.

Billy reaches behind the cooler and hands him the tube of crickets.

Jack turns in the bow and gives him a look. "Forget about it, god-damn it. She'll get over it. So you're tired of playing music, so you played a little hooky. Big deal. I've never seen a grown man fret so much over a woman."

"It's not Jean. I'm just thinking, that's all."

"Well, what you ought to do is stop thinking and start doing."

Billy frowns. He's thinking of doing. He's thinking of the morning after his brush with the woman in red boots, of Jean at the kitchen table, drinking a cup of hot chocolate and reading the paper.

He remembers that she wanted to see a movie.

"Anything special?"

"Nothing very serious. Something ridiculous."

"How about that Chevy Chase thing?"

"I hate Chevy Chase," she said. "He's a clown."

"That's what he gets paid to be. You said you wanted to see something ridiculous."

"Not that kind of ridiculous. I mean something like *Wanda Whips Chicago*. That kind of ridiculous."

She was sitting in front of the picture window, and the bright sun and the glare coming off the lake made it nearly impossible to look at her.

"What would you think about me giving up music?" he said.

"What do you mean?"

"I mean I'm thinking about getting out of music. I don't feel so good about it anymore."

And she looked up from the paper, an odd expression on her face, a sort of half astonishment and half anger. "I think I don't need to go to the movies at all. I think I can just stay home and listen to you."

"And what's that supposed to mean?"

"Exactly what it sounds like. And what are you planning on doing after you get out of music?"

"I don't know. I haven't gotten that far yet."

"You don't know? You mean you're just going to quit your job, and you don't have anything else lined up? You don't even have any plans?"

"I didn't say I was going to quit my job. I just asked you what you thought about me giving up music."

"I think you'd better have something else lined up. That's what I think. God, I don't believe this. What a time to start thinking about quitting your job. God, I can't believe you."

"Listen," he said. "I didn't say I was quitting my job. I only said that I'm getting tired of playing music."

"Do you think everybody in the world enjoys their work? My God, half the people in the world hate their jobs. And most of the rest would like to have any sort of job at all. How can you say that to me now? Do you have any idea how many people would like to have things as easy as you? You think we can afford to give up that income while you sit around trying to figure out what you'll like better?"

"I never said I was going to quit. I just —"

"Good. Because we've got to stop thinking so much of ourselves. As individuals, I mean. And we've got to start thinking more about family."

The wind whips up again from the pines beyond the barn, the smoke drifts, the jon boat drifts, Billy drifts. He closes his eyes. He's thinking now about fire. About a fire in New Orleans. The way a gas leak might explode in a kitchen and burn up a whole hotel. This is the same as thinking about his family. This is what he knows most about his father and his mother. Not their lives, but their deaths. And how, after that, there is only his grandparents and the two cousins who stayed with them during the day while his aunt and uncle worked in the office of Frazer Mills.

And he smiles because thinking about his grandparents, his

grandmother especially, is almost the same as thinking about music, the old and the good music. For Billy the beginning was music, old time gospel, the only music she ever cared about. And he remembers how she taught them the music, not by sitting them all down and teaching them the songs note by note out of the hymnals, but by singing the songs over and over every day of her life. Not knowing she was teaching anybody anything, just singing the songs in the kitchen over bread dough and boiling corn and okra and peas. Singing them as she made the beds and dusted and swept the floors, singing them just about anywhere and anytime, and singing them in a voice just this side of a screech, but putting something into them, something that made them true and good. And he remembers her at the kitchen sink, looking out the window and across the pasture, past the barn and the beagle lots, past the pines at the edge of the pasture and the clouds drifting over the tops of the pines, looking way off into the blue, and warbling in her flat bird voice about a place on a far away strand, a place where we'll never grow old.

And Billy, remember the music at church, the tight harmonies of those gospel quartets? The bass and the baritone, the tenor and the lead voices, all rising in the front of Buelah Baptist, all singing of a home prepared where the saints abide, all singing of a mansion over the hilltop, all ready to meet you in the morning by the bright riverside when all sorrow has drifted away.

A tackle box rattles in the bow of the boat. Jack snaps it open and plunders through it, a soft rattling of plugs and boxes. Then he snaps it shut and lays it easy behind the seat.

"One thing I can say. When the army turned to shit, I had sense enough to get the hell out. And the longer you wait on something like that, the tougher it gets to move."

But Billy is still thinking about the good music, another kind of good music, the music that belonged to his grandfather. And he sees again the little grocery on the side of Lost Mountain road, a two room wooden store with a covered porch, two Pure gas pumps, and a big red Coke sign propped up on the roof. And across the road he sees again the old garage, the long wooden garage that has never been painted, the rusted tin roof, the boards warping out from the studs, the garage his grandfather rents to a man who runs an upholstery business. Rain or shine the door is always open, and Billy hears now floating out of the back of the garage the smooth notes of a fiddle. How in the world does that man make a living? He never does anything but fiddle.

And then the concerts in the living room of his grandfather's house. Every third Sunday afternoon, Mr. Arnold and his fiddle, and sometimes a guitar player to back him up, but more often than not a whole string band, guitar player, mandolin player, bass player. Every third Sunday, as regular as the rent. And Billy isn't so sure those concerts weren't the rent.

What was it about that music? Billy wants to call it something corny like dignity, or honesty, or simplicity. Whatever. It was just something that modern country music isn't. It was what? Family music? And the image comes to him again, his grandmother walking through the house, singing her off-key gospel, a small herd of kids trailing behind her. How old did she live to be, Billy? And she always had that music, and she always had the kids, and she was never, in any sense of the word, alone. Billy, can't you see why Jean was so desperate about all of this family business? Can't you see why she insisted on the tests, why you went through that year of gynecologists and urologists, charts and sperm counts?

Billy remembers how long Jean gave it. A week. Then Marilyn phoned and she told her. What a strange weekend. Strange because he almost grew to like Marilyn. It wasn't a good time for her. Rich husband Roy was beginning to move in political circles, there was talk of a race for the state legislature. At the very least, it was understood that he'd make a move for city council. This was north Atlanta talk, Buckhead talk, businessman talk. His support was solid there, but he was testing wider waters, trying to broaden his political base. And this meant a long string of social engagements. There was a certain strain, as Marilyn would say, and there were certain conflicts, and nothing was more vital than keeping up appearances. No, it was not a good time for her, but she drove down that weekend anyway.

They threw a blanket down by the pond and had a picnic. And Billy remembers a full half hour of various toasts, Taylor Chablis and Coors. Toasts to each other, then to everyone they knew. The standard things, love, health, riches, fame.

Then he remembers how Marilyn shifted, and how for a second, for one or two odd still seconds, he almost felt sorry for her.

"And here's to straight arrows," she said.

Jean grimaced. "Oh, not that."

"He's such a straight arrow, though. He pains me right in the ass."

"He's upstanding," Billy said. "Anyone upstanding would pain you."

"He may be standing, but he's rarely up. Not that I care very much whether he is or isn't."

"Marilyn," Jean said.

"And he's so restrictive. You wouldn't believe it. And he's out four or five nights a week wooing his party honchos. I suppose that's all right, but I detest being his ornament. Not that I don't make a very nice ornament. But I have a life of my own, you know."

"Of course you do."

"He simply hasn't come to terms with that. And he doesn't seem to be trying. If I try to go out, my God! I swear he's had me followed. He's had me followed several times actually. Think about that. I can hardly even go out for a drink anymore."

"So what will you do?"

"Something," she said. "If he doesn't first. He's very tired of having me followed, I think."

"Does he want a separation?"

"Oh, I'm quite sure. But he'll wait until he can put me on the defensive. That's his way. It will all have to be very quiet. He can't afford for it to be anything less than absolutely civil. So he'll find out some little something, then he'll point out why a quiet separation would be much more to my advantage."

"Is he so much like that?" Jean said.

"Oh, yes. A very straight arrow with an extremely poisonous tip." And Billy, remember the way she turned to you? "Men are such strange creatures, Billy. They're so possessive."

"I haven't noticed that they're any more possessive than women."

"I think you're very wrong there. Women are willing to share. Men, I think, all secretly want to be God. They want to own and orchestrate. They want to pull the strings, and if they can't write the script and stage the scene, they're just not very happy."

"Do you want a separation?" Jean said.

"I'm not sure just what I want. Even if I did, I certainly wouldn't make it that easy for him."

"But that wouldn't be manipulation, would it?" Billy said.

"Not in the least. That would simply be taking care of myself."

"That's true," Jean said. "We all have to take care of ourselves."

And remember how Marilyn smiled and patted Jean on the stomach. "Anyway, at least you know where you're going now. And I'm very happy about that."

"Yes," Jean said. "But why are we getting so serious?"

How much later, Billy? Three weeks? Then Jean woke you at six in the morning. You were in your dream again, in the long drift, the jon boat and the red river, and she nudged you on the shoulder and told you to turn on the light. But the light was already on, way down at the end of the river, almost blinding where the voices were just beginning to sing. She nudged you again, and all of those voices became one voice, her voice telling you to get up, to get up and turn on the light.

You propped up on your elbow and stretched for the lamp on the night table, but you couldn't find it, and when you found it, it didn't work. So you got up then and switched on the overhead. Jean was sitting up in bed with both of her arms wrapped across her stomach. She leaned forward, pulled down the top sheet, and opened her legs to a small pool of blood.

"Call the doctor," she said. "The number's in the address book." Then she eased off the bed and into the bathroom. She closed the door and didn't come out for fifteen minutes.

The doctor met you at the clinic.

Part Two

9

They were out there in the canoe. So far out that the canoe looked like a yellow leaf floating off the shore of the island. The pines bristling the hump of that island were towering over them, and the sun, already dropping into those pines, kept turning the clouds above the peaks a deeper orange. Only Nolan was paddling, sitting on his feet in the stern, hitting easy strokes on the starboard side of the canoe, then resting the paddle across the gunwales, letting the canoe drift, and stroking again just before they drifted to a dead stop.

Billy sat in a folding chair on the edge of the dock, and as the canoe slid around the side of the island, he watched them grow smaller and smaller. A wind shook the tops of the pines, and what looked like a heron, tiny in the distance, spooked off the bank and beat his awkward wings into the sky above the canoe. With the sun behind him, he was a deep purple outlined in bright gold, and he looked like he might break into flames at any moment. But he didn't, he only pulled himself higher into the air with each heavy wing stroke, his long yellow legs dangling under him like twigs.

Billy reeled in his line and checked his bait. The worm was still alive on the hook, a nightcrawler puffed up with three bubbles of air. He threw it back out toward the middle of the cove where five or six mud turtles helmeted a cluster of snags. For twenty minutes or so he'd been watching the slow metamorphosis of an oak leaf, how it washed against a rock some ten yards down cove, how it drifted up the edge of the lake and grew, inch by inch, a shiny brown tail, a long string of hourglass bands, hazel and chestnut. He watched it pause in the shallows for a few minutes and take full shape against the floor of broken shells. Then it sidled under the dock and through the shallows on the other side, through a school of minnows exploding like slivers of orange light, and into a patch of reeds. For a long time it lay with only the tip of the brown tail showing. Then the reeds parted, and it swam out toward the deeper water, the island turning purple around the banks, and the sun falling into the pines.

By that time the canoe was almost gone, not much more than a seed washing around the edge of the island, and the sun was only a glare in the lower branches. Suddenly the sun was gone entirely, and Billy saw a lantern flare, no bigger than a star, just beyond the south bank. It floated for a few minutes on the black water, then disappeared.

He thought about taking Jack's boat out. He could've fished the structure on the far side of the island. But that would have been too obvious, and awkward too, with the outboard on the porch and the party all gone inside. So he sat for a while and watched the spot where the lantern had disappeared. The only stars now were in the sky and they were sparse, and there was no moon, so the island itself was almost gone.

Over his shoulder, Billy heard the faint notes of a guitar. Someone in the house or on the porch was running one into tune. He knew then that the last car down the drive had been Jerry Lamberti's. Now they had all gone inside to listen to the music, and they were sure to come looking for him soon. Jerry or Jack, or one of the women.

Jerry hit a chord, then another. He dropped a string and brought it back up to pitch and hit another chord. He hit each string slowly and at perfect intervals, and let them bleed into each other until they made a perfect G chord. Then there was an almost perfect silence, no voices, no laughing, no popping of beer cans, no rattling of ice, and Billy noticed the first crickets starting to open up down cove. A note, a high E, rolled down the hill, and after it something very close from another guitar, something brighter and only a little louder. Billy guessed it was his D18, and he leaned back in the chair and listened to Jerry rolling it up to pitch. It was only a matter of minutes then, so he reeled in his line, cleared his hook of the night-crawler, and walked back up the steps toward the hill, the woods, and the clearing full of cars.

"So there you are," Jack said. He was sitting at the kitchen table, his chair leaned back against the wall.

Billy let the screen door slap once behind him and stood for a second in the kitchen. The cabin was full of people, mostly actor types, some of them students from Nolan's drama class, others locals who hung around the theater. Billy didn't know any of them well, and he didn't speak. But it was more than that. He didn't much like actors. None of the ones he'd ever met could figure out when to stop acting.

Jerry Lamberti played a soft chord. He was sitting on the edge of the sofa in the far corner of the room. Billy gave him a quick glance, then looked back over the crowd. Did Jerry really want to be here? It was all so staged, so sixties, so much like a hootenanny.

"Just a few," Jerry said. "I haven't played any music in a long time."

Jack stood up, picked up his chair, and guided it through the crowd. He sat it down beside the front door. "Right here," he said, and tapped the seat with his finger.

Billy wedged through the crowd and sat in the chair. The room was hot and packed solid, people on all the sofas and chairs, people on army blankets folded into pallets on the floor. They were all closing in on him, all watching him with a little too much curiosity, watching him as if they knew something they thought he didn't know, watching him and waiting for something to happen.

Jerry handed him the guitar, and he took it and laid it across his lap. But he wasn't thinking about the guitar, he was thinking about the crowd, all those eyes and what lay behind them, and about the canoe drifting like a leaf off the point of the island and the lantern sparking like a yellow star fading into the darkness. And he was about to do something. He could feel it. He didn't know what it would be, but he could feel it knotting up inside him, choking out everything else.

Jerry went into a song, but Billy only sat there with the Martin in his lap, Jerry playing right on through his intro and into the first verse, and Billy sitting absolutely still in the chair, his eyes focused on the tiny yellow star growing smaller and smaller, the tiny yellow star tightening like a knot of light, Billy sitting absolutely still, thinking about the breaking point and what happens when light snaps. Then he caught a word. Death. Then a phrase, and a whole line. Death began to form a line across the river when Abel died from his own brother's hand.

Billy had never heard Jerry Lamberti sing a gospel song, and he sat for a minute in a kind of half daze as Jerry's voice, perfectly warm and clean, filled the room. In the Great Beyond over in the land of Eden, I'll meet my friends who left this world so long ago. And Billy stood up then, reached across the bookcases behind him, and switched off the lights, and suddenly the only person in the room with him was Jerry Lamberti, his voice and his guitar filling the darkness around them. And Billy kept thinking how amazing it was that an instrument in the hands of a man like Jerry Lamberti could make so much seem all right so quickly.

Almost an hour later, the kitchen door opened and they walked in, two silhouettes against the faint light drifting in from the yard. They let the screen close easy behind them and pushed into the room just far enough to close the kitchen door. Jerry was playing a bluesy version of an old Albert Brumley song, his bottleneck making beautiful whines on the strings of the National Steel. They edged up a little closer behind the people sitting on the floor. Jerry was singing about a land of beautiful flowers, about the prettiest robes and crowns we'll all be wearing, about the city four-square beyond this world of strife. And Billy, in his heart, was singing with him. Then he actually was singing, a low harmony part. Then the singing stopped, and Jerry's bottleneck slid all the way up the high E string, and the guitar slid easy off his leg and onto the floor.

"Intermission," he said. "Musicians need to take a leak."

Nobody turned on the lights, but Jack lit two candles and sat one on his desk and the other on the coffee table. People started to shuffle, standing up to stretch, breaking off to the fridge or outside to the ice chest, to the bathroom and outside to the bushes. Jean was still standing beside the kitchen table, Nolan behind her. Then she struck a path through the bodies on the floor and crossed the room. She picked up her pocketbook from the corner of the coffee table, sat down on the floor at the end of the sofa, and used the candle to light a cigarette.

Billy watched her for a few seconds, but she didn't look at him, only took a magazine from the coffee table and spread it on the floor in front of her. He didn't say anything, just sat there with the Martin in his lap.

Jerry leaned his guitar against the wall and stood up and stretched. "How about a drink?" he said.

"Beer."

Jack came through the front door, a beer in each hand, a little tipsy, almost stumbling over a couple on a blanket. He picked his way across the room and sat down on the floor beside Jean.

The candle on the table was sputtering, and Billy watched the odd shadows it threw against the walls. How could she read that magazine? He could hardly see the toe of his boot, and she was reading a magazine? A prop, he thought. Just a prop. All actors have to have them.

"So the play," Jack said to her. "How's it going?"

And Billy could feel the tiny knot tightening again, a tension that never quite went away, a tension that had been there for months, tightening, always threatening to snap. At first he'd blamed Jack too. But that was a mistake. Sure, he'd given her the biggest push, but what happened after that wasn't his fault. The whole thing started too crazy. An old movie, *The Snows of Kilimanjaro*. Jack had hated it, typical Hollywood. But it convinced him that someone might turn the story into a decent one act play. And he convinced Nolan, who said the workshop might be willing to produce it. But Jack had accepted a teaching assistantship and was too busy with his courses, so what do they do? They convince Jean that she should get back into school spring quarter and try it. If it worked out, she could use the script as a master's thesis. And Billy, you were all for it too.

"Actually," she said. "It's going very well. We've finishing casting, and we're already into the first week of rehearsals."

"Already?" he said. "You're not talking about the Hemingway thing?"

"Oh, that. God, no. I'm still mapping out my strategy. I thought you meant the Williams play."

"Not me. I could care less about Tennessee Williams. Besides, another Williams play? Nolan's liable to wear us all out on the decadent South."

"Oh, I don't think so. It's going to be a super production. God, you've got to see the woman who's playing Serafina. Boobs like balloons. She's absolutely wonderful."

"But is she Italian?"

"Is pasta?"

Jack took a cigar from his shirt pocket and lit it with the candle. "Dark eyes?"

"Like the night."

"Well, why didn't she come over?"

"Sunday. Something at her church tonight. She's religious."

"Religious?" he said. "Good material there. If Nolan wanted

another Williams play, he should have done *Night of the Iguana*. I'd have made a perfect Shannon. Don't you think I'd look rather handsome in a collar?"

"Absolutely," she said. "And how would I look with a rose on my chest?"

"How's that?"

"Nolan wanted me to audition for Estelle. I said, Nolan, I haven't acted anything but silly in years. He didn't care about that. Just thought I'd look good with a rose on my chest. Imagine that." She laughed, closed the magazine, and laid it back on the coffee table. "What do you think, huh? Maybe just a little one?"

A hand touched Billy on the shoulder, and he turned and saw Jerry Lamberti's girl offering him a beer. What was her name? Jerry had introduced them a couple of times at The Under Thing, but he'd never been able to put his finger on the place he'd seen her before. But as she handed him the Coors, he remembered her as the girl in the restaurant commercial with Nolan Hughes. She was the blonde in the elegant black evening gown who sat across the dinner table from Nolan, the sophisticated young lady in pearls who during the entire commercial did nothing but gaze admiringly through the candlelight into the eyes of Nolan Hughes. Only her hair wasn't blonde now, it was black. And it wasn't swept up from the back of her head, it was long and straight, and it hung down well below her shoulders.

"It just came to me," Billy said. "That Brother's Three commercial."

"Ah," she said, without much enthusiam. "The portrait of the perfect couple. Do they still show that thing?"

"On weekends sometimes. Mostly during the late movies."

"Didn't we make a sweet pair?"

"I suppose."

"Well, I'm a good actress."

She was already moving away toward the kitchen, and Jerry

111

wandered out of the crowd at the same spot she wandered in. He had a drink in his right hand, his left cupped over the top to keep it from spilling. He walked on by Billy, opened the front door, and stepped out onto the porch.

The room had gotten hot and smoky, and the breeze from the door felt good. Billy sat there for a minute drinking his beer, then Jean and Jack started talking about Nolan. He didn't want to hear that, so he leaned his guitar against the bookcase, got up, and followed Jerry out.

The breeze was coming up off the water, and it had turned just chilly enough to remind Billy that good night fishing was still a few weeks away, just chilly enough to make you want a sweater if you were planning on staying out for a while.

Jerry stood by the screen, looking across the yard, the tops of the shrubs, and out into the middle of the lake. There wasn't much out there to see, only the black water. But someone had turned on the lights of the fishing camp, and you could see them through a break in the trees. They were far off, hardly more than two dots, and they reminded Billy again of the lantern flaring like a star on the water.

"So what are you working on now?" He closed the door behind him and leaned against the frame.

Jerry didn't turn around, only took a swallow of his drink. "We're still on that Call Street house."

Billy tried not to look at the two lights, but his eyes kept moving toward them. They winked sometimes, then the wind came up the hill and across the yard. "Is that thing Victorian?"

"I don't think so. Maybe turn of the century. And I don't think anything's been done to it since then."

Billy stepped over to the metal glider and sat down. The seat was cool, but he leaned back anyway. "So who bought that thing?"

"A doctor named Millhollan. Some kind of eye doctor. His office is down in the med center behind the hospital. This is about the third or fourth one he's restored."

Billy took a sip of the beer, sat it down on the floor, and wedged his hands under his legs. "So what does he do with those things? Sell them?"

"I suppose. But I think he's moving into this one. And it'll be some fine house when we finish it. Some beautiful walnut mantles, some nice stained glass too."

"You like that work?"

Jerry looked back over his shoulder, then he turned around and looked out toward the water. "It's okay," he said. "Don't get me wrong. It's work, and I've got to be careful with my hands."

"Well, I can't tell that it's hurt your music any." He pushed the glider back on its track and it squeaked a painful little squeak.

Jerry didn't say anything, only stood there looking out across the yard and the lake, watching the light at the fishing camp. He took another sip from his drink. "No, I'm real careful with my hands. I wear gloves when I can. They still get beat up a little, but I try to be pretty careful. Wouldn't want to bust any bones." Jerry turned around and stared through the window of the door. Then he sat down in a folding chair in the corner of the porch.

They sat like that for a few minutes and listened to a dog barking across the cove. Someone was laughing down the hill, and they listened to the laughter move off toward the dock. For a moment it was very quiet inside, and the laughter faded and there was only the barking of the dog.

"Wild dogs," Billy said. "Jack's planning a hunt. Whole pack of them run the woods across the cove."

"I hear you're looking for a job?"

Billy turned and looked at him. "Who told you that?"

"I don't know. Leon maybe. Or maybe Jack mentioned it. I don't recall. Just something I heard."

Then there were two or three dogs howling across the cove, and Billy thought their voices coming across the water made an incredibly clean and eerie song.

"No," he said. "I'm not looking for a job. If I said something like that, I was only talking. I get a little itchy sometimes."

"I understand that. It's only natural." Jerry propped his legs up on Jack's outboard and sloshed the drink around in his glass.

"Besides," Billy said. "Have you looked at the want ads lately?"

"Not since yesterday."

"Then you know it's all electronics and computers."

The noise inside had started to pick back up, someone banging out a few rough chords on a guitar, someone else blowing into a mouth harp. Jack shouted "Music!" Then a glass shattered in the kitchen and his voice died off into the general commotion.

Jerry looked back out toward the lake and the two lights shining like tiny eyes across the water. "I thought once about going back to school. Maybe in data processing or something like that. That's spooky, isn't it? Me in data processing."

"Spooky enough."

"Then I thought about some kind of business school. Accounting or something like that. I even thought once about trying to open up a music store. Maybe just a guitar store. But even that would cost a fortune. Hell, just the franchises you'd need would cost a fortune, even if you could get them."

The guitar picked up again, someone beating out a fairly rough version of what sounded to Billy like "Greenback Dollar." He looked at Jerry. "I hope that's your guitar."

Jerry didn't say anything for a second, only looked back out across the water. Then he said, "You know, in a lot of ways a guy like Leon has a great thing going."

"Leon has to put up with a lot of shit. It's no easy trick running a place like that."

"I never said it was. But at least he's his own boss. And when something belongs to you, you don't mind putting in some time with it. I mean putting in some real time. And you feel like you're doing something for yourself, not just for the other guy. And you are."

"And when business slacks off, you're the first one to start eating beans and shitting bills."

"I eat a lot of beans anyway," he said. "And who doesn't have bills?"

"Well," Billy said, "it costs a lot of money to open a bar too. And it's not real easy making something like that go. It takes a long time to build up a string of regulars."

Jerry took a swallow of his drink. "How much you figure they had when they opened that place up?"

"I don't know, they had some money. But I don't think it was anything like a fortune. They just happened to be in the right place at the right time. They could've started that place on nothing. There wasn't anything like it around then. You couldn't do something like that now."

Someone inside was singing, but it wasn't "Greenback Dollar." It was "Boots of Spanish Leather," the guy on the mouth harp doing a poor imitation of Dylan. Billy kept wondering if the harp was in the right key. Nobody else seemed to care.

"You know," Jerry said, "I heard that Harold Wright is looking for somebody."

"I don't think I'd make much of a salesman."

"I don't know," Jerry said. "I worked in a music store once. It really wasn't so bad. Every once in a while you meet a decent picker."

"Where was that?"

"Memphis. I sort of liked it. You get used to buying things wholesale, and you've still got enough time to play a job every now and then, if you want to."

"I didn't know you lived in Memphis."

"Went to Memphis State for a while. Then I dropped out and went to work full time. That's where I got stage happy, at the store. And I was just a kid, twenty-one or twenty-two, so I quit. But it really wasn't that bad."

"You ought to check into that," Billy said.

"I already got a job. I just thought you might be interested."

"No," he said. "I don't think that's for me. I'll just keep on playing

115

for Leon. He's not sick of me yet."

When Jerry sat back down on the sofa and picked up his guitar, Billy walked into the kitchen, flipped on the light above the stove, and looked over the whiskey bottles. He picked up a nearly full pint of George Dickel, took a paper cup from the stack on the cabinet, flipped off the light, and walked back out onto the porch. He closed the door behind him, sat back down on the glider, and poured himself a drink.

Inside, Jerry was playing a few soft chords on his Gibson, and things were starting to quiet down. Across the cove the dogs started up again, and Billy closed his eyes and listened. He could pick out three voices now, one much higher than the others. They started off barking, short sharp yelps, then the yelps grew longer and turned into howls, the high voice almost piercing as it came across the water, and Billy thought of a good high tenor in a bluegrass band, his voice cutting right through the lead, the baritone, and the bass. And he thought of Jack and Nolan tramping across those hills. Jack and Nolan with rifles in their arms. And that thought bothered him all the way through the first whiskey and into a second.

What bothered him after that was Jerry, what Jerry had said about looking for work. What business was it of his, anyway? What business was it of anybody's? And then the business about Harold Wright. Why in the world would he want to work for Harold Wright? Why in the world would he want to spend his life selling guitars?

He noticed that the barking had stopped, and there was only the Gibson and Jerry's voice rising in the room behind him. It was a blues tune. Something about a woman so mean she'd make your blood run cold, so mean she'd turn sugar into salt. Jerry got into the blues then, his voice rising at times to a full shout. And Billy listened to him for what must have been an hour, the Dickel going steadily down in the bottle, the porch growing steadily warmer. Then suddenly he'd had enough of the place and enough of the

116

people, and he was ready to go.

He stood up, but his legs weren't working very well. He leaned for a minute against the arm of the glider and tried to steady the sway of the porch. When he got his balance, he stepped over to the door and pushed it open.

The room was still dark, only the candlelight, and he couldn't see Jean. Jerry was singing something quieter now, some kind of ballad, and Billy leaned into the door. "Jean," he said. "Let's go."

"Ssssh," somebody said from the kitchen.

"Jean," he said.

"Ssssh," somebody said again.

Jean stood up and made her way across the room, and Billy backed out of the doorway. She walked out onto the porch and closed the door behind her.

"What's wrong, Baby," she said. "You lonesome?"

"I'm ready to go. Get your stuff and let's go."

"Not just yet, Baby. I'm having a good time."

"Well, I'm not. I've had enough of this. Let's go."

"It's early yet. It's not even twelve."

"Well, listen," he said. "I'm leaving. You hang around as long as you want to. Maybe Nolan'll give you a ride home."

Her expression changed, and he thought she looked almost pale against the dark wall of the porch. "So what do you mean by that?"

"Nothing. Not a thing. Only that Nolan's been getting pretty good about carting you around lately."

"Oh, I see," she said. "You're being rather silly, don't you think?"

"You're pretty goddamned determined, aren't you. I suppose nothing else in the goddamned world accounts for anything."

"I'd really rather not start this, you know. I thought we'd settled that."

"You thought, huh?"

"Let's not be silly," she said. "This isn't the place for it. And lower your voice."

"Lower my voice? You think I'm the one who's attracting

117

attention?"

"Let's not be foolish, Billy. You've had too much to drink."

"I've had too much of a lot of things."

"I'm sure I don't know what you're talking about. And this —"

"For one damned thing I'm talking about Nolan Hughes carting you around all over the goddamned place."

She looked away from him and stared out into the dark. Then she raised her eyebrows and turned back. "I see," she said again.

"And I see too. I'm not half as goddamned blind as you think I am."

"You know," she said. "Sometimes you are very stupid and foolish, and this is one of those times."

"That's not very convincing."

"I really don't care whether it is or isn't."

10

The thunder woke him. The rain sounded like someone washing the side of the house with a pressure hose. It was still dark, then half the room went alive with lightning, the corner of the chest, the corner of the bed, the rocking chair, the quilt rack, the open door of the closet. Jean was moving around in the bathroom. He could hear her brushing her teeth, rattling through the things on her makeup shelf. He thought about saying something to her, but he couldn't think of anything to say. He thought about asking her what time it was, or how she felt, anything. But he only lay there until the front door closed, then he reached down and pulled up the spread.

When he woke again, it was after ten-thirty. The rain had let up some, but it was still coming down at a steady pace. The house was a little chilly, so when he dressed he put on a long sleeve shirt. He checked the thermostat to make sure Jean hadn't turned on the air, then he fixed himself a bowl of Cheerios, opened a can of Pepsi, and sat down at the kitchen table.

Crazy things were happening on the pond, the wind whipping the water one way, then another, suddenly turning the pond into a big whirlpool that spun for a minute in the center, then ran off into the cove, under the barbwire fence and into the brush leaning over the bank. The jon boat was half full of rain, a beer can floating on its side between the seats. The yard looked like a swamp. And none of this bothered the ducks. They paddled around in the shallows like it was the best of days.

Billy hadn't slept well, and he had a headache that bordered on a hang-over. He'd spent a lot of the night thinking all of the obvious things about Jean, things he'd gone over in his head time and again, knowing all along that thinking about them would do absolutely no good because they were inevitable and, in many ways, had little to do with him. And he thought too about Jerry Lamberti sitting out on Jack's porch, about Jerry sizing up his future. And that still bothered him. At least he could still play music, he could still draw a decent enough crowd. And that was something. He wasn't smashing his fingernails blue with a hammer. And he never had to worry about slicing off a finger with a power saw. And he drew a decent enough check. All of that accounted for something, didn't it? And then what bothered him was the way he felt. How could he feel that way about Jerry Lamberti?

When the phone rang Billy didn't get up to answer it. He just sat in front of the window, eating his cereal and watching the ducks cut up in the rain. But it kept on ringing, and he thought it might be Jean.

It was Jack. He wanted to know if Billy was coming into town today.

"I hadn't thought about it. What's on your mind?"

"Nothing terribly serious. I thought we might have a chance to talk last night, but it didn't work out."

"So what's the mystery?"

"No, nothing like that," Jack said. "I've just come across a piece of information that might be worth mentioning, and the telephone's no way to talk it over."

Billy felt his heart sink, it was like a flurry of requests, and behind his eyes the little knot of light glaring like the lantern flare tightened enough to make him wince. So Jack knew. Well, of course, he knew. He had to know. And the last thing Billy needed was an hour or so of awkward, trite advice.

"So what time are you talking about?" Billy said.

"I'm in class until three-thirty. How about four at The Under Thing?"

"No, let's not go down there. I see enough of that place."

"All right," Jack said. "Four o'clock at The Brew and Cue."

As soon as Billy hung up, he thought about calling back and saying he couldn't make it. Why should he talk to Jack about it? What business was it of his? But, of course, it was too late for that. It would look too funny. Still, it bothered him. What business was it of Jack's? And what did Jack expect him to do?

After Billy cleaned up his dishes, he went upstairs to take a shower. There was an envelope taped to the door of his room. He took it down and pulled out one of Jean's note cards, a watercolor on the front, a marsh hen standing in tall grass beside a wallowed-out nest. In the nest was one brown egg. He opened the card and read it.

> I love you, Billy.
> Don't be silly.

He folded the card, slid it back into the envelope, and laid it on top of a speaker. Then he went into the bathroom and turned on the water in the shower. Out the window he could see the rain coming down hard again on the pond. The ducks were huddled along the muddy edge of the yard, the rain trying to wash them clean. Of all things, he thought of Marilyn McKinley, of something she'd said once right out there by the edge of that pond. And then he thought about Nolan Hughes. Jean, of course, didn't love him. Nolan was only a convenience, as Marilyn would say, someone to be shared, to be borrowed. Then the window started to fog over, and he said the hell with it all and took a shower.

Jean came home around one-thirty. Billy was up in his room with the guitar, trying to recall a few of the gospel tunes Jerry Lamberti had sung at Jack's house. She rang the bell five or six times as fast as she could, and by the time Billy got to the top of the stairs, she'd rung it five or six more times.

When he opened the door, a huge grocery bag slid into his arms, then another. She was standing under an umbrella and balancing a third bag against the frame of the door.

"Put these on the cabinet," she said. "And there's another one in the back of the car."

Billy put the bags in the kitchen, took her umbrella and walked out to the car to get the other bag. The rain was still coming down hard, and the front yard was starting to puddle, two wide streams of water washing down the shoulders of the street. He pushed the umbrella into the wind, but the rain blew under it, and by the time he wrestled the bag out of the back seat, the legs of his pants were soaked.

He left the umbrella and the boots in the hall and carried the bag into the kitchen, sat it down on the stove. He leaned against the wall, pulled off his socks, and draped them across the arm of a chair. "I'm going to have to change my pants."

"Don't be such a baby." She had already emptied two bags and was working on the third. "They'll dry. You had any lunch?"

"I had some Cheerios about ten or so."

"Can you eat a sandwich now, or do you want to wait a while?"

"Are you eating?" he said.

"I'm starved. All I've had all morning is coffee."

"I'll have a sandwich then."

"What about a B.L.T.?"

"Whatever." He started emptying the last bag. Milk, eggs, Swiss cheese, cheddar cheese, skim milk, bacon. He was laying out a whole dairy case on the cabinet.

"Listen," she said. "If it's dry tomorrow, I'd like you to help me break up the dirt in those back flower beds. We've been putting that off for two weeks."

"It'll be too wet," he said. "Even if it stopped raining right now, the ground would still be too muddy."

"Well let's give it a try, all right? I'm getting tired of putting off things that need to be done."

He was right, but he didn't want to argue. "So how was class?"

"Class was fine. We worked on set designs. What have you done today?"

"Not much."

"You think you might help me with the vacuuming?"

"Sure," he said. "Then I've got to run into town later." It depressed him to think about it.

"What for?"

"Leon's got somebody playing in there tonight, and he's having some trouble with the P.A. I told him I'd meet him about four." Billy took two plates out of the cupboard and sat them on the table. "You got rehearsal tonight?"

"Always, Baby. You know that."

"Try not to be so late."

"Don't forget the place mats." She folded the grocery bags and put them in the basket behind the table. "Why doesn't he ever ask Jerry to play in there? I think it would do Jerry some good to get out in public once in a while."

"I think Jerry's through with music. Anyhow, that's his business."

"No, he's just taking a break. No one who plays as well as Jerry is ever through playing music."

"Maybe not. You know, he said something sort of funny last night."

"What's that?"

"He told me that Harold Wright's looking for somebody at Tallahassee Music."

"Why is that funny?"

123

"I don't know. Only that he'd mention it to me, I guess."

She took a frying pan from the cabinet underneath the counter and sat it on the eye of the stove. Then she turned and looked at him over her shoulder. "Are you going to call him?"

"I don't think so. I don't think I want to spend the rest of my life selling guitars and banjos."

She started peeling off strips of bacon and laying them in the pan. After a few seconds they started to sizzle. She let them fry for a minute, then flipped them over with a fork. "It might be a change," she said. "A nice break. If it paid as well as The Under Thing."

"I don't think so," he said. "I don't see myself behind a cash register. I don't think I'd like it."

"Who knows? It might be a nice break."

Billy took two glasses from the dishwasher and put them on the table. He opened the fridge, took out a can of Pepsi, and sat it on the table beside his glass. "You having tea?"

"I'll fix it. Want your bread toasted?"

"I don't care," he said. "Whatever you're having."

"Toasted."

Billy looked out the window again. She was standing near the edge of the yard, the rain pelting her umbrella and raincoat. The ducks had made a semicircle around her feet and were climbing up each other's backs to get to the crackers she dangled over their heads. Then she squeezed the stack and a curtain of crumbs rained down under the umbrella. She took a couple of steps back so they wouldn't maul her legs, then held up another stack of crackers. She liked to see them go crazy like that, pecking the grass into a puddle of mud, wobbling around her feet in a frantic parade, turning her around and around, the umbrella spinning off circles of rain. She had a whole box of stale honey grahams, and Billy figured she'd be out there until every cracker was crumbled and gone.

He opened the phone book on the kitchen table and leaned over it for three or four minutes, watching her tease the ducks. Then he pushed off the chair, walked over to the phone, and dialed the number.

Out the window he could see the wind beating the trees on the far side of the pond, leaves and pine needles flying down the bank like confetti. The wind shifted suddenly and the window was drenched with a curtain of rain.

"Tallahassee Music."

"Is Harold around?" he said.

"In Jacksonville on a buying trip. Won't be back till Friday morning. Can I help you with something?"

"Is this Wayne?" he said.

"Sure is."

"Wayne, this is Billy Parker."

"Right, Billy. What can I do for you?"

"Listen," he said. "I heard that Harold might be looking for some help. You know anything about that?"

"Yeah, Harold's been talking that way. That's about all I can tell you. But you know how Harold is. He might talk about it for a year before he decides to put anybody on. Why? You interested?"

"I thought I might check it out."

"Well, I don't much know what to tell you. We could use some help, but I don't have any idea what Harold'll do. He needs to do something before summer, though. Be a big jump in lessons then."

"You like it there?" Billy said.

"It's five days a week. Nine till six, and everybody works on Saturday. But it's all right."

"That's pretty long hours."

"But the work's easy enough."

"Well," Billy said, "I might call him back on Friday."

"You ain't playing anywhere now?"

"I'm still down at The Under Thing. Jerry Lamberti just mentioned that Harold might be looking for some help. Thought it might be worth looking into."

125

"Jerry was in here a week or so ago. First time I'd seen him in months."

"He stays pretty busy."

"That's what he said. He looked real good, though. Must be liking that carpenter business."

"He says it's tough, but I guess he likes it okay."

"I tell you what," he said. "Harold's supposed to call in sometime this afternoon. I'll tell him you called and get back with you. No sense walking around in the dark all week."

"I'd appreciate that," Billy said. "I won't be here this afternoon, but I'll be around tonight."

"Tonight?"

"Anytime's okay."

When Billy hung up the phone and stepped over to put the book away, he stood for a minute by the table and stared out the window. Jean had folded up the umbrella and laid it down beside her on the grass. Her hair was plastered to her head, and she was sitting on her raincoat in a puddle of mud, her legs crossed under her Indian-style. There were ducks all around her, ducks in her lap, ducks trying to crawl up her back. It irritated Billy to see her wallowing like that in the yard, and he leaned across the table and rapped on the window. When she didn't hear him, he rapped again. Then he gave up. She couldn't hear anything. She was surrounded by a flurry of wings and splashing mud, the ducks honking like bad traffic, all flapping for the honey grahams she held as high as she could above their heads.

11

Turner Kay racked the balls into a tight diamond while Billy wandered around the room, looking for a cue. Over the last few months they had let the place go down considerably. The problem was the new bar across the street, The Seminole Room, complete with pool tables, dart boards, bumper pool, and video arcade. The upshot was that The Brew and Cue lost practically all its fraternity business, which seemed to Billy a great improvement. Unfortunately, that also made it hard for the owners to keep the room up. Now the only people who ever came into the place were the old hard-cores, the guys who had been coming in regularly for eight and ten years. Nothing had changed for them. They came in, as always, with their cues tucked under their arms. They shot the same games at the same tables and griped only occasionally if there was no chalk on the tables or no powder in the dispensers. Or if anything had changed for them, it was for the better. There was no waiting for a table now, and there were never any loud drunks or rowdy crowds.

For Billy things were not that convenient. There were, for instance, no decent cues. They had stopped trying to repair them months ago, and half of those hanging in the racks looked like something W.C. Fields might use in a bad skit. Most of the others had busted tips. Billy took one off the wall and rolled it across a table. It hopped like a frog.

Turner Kay unzipped his case and screwed the two sections of his cue together. Billy motioned for him to go ahead and break, then he tried a few more cues. When he found something almost straight, he walked over to check the damage.

A typical game of nine ball with Turner Kay. Billy gets in a shot, sometimes two, Turner drops the nine. Billy pulls out a buck and drops it into a corner pocket. In two years of shooting pool with Turner Kay, he could count the games he'd won on his left hand. But he liked Turner, sort of the disreputable member of an old respectable Tallahassee family, a regular in the place, a gambler, divorced, nothing better to do than watch ball games and shoot pool. Billy thought of it as an education. And the tuition was cheap enough, so he kept coming back.

"You know what you oughta do?" Turner said.

"What's that?"

"You oughta give up pocket billiards and get something down on the game this weekend."

"Oh yeah? You got the latest?"

"Seminoles. Three runs."

It was the first home game for Florida State. They had a new coach, an ex-Brave who had managed Richmond to a Triple-A pennant, and they had won their first five on the road.

Turner helped him clear the pockets.

"What do you think?" Billy said.

"I don't think the Gamecocks'll leave here the Lamecocks."

"You don't, huh?"

"I said it."

Billy racked the balls tight, eased the rack off the table, and hung it on the wall. "How you figure that?" he said.

Turner set on the cue ball, then whack. Colors all over the table.

The four ball dropped into a corner, then the balls rolled to a slow halt. "They gonna bring that Lopez kid back. Been hurt. He's the lefty that pitched the no-hitter last year." He leaned over the table and cracked the one ball into the side pocket. "Seminoles got too many left-handed hitters in the line-up. Can't substitute, all their power's on the left side. They won't do nothing with him."

"I don't know."

Turner chalked the tip of his cue, set on the cue ball, and eased the two by the seven and into the corner. Then he dropped the three and the five, one in each side. "Three runs don't even make it gambling," he said. "You better get down twenty or so. You ain't gonna make no money here."

When Jack came in, he hung his umbrella on the coat rack and walked to the bar. He bought two bottles of Bud and took them over to a booth. Billy watched Turner Kay crack the nine ball into the side, then he pulled another bill from his pocket, folded it twice, and dropped it on top of the nine. He nodded toward Turner, hung up his cue, and walked up front.

"So how'd you fare?" Jack said.

Billy sat down in the booth and took a swallow of the beer. "I got my money's worth."

"Sorry, I'm late. Got caught in a conference."

"Female?"

"One of the more attractive ones in my class."

"Sounds interesting."

"Not as interesting as I'd have liked it to be. Then again, they're only kids. I have to keep reminding myself of that."

"No, they're not," Billy said. "I think they're calling them young women now."

"When you're twice their age, they're kids." He took a swallow of the Bud. "You know," he said, "You used to be able to get a Watney's in here, or a Bass."

"They stopped carrying imports. That new joint across the street got all their college business."

"Well, there's a curse behind every blessing."

Billy took a deep breath and let himself settle. "So what's the big mystery?" he said. He didn't really want to talk about it, he only wanted to get it out in the open and over.

Jack took another swallow of his beer, then leaned across the table. "No mystery, really. I've just got something to ask you, and I've been trying to think of the right way to approach it."

"Now I'm supposed to say something like 'Why don't you just come out and say it?'"

"Maybe. And I intend to. But it's the sort of thing that requires a little prefacing."

Christ, was it going to be that hard? Billy smiled a little. "So preface," he said. "Let's get it out."

"All right. But what I've got to say—Listen, I know we haven't known each other very long, but I sort of feel like we know each other pretty well in a number of ways. Am I wrong?"

"No."

"Then you think we're close enough to share a confidence?"

Billy's heart sank. "I hope so," he said.

"Good," Jack said. "That's very important to me. I tell you what. I'm going to ask you a question, and I want you to think before you answer it. It might sound a little silly, but think about it anyway."

"This is starting to sound a little bizarre." He wasn't smiling anymore.

"I'm sorry. I hadn't wanted it to sound like that."

"Okay," Billy said. "What's the question?"

"The question is this. Do you trust me?"

"That's it?"

"That's it? Do you trust me? And do you believe I'd ever do anything to harm you, give you any bad advice?"

Billy looked at him hard. He looked at every line in his face, every gray hair in his beard. He looked at his lips pressed together tight, half hidden under his moustache. He looked at his eyes. Jack's expression never changed.

"Sure," Billy said. "I suppose I trust you."

"And you believe I'd never do anything to cause you any harm or put you in any real danger?"

"I don't suppose you would. At least, I hope you wouldn't. What the hell are you driving at?"

"Just this one more question. Could you use some money?"

What did this have to do with Jean? Where was he going with this crazy stuff about money? "Who couldn't use some money?"

"No, let me start again. Think about it this way. I know you're still torn up about this music shit, and what I want to know is this. Would money make any difference? Think about it seriously, because if it's the sort of thing money can't help I won't go any farther."

What was all this business about money? Then it occurred to him that Jack had never intended to talk about Jean at all. This was something totally different, totally out of left field. And when his head cleared he started to think, and the two people he thought about were Jerry Lamberti and Leon Thibodeaux. What was the real difference between them, between the situations they found themselves in? Only that one had had the money he needed and the other hadn't. No, that was too simplistic.

Billy took a sip of his beer. "Listen," he said. "I don't want to borrow any money from you."

"Good, because I don't have any to lend you."

"I don't get it."

"I'm only asking if money would help."

"Well money always helps, doesn't it?"

"Not always," Jack said. "But sometimes it tends to make things more convenient."

"I don't see what you're getting at?"

"Suppose I told you how you might come across a good bundle of money fairly quickly?"

"I'd be interested. Then I'd be suspicious. I hope you're talking about something legal."

"That's sort of a gray area," Jack said. "But I think you can say that we're talking about something absolutely moral. Something that is without question incredibly moral."

"Listen," Billy said. "I can tell you right now that I'm not interested in getting mixed up with the law."

"Me either, that's the last thing anybody needs. And you can put that out of your mind. There's really very little to worry about there."

"So what are you getting at?"

Jack wasn't looking at him then. He was looking over his shoulder toward the bar. Billy turned sideways and saw Turner Kay, cue case under his arm, walking toward the coat rack directly behind him. Turner didn't say anything, only stopped at the door and slipped on a raincoat and a hat.

"Take care," Billy said.

Turner said, "You too, kid. And about Saturday. Don't say I didn't give you the tip."

When the door closed, Billy turned back around in the booth. "You were saying?"

Jack cleared his throat, leaned forward, and propped an elbow on the table. "Suppose I told you I had a friend, absolutely reliable and trustworthy, who possessed good information about the goings on of some folks involved in a somewhat shady trade."

"Namely?" Billy said.

"Namely, the distribution of various controlled substances to certain small-time toughs in south and middle Florida."

"Then I'd start to get a little nervous."

"And I'd say that was a reasonable reaction. But suppose I told you that what he proposed was just about foolproof and not quite as dangerous as crossing Tennessee Street on a Friday night."

"I'd say Friday night on Tennessee's no trick."

"Maybe not," Jack said. "And that's part of the point. You'll do a lot of things in your life that are just as dangerous and not nearly as profitable."

Billy smiled. He didn't know how to take this. "So, just out of curiosity. What's this friend proposing?"

"All right, suppose again, and we're supposing in strict confidence."

"Sure."

"Then suppose a certain group of small-time toughs in south Florida are about to make a major purchase from a group of small-time toughs from north Florida. And suppose my friend has very reliable information as to the time and the place of this exchange and has studied this operation very carefully and determined that it's quite possible for a small appropriately armed group to intercept these guys before the exchange is made and relieve them of their cash without meeting any noticeable resistance."

Billy didn't say anything for a minute, only took a swallow of his beer. "You're serious about this, aren't you?"

Jack's face didn't change its expression. "Of course."

"Do you have any idea how something like this sounds to somebody like me?"

"Yes, I do. And that's why I want to be very careful to point out that the risk here is actually much smaller than it might seem. Actually, for you the risk would be very small. To make a long story short, we need a fisherman who knows how to handle a small boat, and when the time comes to stand watch, be a lookout. Your part in this business wouldn't go any farther than that."

Billy leaned back in the booth. "Who exactly is the *we* here?"

"There'd be four of us."

"Okay, that's you and me. Who're the other two?"

"Well, I'm not sure I can —"

"Is one of these guys Nolan Hughes?"

"I suppose that's obvious."

"Then one of these groups of toughs must be the Generals?"

Jack raised his eyebrows, then he took a swallow of his beer.

Nolan Hughes. Billy wasn't surprised. "So," he said, "Nolan's crossing his biker pals?"

"Not quite. That'd put everybody in too much jeopardy, Nolan especially. The Generals are making the sale. We intercept the buyers before the sale is made."

"And nobody is the wiser?"

"Probably not."

"Do Nolan and this other guy know you're talking to me?"

"We discussed it."

"Why me?"

"Well, the operation calls for four guys. Too much could go wrong with three. Five would be safer, but the profit wouldn't justify the risk."

"But why me?"

"Actually we had somebody else, but he had to drop out. So why not you? We'll have to take somebody. And you're stable, you can handle a boat, you can be trusted, and you can put the money to good use."

Billy peeled half the label off his Bud bottle, wadded it up, and dropped it into the ash tray. "How many boats?" he said.

"Two boats. Just a short trip up river. It'll be just like a fishing trip. You'll hardly know the difference. In fact, that's the whole point. You may even catch a few."

"You've done this sort of thing before, haven't you?"

"Listen," Jack said. "I just saw an opportunity for you, and I thought it might be worth mentioning."

"It's not the risk," Billy said. "I don't think of myself as a coward."

"Nobody else does either. Mentioning this to you at all is proof enough of that."

"Sure," he said. "It's just that this isn't my sort of thing. I just don't think in terms of something like that. This kind of business is just a little drastic for me."

"For anybody, I suppose. But some people do drastic things. It all depends on what it's worth to you."

"And that's my point. Some people might do drastic things, but I don't. It isn't worth that much to me. My situation isn't quite

134

that desperate."

Jack wrinkled his eyebrows and looked straight at Billy. "You say that as if it were bad news. I'm really glad to hear it. I didn't know if it was or not."

"Well, even if things turned that rotten, there are lots of other options."

"For instance?" Jack said.

"For one, I could get a job."

For the first time, Jack broke into a smile. He leaned toward Billy. "And that's not drastic?"

"No, you're right," Billy said. "For me that would be fairly drastic. But a lot less drastic than your idea."

"You got anything lined up?"

"Not really. But Jerry Lamberti put me onto something. A job at a music store."

"Downtown?"

"Governor's Square. Tallahassee Music, down by Burdine's."

"You looked into it?"

"I gave them a call. The guy who owns the place is out of town. He's supposed to call me back."

"I suppose this is a selling job." There was a slight touch of disapproval in his voice. "That's tough work."

"Probably selling," Billy said. "Guitars, amps, banjos, whatever. Maybe doing some repair work too. I don't know."

"Well, you're good at that. And you could sell, you're good with people. It's tough work, but I've known folks who could make a decent living at it."

"I don't know. And I don't even know if I could do it. I'm just thinking about it, that's all."

"Let me ask you something," Jack said. "What would you like to do? I mean in a perfect world where you could do anything you wanted, what would you like to do?"

"Who knows?" Billy said. "And I don't think it does much good to think about things like that."

"Maybe it does. What would you do? I'm just curious?"

"In a perfect world?"

"Sure."

"I suppose I'd play perfect music for perfect people."

"Well," Jack said, "in a world a little less perfect. Playing music aside."

"Who knows? I like the notion of doing something for myself. But I don't know what it would be. Maybe I'd go back to school, get some kind of degree you can do something with."

"You went to Georgia, didn't you?"

"Three years. Folklore major." He smiled. "Can you imagine all the opportunities waiting on a folklore major?"

"Or an English major," Jack said. "But whatever you decide to do, seventy or seventy-five thousand dollars would make it a lot easier."

"That much?"

"Maybe. Maybe a little more."

Billy smiled again. "But that's not the point, is it?"

"It's something to think about. It's something to think about very carefully." Jack finished his beer and sat the bottle on the table. "You want another one?"

"No," Billy said. "I don't think so."

It's raining in Korea. A Jeep rolls by, mud halfway up its tires. The rain has been falling for days and the tents look gray and soggy. The wind looks like it might blow them all down. A man in a gray parka comes out of a tent and walks across the compound toward the latrines. You can't see his face, and in the rain and mud he looks like an old cartoon of death. You wonder where he's left his scythe. He stops for a minute at the edge of the road, stands absolutely still, then tilts his head as though he's listening to the sky turn the road into a river. Some trash blows by his feet, wrinkled gray paper tumbling in the wind, and he stands there all alone in the rain, his head tilted toward the mountains. Any minute now, the choppers.

When the phone rings, Billy leans up in his chair and turns down the TV. A little dizzy on Irish, he gets up and walks into the kitchen to answer it.

"Saturday," the voice says. "One o'clock."

"What's that?"

"Saturday," the voice says. "Harold says to come in on Saturday and talk to him. One o'clock. Things look good."

"Saturday," Billy says.

The kitchen is dark. The porchlight is off and the deck is dark. There are stars out on the pond, and the lights from the houses across the pond are floating with the stars. The hands on the clock above the stove are shining. They say nine-thirty. Jean is across town at the theater. She is helping Serafina remember her lines. Billy can see her sitting on a stool off stage, the script folded open in her hand. She is smoking. Prop men are milling around backstage. A few more people in the audience. Nolan Hughes is studying the actors from the second row, his legs draped across the back of the seat in front of him. There is a dazed look on Serafina's face. Jean is trying to whisper. The words are hovering somewhere in the air between them.

At one o'clock Billy switches off *The Avengers* and goes to bed. Where is Jean now?

12

All the cars in front of Billy had followed the detour signs and turned left onto Tennessee Street. Billy was about to turn left himself when he looked through the thin crowd gathered on the curb and saw a Seminole Indian riding a pinto horse, a Seminole Indian in war paint and buckskin pants and mocassins, strands of red and gold beads hanging across his bare chest, and in his headband two feathers like the ones on the tip of his spear, red and gold feathers that bobbed up and down with the gait of his horse.

Behind him marched a chorus line of Indian princesses dressed in buckskin bikinis. Their spears were shorter, and they were twirling them like batons, the feathers on the tips making red and gold circles in the air. As they approached the street corner a few whoops and whistles rose out of the crowd, drum rolls thundering at the end of the street. Billy was a little early, so he pulled over onto the lot of a Gulf station and parked the truck beside a phone booth.

The first thing he thought about was Homecoming. But they'd already had one of those this year. A banner went by between two spears. "Go Noles!" Then the parade hit the corner of Monroe and the whole intersection exploded into a march, people yelling and throwing confetti, Indians doing war dances up and down the street, three bass drums pounding like tom-toms, cymbals clanging. Billy sat in the truck and watched it pass. Not much more, only a few flatbed trucks loaded with cheerleaders and baseball players and in the last truck, a Seminole with an electric megaphone. Go Noles, Go Noles, Go Noles.

They moved down Monroe toward the middle of town, and Billy sat waiting for the traffic cop to move the sawhorse that was blocking the street. Small as it was, the parade seemed like a lot of trouble to go to for a baseball game. This was the sort of thing that would have annoyed him on any other day, but today was too nice for that, too promising. The sky was absolutely clear, not a trace of anything like a cloud, the temperature holding in the mid-seventies.

If it looked like a good day, it looked like an even better night. Billy was already making plans. He'd have Jack or Leon drive over to the theater and pick up Jean, bring her down to The Under Thing. They'd break open a bottle of champagne. Did Leon have any champagne? They'd send out for a bottle. He wanted it to be a good party. Who could tell how Jean might react? Even if it had been her idea, she'd certainly never expect him to do it. So who could tell how she might react?

He tilted the rearview mirror toward him, turned up his collar, and put on his tie. He smiled at his little deceit. On his way out of the house, she'd caught him coming down the stairs.

"So where are you off to?" she said.

"Into town. You need something?"

"No, thanks. What's in town?"

He held up the bag he'd stuffed a good pair of slacks and a tie into. "Radio Shack. Need to get some mikes checked out."

When the last truck in the parade was out of sight, the cop pulled the sawhorse to the curb and motioned the traffic on. Several other folks had stopped to watch, and the cars had stacked up into a major jam. Billy had to wait a few minutes before anyone would let him pull back in.

It was strange to see downtown crowded. It looked like something you might see on Peachtree in Atlanta, people elbow to elbow on both sides of the street, ignoring crosswalks, stepping out into the traffic, banging on hoods to make cars stop. And all for what was literally a one-horse parade? Maybe something else was up. The Chamber of Commerce was always throwing stunts of one sort of another to draw folks away from the malls. Street dances, carnivals, festivals to celebrate everything from Flag Day to National Education Week. Not much escaped them.

Off Apalachee Parkway he turned left onto the access road, climbed the long hill, and passed under the marble arch of Governor's Square. The top of the hill leveled off into a gigantic paved plain, fifty or sixty acres of asphalt parking lot, and at the center a huge mall of marble, brick and steel, roofed with rows of glass geodesic domes. It looked to Billy like something out of a science fiction movie, something meant to dwell in the sky. It dwarfed everything else in Tallahassee, even the state capital building, and beside it the cars parked in their yellow stalls looked shabby and old. Even the bright new Cadillacs looked absolutely primitive.

The parking lot wasn't full, but it was already becoming crowded and there were no spaces very close. Tallahassee Music was on the far side of the mall, but Billy parked the truck by the Sears entrance so he could stop by the men's room and change his pants.

His knowledge of Governor's Square didn't go very far beyond Sears. Since Marilyn had opened her shop and Jean could buy whatever she wanted wholesale, she rarely bought any clothes anywhere else. Billy rarely bought any clothes at all, and most everything else they needed could be found in some department at Sears.

In the restroom he straightened his tie and combed his hair. The gray slacks fit a little tighter than they had the last time he'd worn them, but they looked all right, and he'd folded them carefully so they wouldn't wrinkle. He stuffed the jeans into the bag and stuck it under his arm.

The inside of the mall was just as striking as the outside, all brass and polished tile. Everything shined — the railings, the walls, the floors, the windows. In fact, the mall was so bright that from the center of the Sears store, the entrance looked like one huge wall of light.

When Billy stepped into that light, something strange caught his eye. He glanced up at the roof. Three single-engine airplanes hung on cables from the cross beams. Their props were bright polished wood and their wings and tails were canvas, bright green and yellow on one plane and green and orange on the other two. They were single seaters, the seat wedged just behind the engine, and their frames looked like they were made out of bicycle tubing. Underneath each frame hung three bicycle tires, spokes painted to match the wings. The airplanes looked like something Orville and Wilbur Wright might have smashed off some cliff at Kitty Hawk, but hanging against the glass domes they seemed strangely futuristic.

An orange booth made out of the same canvas sat on the floor in the center of the mall. It was sandwiched between two signs on metal easels, one an enlarged aerial photograph of a woman flying one of the planes over an open field, a farm house just off the tip of her right wing. She was wearing bright red goggles, and her hair blowing behind her like a scarf reminded Billy of a World War I flying ace.

Several people stood milling around the photo, talking with the salesman inside the booth, picking up pamphlets. A kid with patches on his jeans, a gray-haired man in a blue suit. Mostly unlikely types, but they were looking at the photo, going through the literature. Billy understood that, but he resisted the urge. He walked by just close enough to read the other sign. The letters were a deep blue, like the sky:

ICARUS RISEN
Wilson Ultra-light,
The Plane Pilots Fly For Fun

When he reached the music store he stopped to check out the windows. The right one held a couple of cornets, a silver trumpet, a French horn, a trombone, a saxophone with pearl buttons. They were displayed without much imagination on three red velvet risers.

The left window was all strings. Up front a Gibson F5 mandolin and an Ode teardrop, and three Gibson banjos sitting on guitar stands. An old Martin D18 or D21 leaned against the side wall, and above it hung three fiddles, two of them old and deep red, the other one new and Japanese and very blond.

The front of the store was a little misleading, only the two windows with a single glass door between them. But inside, the store opened up onto a huge sales floor. The place looked like a supermarket of musical instruments, and the only thing that softened the effect was the gold carpet on the floors and walls. All along the right wall were tall glass cases of band instruments, horns, flutes, clarinets, oboes. Two electric pianos and a xylophone sat on the floor in front of the horn cases, and behind them four or five sets of Slingerland drums, a rack of cymbals, and more high-hats.

The racks on the left wall held a dozen or so banjos and two long rows of guitars, acoustics toward the front and electric and bass guitars toward the back. Billy immediately picked out eight or ten Martins of different sorts, then there were Gallaghers, Gibsons, Washburns, Guilds, Yamahas, Fenders. A pretty good selection. And in front of the guitars, two glass cases full of mandolins, mostly Gibson F models, or imitations. On top of one of those cases sat an autoharp, a tiple, and a four stringed dulcimer, and on the floor in front of them, a half dozen dobros on guitar stands, and three pedal steels. Being around all of those instruments excited Billy, all of that possibility made something crawl along his spine, as though at any second one of those instruments might jump up and play the very best music anybody had ever heard.

Several folks were looking around, but it wasn't the sort of crowd he expected on a Saturday afternoon, and Billy wondered if everybody worked on a commission. Then it occurred to him how many people it would take to make that room look crowded. And there were probably some people in the back room too. He could see the tops of the amps through the glass divider. That was a smart idea, to have the amps in a separate room. That would save the salesmen a lot of noise.

Wayne Dobson walked around one of those amps and through the glass door. He had a guitar chord in his hand and was rolling it into a coil. Billy took his hands out of his pockets and walked back to speak to him.

"All right," Wayne said, and held out his hand.

Billy gave it a firm shake.

"Harold's downstairs with a customer. He'll be up in a few minutes. You know everybody else?"

"Just you and Harold," Billy said. "You know I don't get in here much."

"Trading with the competition." Wayne smiled and pushed his glasses up the bridge of his nose.

"Not really. I just don't need much, and I still get my strings wholesale out of Atlanta."

"I'm the same way," Wayne said. "If I didn't work in a music store, I don't guess I'd ever go around one. Too much stuff to see and I can't afford none of it." He glanced around the room. "When things free up, I'll introduce you to everybody. Right now, there's only six of us. That's sales people. We got one other guy in the shop. He just works on horns. Pads, valves, and whatever goes on horns. Another guy comes in twice a week and works on amps and heads."

"So all the repair work's done right here?"

"Every bit."

"And who's doing the guitar work?"

"That's me, right now. But we got plenty enough to pass around." He nodded toward the front of the room. "That guy up there with the trumpet is Bill Myers. He mostly handles the band instruments, and two days a week he's teaching piano. The guy with the banjo is Lamar Pierce. You don't know Lamar?"

144

"I don't think so."

"Teaches banjo. Plays a good mandolin too. Everybody else is in the back or downstairs. But they're pretty easy going. You'll fit right in here."

"You think so, huh?"

"No question," Wayne said. "And we could use another picker around here too. Right now it's only Lamar and me. Everybody else is into jazz and pop, all keyboards and horns. And damn if Harold ain't trying to learn how to play the vibes. I have to listen to that shit all the time."

"You playing a lot now?" Billy said.

He shook his head. "Not a lot. I sold my upright, bought me a Fender. Nobody wants a upright bass anymore."

Wayne threw his hand into the air, and Billy turned and saw Russell Reed coming through the front door. Russell was sporting a huge smile. He gave them a nod and walked on back.

Wayne looked glad to see him. "So," he said, "how's that banjo?"

"Still loving it," Russell said.

Wayne turned to Billy. "You seen this man's White Lady?"

Billy looked at Russell, who looked like a kid who'd just had a big Christmas. "What happened to your Mastertone?"

"It's on the wall over there. I came in here last week and Lamar was playing this Vega. 1949 White Lady with a Tree of Life inlay. I swear, the prettiest banjo I've ever seen, and a tone like the angels."

"We bought it off Claude Franklin," Wayne said. "You remember him?"

Billy shook his head.

"Used to pick with Carl Story. Lives over in Panama City now."

"Anyway," Russell said, "I picked one tune on it, and I knew I had to have it. Lamar beat me out of my socks, but I had to have that banjo. What can I say?"

"Lamar didn't beat you out of nothing," Wayne said. "You walked out with the best banjo, didn't you?"

"And I never regretted it." He turned to Billy, "So what's

happening with you. You still down at The Under Thing?"

"Still there. Haven't seen you around lately."

"I been working with this group, trying to get something together. It looked like it might work out for a while, but I don't know. They're pretty traditional."

Wayne took off his glasses and wiped them on his tie. "Didn't you say you all were playing around here somewhere?"

"Not us. We're just trying to put something together. Haven't practiced in two weeks, though, and it looks like it might fall apart. The biggest bitch is the miles. They all live down in Perry."

"You got to love it," Wayne said. "It's bad enough to have to practice at all, without having to drive to do it. You got to love it, that's all."

"Listen," Russell said. "What I got to do is run, and I need a couple of sets of strings, Gibson light gauge." He tapped Billy on the arm. "Let's get together and do some picking."

"You know where I am," Billy said. "I'd like to see that Vega."

"You down there tonight?"

"Just like always."

"We're supposed to practice, but I might drop by." He was already following Wayne toward the cash register and the wall covered with strings.

Harold sat down on the other side of the desk and took a paper bag out of the bottom drawer. From the bag he took two plastic Tupper Ware boxes and a sandwich wrapped in aluminum foil. "You don't mind if I dig in here, do you? I haven't had a minute all day."

"Sure," Billy said, but Harold was already lifting the tops off the Tupper Ware. One box was full of sliced carrot sticks, the other was full of apple slices that had started to yellow a little around the edges.

Harold crunched into a carrot stick, and Billy looked again at the three fish hanging on the wall above the filing cabinet. Three bass, largemouth. The two on the top were respectable bass, but the one on the bottom was a real lunker. Billy guessed it must have gone eight or nine pounds.

"So tell me something about yourself," Harold said. "I mean, why you're interested in Tallahassee Music."

"I'm looking for something steady, I guess."

"Playing music isn't steady?"

"It's steady work, I suppose. But maybe that's not the sort of steady I mean."

"What sort of steady do you mean?" He looked at Billy like he'd just asked a profound question.

Billy looked down at the desk calendar in front of him, one of those large blotter types. Harold had already torn away March and jotted in all his events in April. Maybe they were playing dates. Then Billy looked at the wall behind the desk, the autographed pictures of Duke Ellington and Jack Benny. Duke Ellington he could figure, but Jack Benny? And something about the picture bothered him. It was that famous Jack Benny expression, that look of mild astonishment he assumed when he crossed his arms and put his hand against his cheek. "I really don't know," Billy said. "Just not playing music. I guess I'm sort of burned out on playing music."

Harold was about to take a bite of his sandwich, but he stopped. "What makes you think you won't burn out on working in a music store?"

"I don't know," Billy said. "I honestly can't say that I won't."

"That's fair enough." He took a bite of the sandwich and chewed it like he was in a race. "You ever sell anything before?"

"Not a thing."

"It's not hard. Most of the people who come in here know exactly what they want. Sometimes they need some advice, a kid wants to learn how to play the guitar, he doesn't know anything about guitars, so you help him. But you don't have to sell him. He's sold before he ever walks in the door. Ted Nugent's already sold him, all you got to do is help him along. And you know strings so you won't

147

have any trouble."

"What about the hours?" Billy said.

"The hours aren't terrible. Everybody works five days a week, nine to six. Everybody works on Saturday. You can pick your days off, but you'll have to get with everybody else on that. We can't have four or five guys off on the same day. You'll also need to get with the other guys and go over the studio schedule. We got three nice music rooms downstairs. I think it's Wednesday that's open. The last guitar man we had taught on Wednesdays."

Billy was watching Jack Benny staring down from the wall. He shifted a little in his chair. "You know I've never taught any guitar."

Harold swallowed a bite of sandwich and sipped at his coffee. "There's nothing to it. You just grab you one of those Mel Bay books and go to it. You may have a few problems at first, with the beginners, I mean. Most everybody gets a little impatient. But you just have to lay back and be cool. You won't teach anybody anything overnight. Just remember that and you'll do okay." He sat his mug down on the calendar and looked across the desk at Billy. "You do read music, don't you?"

"Actually, I don't. The sort of stuff I play, I just play by ear."

Harold wrinkled his eyebrows. He didn't say anything for a few seconds, then he leaned forward and put his elbows on the desk. "Wayne didn't ask you that before you came in?"

"Never mentioned it."

"Billy, I'm sorry," he said. "I really am. But we've just got to have somebody that reads. We get calls in here every day about guitar lessons. And it's not just the lessons, it's what they buy when they get in here. The bottom's dropped right out of our guitar business. That bunch across town has started teaching and they're getting all the business."

"Sure," Billy said. "I understand. I just thought I'd check it out."

"Really, I'm awful sorry," Harold said again. "I should've had Wayne ask you that over the phone. If it wasn't for that, you'd be perfect."

148

"Sure, Harold. I understand." Billy had a hollow feeling in his chest. He thought for a second about saying he could learn how to read, but he didn't say it.

Billy leaned the guitar cases against the bar, picked up the glass of Irish whiskey, and took a sip. The room was considerably less than half full, a few people sitting around the stage, but most of the others sitting at the tables in the back. He sat on a bar stool and nursed the Irish. Oddly enough he didn't feel nearly as low as he might have. Only dull and a little hollow, the way he felt sometimes after he'd slept too long.

Leon came out of the office and drew himself a beer. "Might be a little thin tonight," he said.

"Because of a baseball game?"

"Ballgame, fireworks, lottery." He poured off the head and took a sip of the beer.

"Lottery?"

"Somebody's giving away a Toyota. Your pal Nolan Hughes is supposed to draw the winning ticket."

"What's the occassion?"

"Who knows?" Leon filled the glass to the top and walked back into the office.

Nolan Hughes giving away a car. The guy's everywhere. Well, maybe he'll rig it so that Jean wins.

Billy took a shot of the Jameson. He wasn't going to let himself fall into that attitude. All in all, he'd handled the day pretty well. The only thing that really plagued him was that photo. He could still see that face grinning at him from the wall behind Harold's desk. Not that it was anything ominous. More comical really, the sort of expression you have when you hear a good joke and suddenly figure out that it was on you.

He finished the Irish and set the glass on the bar. In the office Leon had turned on the radio. Billy could hear the announcer say something about a southpaw. Then the crowd drowned him out, and Leon rapped his fist on the wall.

"What happened?" Billy said.

"Walked a run in."

"What's the score?"

"FSU, six to zip. Bottom of the second."

Sarah Libby Cook came around the back of the bar, took the Jameson bottle off the shelf, and poured Billy another drink. She'd had her hair cut. It was flipped up and bouncy, parted on the side.

"When did that happen?" Billy said.

"This morning. I took it down to Head Hunters. Felt like something different. What do you think?"

"Looks good."

"It's cooler, anyway." She left the bottle on the bar and walked off to wait a table.

Billy felt like something different too, but he didn't know what until he'd started the first set. He cradled the D28 in his lap and looked out across the half-empty room. In the dark place behind his eyes there was still that faint but steady glow, that little knot of light like the lantern flare bobbing on Lake Talquin. He was trying not to think of all the things that fired it, of Jean, Nolan, of Tallahassee Music. He hit a D chord, then an A. The knot tightened. He strummed through an A minor and back to a G. He was thinking about how to loosen it up, make it fade, and he remembered Jerry Lamberti playing in Jack's cabin, Jerry's voice pouring out into the dark, the warmth of it and the clarity. He played through a slow intro in G, then went into a laid back version of "When I Take My Vacation in Heaven." Halfway through the first stanza, everybody in the back stopped talking, every eye in the room stared at him, mostly in disbelief. When I take my vacation in Heaven, what a wonderful time that will be. Hearing concerts by the Heavenly chorus, and the face of my Savior I'll see.

Leon came out of the office and stood with his hands on his hips at the end of the bar. Sitting down by the banks of the river, 'neath the shade of the evergreen tree, I shall rest from my burdens forever, won't you take your vacation with me? Then through the second verse and another chorus, and when Billy finished, not a soul in the place clapped a hand or said a word. Leon raised his eyebrows and walked back into the office. Sarah Libby Cook set a pitcher under the Stroh tap and jerked the handle. A faint roar, like static, came from the radio. A few glasses rattled in the back of the room.

Billy played a slow G chord and let it ring into the mike. Then he slid down to a D and played a slow turn-around. Why do you have a holiday religion and only go to church twice a year? Christmas Day and Easter Sunday morning are the only times that you are here.

Sarah Libby Cook sat down at a table near the stage, and Leon came back out of the office with an odd smile on his face, and every eye in the place looked at Billy like he was something strange.

You complain the church is crowded when it's Christmas Day. You come late and you leave early, that's the way you pray. And all through that, slow and easy, the Martin ringing like church bells, and when the last note died and there was nothing but silence, a guy in the back of the room said, "Play another one." And Billy did. And after that he felt as good as he'd ever felt at The Under Thing. He played some old Hank Williams gospel, "House of Gold" and "I Saw the Light." Then just some old Hank Williams, and half the people in the back got up and moved to the front, and all the rest leaned back in their chairs and listened.

It went on like that, sort of a private party, until almost eleven-thirty when people started to drift in. From the looks of them, the Seminoles had stayed on top. They were happy and rowdy and ready to celebrate. Billy thought about Turner Kay hustling the pool room, trying to scrap up enough cash to cover his bets. A strange day all right. When Turner Kay loses a bet on baseball, the world is truly upside down.

Jack Giddens came in and with him, of all people, Nolan Hughes. They sat down at the bar and gave Billy a smile. The knot tightened slightly, but Billy ignored it, nodded back, and went into a song. Each night I leave the barroom when it's over, not feeling any

151

pain at closing time. But tonight your memory found me much too sober, couldn't drink enough to keep you off my mind.

Halfway through it two Generals sat down at a table near the stage. Billy thought one of them looked slightly familiar, a big guy with a black beard, but the other guy, smaller and clean-shaven, he'd never seen before. Nolan Hughes slid off his barstool, walked over, and sat down at their table. Sarah Libby Cook brought a pitcher of beer and three glasses.

When break time came, Billy walked over to the end of the bar and sat down by Jack. Leon sat a snifter on the bar in front of Billy, then brought up a bottle of Martel and set it on the bar between them.

Jack poured the drinks. "You see those guys with Nolan?" he said.

"Sure."

"You know anything about them?"

"Not really. I've seen the big guy in here before. And sometimes a few other Generals wander in."

"What do you think about guys like that?"

Billy took a sip of the Martel. He looked at Jack's face. It was cool and expressionless. "I don't know. They get a little loud sometimes, but I got nothing against them."

"You know where those guys get their money?"

"Who cares?"

"Their women suck cock for it."

"So?"

Jack turned and looked at the three men sitting at the table. Then he turned back and took a swallow of the Martel. "And then they sell dope to high school kids."

"I don't think you like those guys."

"Not much. They're essentially scum. Not an ounce of virtue in any of them, which makes it almost moral to take their ill-gotten bucks."

"You're still set on that?"

"Two weeks," Jack said. "If nothing changes."

"I don't want to hear about it."

"All right."

Billy watched him swirl the Martel in the snifter. He held it in his hand the way he might hold a woman's breast. "You know," Billy said, "I worry about you. I really do."

"I appreciate that. In fact, if that's the case, you might think about loaning me your boat. You don't want us cramming everything into mine."

"You bought a boat?"

"This morning. Twelve foot Alumacraft. Noisy, but light. We'll carpet the bottom, it'll do fine."

"Shit," Billy said. "You really are serious. You get anything to push it?"

"Nine-and-a-half Johnson. The motor's used, but it looked good to me. And Nolan looked it up and down, inside and out. And he knows more about motors than anybody I know."

"Where'd you buy it?"

"Sam's Southside. Nolan says he's good about backing up what he sells. And the price wasn't bad."

"What'd you have to give for it?"

"Six hundred, boat and motor."

Billy took a sip of his drink. "You could've done worse, I guess."

"Well, I don't want to buy another one. I know that. But we can't take Nolan's canoe."

"But my boat would be just the thing?"

"You got it."

"I suppose you'll need the motor too."

"What is it?"

"Four-and-a-half Johnson. But it'll push that jon boat pretty good."

"Okay, but what I really need is a couple of trolling motors."

"Well, I don't have any of those."

"What do they cost?" Jack said. "You know?"

Billy looked across the room and saw Nolan Hughes heading for

153

the door. "Southside didn't have any?"

"He had one, and he wanted two-fifty for it."

"You can pick up something at K-Mart for a hundred or so."

"We need something dependable. And quiet. The last thing I want to worry about is a boat motor."

"Call up the other marinas and see what kind of deal you can get. I'd get something with some thrust, though. Especially if you're planning to put some weight in those boats."

He was three songs into the last set when Russell Reed came in, and as soon as the crowd saw the banjo case, they started whistling. Billy had forgotten all about Russell, and he tried to force a smile as he made his way across the room.

Russell set the case on the edge of the stage, opened it, and took out the Vega. It was a beautiful banjo, a large scrolled head with a pearl star in the center, and all down the neck pearl inlay in the shape of a tree. There was so much pearl on the resonator that it looked like it was made out of marble. Billy dropped the last verse of the song he was singing, wrapped it up, and waved Russell onto the stage.

A short burst of applause and a few whistles, and Billy slid his voice mike over to his right and pulled down the goose neck. He played a G chord so Russell could check his tuning. Russell did, then he took off on a Don Reno tune called "The Chinese Breakdown." He played it pretty straight, not a lot of chromatic jazz, and his timing was good. Billy was impressed. Somewhere over the last few months Russell had picked up a hint of taste. Maybe it was those guys from Perry.

The applause was the real stuff too. Real whoops and whistles. Somebody in the far back shouted "Bill Cheatum," and a guy at a table to the right of the stage yelled for "Cripple Creek," everybody else still whistling and clapping.

Russell took off on "Bill Cheatum," a little fast but controllable. He played through it once, then looked Billy in, and Billy played through it on the Martin. Behind him he could hear the Vega popping out the rhythm. It was clean and sharp, and it cracked like a rifle. Russell caught the last note of Billy's lead, and Billy fell back into the rhythm. And so did just about everybody else, hands clapping, feet stamping all over the room. Russell ended it on an open chord and let the Vega ring into the mike.

Whoops and shouts again, tables rattling in the back of the room. Billy looked over at Russell and gave him a nod.

"Cripple Creek!" the guy shouted again. It was one of the Generals, the one with the clean-shaven face. "Hee-Haw! Hee-Haw! You're a-picking and I'm a-grinning!" He was slapping his friend on the shoulder. They were both all grins. "Hee-Haw, goddamnit! Hee-Haw!"

Russell backed away from the mike and checked his tuning. Then he took a step forward and kicked off "Little Dave." It was too fast again, but smooth, and the hands and feet started quickly in the back of the room and ran toward the front like a great wave, everybody in the place slapping tables, clapping, stamping feet until it was almost a race, their rhythm against the rhythm of Russell's Vega, and Billy caught somewhere in the middle trying to keep them both together.

Russell looked at Billy to see if he wanted to take a break, and when Billy looked him off, he went through it again, the crowd right behind him or maybe in front of him, and nobody caring which. He cracked it to a halt and the crowd went happy again, half of the folks in the back standing up at their tables.

"Salty Dog," somebody shouted.

"Cripple Creek!" the General shouted.

Then his buddy started too. "Cripple Creek, goddamn it! Cripple Creek!"

Russell backed away from the mike again to check his tuning, and when the noise died down Billy leaned forward and checked the Martin. He played a G for Russell to tune to.

When they were together again, Billy pulled his guitar mike up so it would catch his voice. "We'd like to slow it down a little bit now and play an old song that—"

"Cripple Creek!" the General shouted again.

Russell leaned over toward his mike. "I believe we played that one last year, friend."

"Then it's about time to play it again!" He laughed loud and slapped his buddy on the arm. The buddy thought it was the joke of the year. They were all laughs and slaps.

Billy leaned into the mike. "We'll get to that one a little later. And maybe a few more of those big tip songs." He ran through an E chord. "Right now, though, here's an old Lester—"

"Here's a tip for you!" the guy yelled. And he picked up a couple of quarters from the change on his table and threw them at the stage. One of them hit Billy's D28 and cut an inch and a half gash just below the pick guard. That was the biggest hoot of all. They were all laughs and slaps.

The room went quiet then, and Billy turned the Martin up in his lap. The gash was deep, almost all the way through the face. His head throbbed with a white light. He looked around the room for Leon, then back at the Martin. The place had gone dead, only the laughs and the slaps at the one table. "Break time," he said.

He sat the guitar down easy on the stage, face up, stepped down and walked toward the bar. The two Generals were still laughing, huge drunken grins plastered across their faces. Billy didn't pause a second when he reached their table, only picked up a long-neck Bud and swung it as hard as he could into the grin of the big tipper. The guy went straight to the floor, screaming like he was dying, and Billy just stood there over him, throbbing with adrenaline, watching the blood spurt through the guy's fingers and onto the floor, and seeing out of the corner of his eye the huge black jacket rising above the table, the red fist cocked above the shoulder, Jack Giddens shoving away from the bar.

13

All the neon on Tennessee Street was either red or blue. They passed the Travel Lodge with the big bear sleepwalking on the side, and Billy watched the rowdies leaning over the second floor rail, throwing beer cans into the pool. Why did they let them do that? The swimming pool looked like a fountain full of bent coins, all the rowdies crowded against the rail, making their wishes. The neon around the roof throbbed blue and red, so did the neon on the sign at Bullwinkle's Tavern, and the lights in the windows of The Brew and Cue. Billy thought about Turner Kay hunched over a pool table. He thought about the nine ball sitting dead in a corner, all that open green, and Turner Kay leaning over the table to set on the cue ball, standing up and shifting to another stance, Turner Kay already hustling to pay off his bets, shuffling around the table, eyeballing his shape, powdering his hands, chalking his cue, cursing Florida State, cursing southpaws, cursing baseball. The world was truly upside down.

Then they crossed Monroe Street, and Billy looked down the long tunnel of lights moving off toward the State Capital. The street was full of trash, people wandering in and out of bars, people hanging out on the sidewalks, drinking, whooping it up. And he thought he saw the Seminole Indian again, way down at the end of the street, the head of his pinto tossing above the heads of the crowd, the tip of his spear drawing red circles under the street lights.

Jack stepped on it and beat the caution light across Call Street. The lights were on behind the red and green stained glass windows of the eye doctor's house, and Billy thought about Jerry Lamberti's hands, about saw blades and hammers, about Jerry Lamberti moving in and out of those rooms, his hands tucked carefully into his gloves. They passed Seminole Liquors, One Hour Martinizing, Gibson's Texaco, the Waffle House. They passed Rose's Cantina, the electric sombrero lit up like fiesta, red hatband throbbing.

Billy eased the towel away from his eye and tried to fold it.

"Keep that thing pressed tight," Jack said.

He could feel the slow trickle of blood oozing again out of the throb. For the third or fourth time he said, "How bad does it look?"

"You ever see Scott LeDoux fight?"

Billy put the towel back to his eye and pressed hard.

The Walk-in Med Center was empty, and when the nurse saw that Billy was bleeding she motioned them back. They walked down a narrow hall and into a small examination room. Two of the walls were covered with cabinets, the other two blank and white. A metal table covered with white butcher paper sat against the far wall. The nurse motioned for Billy to sit down on it, then she handed him a yellow form attached to a clipboard. Billy handed it to Jack, and Jack filled it out.

A minute later the doctor came in, a young guy who looked like he was just out of med school, white lab coat draped over blue jeans and running shoes. He was lean and tan, but there was a tired expression on his face. Billy thought he looked like a failed tennis pro.

"Let's have a look," he said. He lifted the towel away from Billy's eye and laid it on the cabinet. The blood started to trickle again, and he dabbed it away with a swab. "So what does the other guy look like?"

"Considerably worse," Jack said. "Both of them."

The doctor dabbed again at the eye and tossed the swab into the waste basket. "I think you'll live," he said. "But you'll have a nice shiner. Lie down on the table and I'll check that blood pressure."

Billy stretched out across the paper, and the doctor rolled up his right sleeve. The bright lights against the ceiling reminded him of the stage lights at The Under Thing and then as he squinted his eyes, of the tiny lantern flare bobbing on Lake Talquin. The doctor pumped the bulb five quick times and the flare brightened.

Billy felt the wrap loosen and fall away from his arms. He closed his eyes and listened to the paper crinkle under his body.

"You have any allergic reactions to drugs?" the doctor said.

"Not that I know of." He opened the good eye and saw that the doctor had taken a hypodermic from a drawer. He was jabbing it into a small bottle.

"What about Xylocaine?"

"I don't even know what that is."

"Local anesthetic." The doctor turned and said it like a jingle, "Erase your pain with Xylocaine."

Billy didn't say anything. Neither did Jack. Only the nurse smiled, as though she'd heard it a hundred times.

"Okay," he said. "Turn your head slightly to the left and close your eyes."

The doctor stuck the needle in twice, then he swabbed the wound with something that smelled like alcohol. Billy could feel it run down his head and into his ear. It tickled, and he had to wipe it away with his finger.

When he opened his eyes, the doctor was bending over him with a curved needle in his hand, a tail of black thread hanging from it. Billy closed his eyes tight and tried to put himself somewhere else. He tried to think about something pleasant, but all he could see was the huge black jacket rising above the table, and when he tried to

159

put that out of his mind, all he could think about was Nolan Hughes. Then he felt the needle passing through the skin, and he thought about that. It didn't hurt, but he could feel it passing through his eyebrow, could feel the doctor's hand tugging on the other end. The needle went through again, then another tug and the loud snip of the scissors.

"Well," the doctor said, "that should keep your brains from falling out."

"I don't feel like I've got any brains. Just a big headache."

"Don't worry about it. Not much of wound. You'll live and you'll prosper from it."

"I suppose."

"Sure you will. That's the sort of wound that either knocks some shit out or some sense in. Either way, you're better off." He laughed. He thought it was funny.

Billy was surprised to find Jean's Fiat in the driveway. But there it was parked outside the garage in the shadow the moon threw behind the house. He pulled the truck down beside it and sat for a few minutes staring across the back yard. The night was absolutely clear, stars booming in the black sky and bouncing off the surface of the pond. He thought about rowing into the cove and dropping a line outside the fence. Maybe lay back with his knees over the seat and float for a while. Let things clear. But his head still rang like a bad note, and every time he winced he thought his eye might rip open.

He stepped through the front door and stood for a second in the hall. The TV was on in the living room, and Jean was sitting on the end of the couch, her legs stretched out across the cushions. She had a blanket draped over her feet, and she was eating a bowl of ice cream.

"You're home a little early," she said.

"So are you." He didn't say it in a nasty tone. He was too tired for that. "What's on?"

"Classic horror, *The Island of Lost Souls*. Want to watch?"

He sat down in the rocker and stretched his legs out in front of him. The woman in the television commercial was stretching hers into a pair of black panty hose. "Rehearsal break up early tonight?"

"I skipped it. I wasn't feeling very sharp. Besides, they only had half a rehearsal. Nolan had to be somewhere. He turned it over to Amy Eliot."

"Who?"

"Amy Eliot. You remember. Jerry's Amy."

Billy kicked off his boots and propped his feet on the coffee table. His legs felt like he'd walked home from a war. "I saw him tonight. He and Jack came into the club."

"Jerry?"

"No. Your buddy Nolan."

"Oh?"

"But he didn't stay long. He had a woman with him."

"Oh." She didn't look away from the television.

"A tall blonde girl. Never seen her before. I figured she was with the play."

Jean finished the ice cream and sat the bowl on the floor. "I'm sure Nolan has a lot of women, don't you think?"

"Who knows?"

"But then why should either of us care about Nolan's women?" She turned on the couch and looked at him. "Would you hand me my cigarettes. There on the magazines at the end of the table." Then her jaw dropped. "My God," she said. "What happened? Are you all right?"

"A misunderstanding," he said.

"A fight?"

"Only a short one."

"At the bar?"

"The last set. Some joker kept ragging me."

She slid off the couch, stepped over, and turned his head toward the light. "Oh, Billy," she said. "I'm so sorry. Does it hurt much?"

"It hurts a good bit."

That was the night he had the dream again. Or the night after. He was in the jon boat on the same narrow river. The trees on both banks were tall, and the sun shot down through the branches and trapped itself between the fog and the water so that he and his father were trolling their lines through a tunnel of orange light. His father steered the motor with his elbow and guided his line around the underbrush and snags. Billy listened to the motor purr quiet and steady. The cold smelled like rich dirt. It hurt his nostrils and the back of his throat. He looked down at his fingers and saw that all of his fingernails had been bruised by hammers. He wedged the rod between his knees and slipped his hands under his legs.

The jon boat cruised down the tunnel of orange light. The trees on the banks leaned out farther over the water, and the fog looked like gold smoke rolling under stage lights. This is the wrong dream, he told himself. And suddenly his father cut the engine and the boat slowed. The sun was coming up behind the trees at the end of the river, and the boat caught the current and started to drift.

Then the voices came again, rising in a chorus out of the darkness that was really the light. And it was the right dream because it was like being in church, the waves of voices becoming a hymn caught in phrases as the jon boat swung around sideways and his father caught the arm of an oak and pulled them to the bank where they sat quietly under the trees as the bodies sloshed down into the water where the river bent like a question mark and the fog opened in a flash of yellow light that clothed those bodies in gold filament. A head went under the water and came back up. Then a few more bodies waded into the water, and they all waved their arms like wings until they became the great bathing flock of golden birds, and the yellow light beyond them sang hallelujahs. Let's go closer, Billy said to his father. But the boat didn't move. Let's go closer, he said, then turned to see if his father had heard him. Only it wasn't his father in the back of the boat. It was Jack.

162

14

It rained for a week, a hard steady rain, and every morning Billy sat at the breakfast table and watched the rain come down on the pond. After a day and a half, the yard went to puddles and the jon boat filled up with water. Sometimes when the rain came down very hard, the ducks huddled together on the bank or wallowed in the yard. The wind would blow patterns on the pond, ripples and swirls, and the boat would wash back and forth on its rope. Finally the boat filled up entirely and sank in the shallows, and there was only the stiff blue rope rising out of the pond and wrapping itself around the tree. The want ads were already a habit, and Billy sat there every morning with his bowl of Cheerios and the morning paper and poured over the job listings and watched the rain.

All of this business in the news about unemployment, and pages and pages of jobs. Jobs for file clerks, legal secretaries, inventory analysts, keypunch operators, addiction counselors, leasing agents, medical assistants, paste up artists, backhoe operators, registered nurses, roofers, robot operators, reservations agents, listings for every kind of honest work imaginable. Still, most of the ads said only experienced persons need apply. For Billy that seemed just as well, since only one ad in the whole Classified Section really interested him. It was listed under Business Personals:

Wanted immediately guitar or bass player with tenor voice for working gospel quartet. Must be dedicated musician and Christian. Must travel. Bookings through July. Call Arthur Webb (205) 577-3317.

It was an Alabama number, probably south Alabama. He thought about it, but he didn't call. No, he thought about it very carefully, but he didn't call. First off, he couldn't sing tenor, not the sort of tenor they would want anyway. He could strain for the notes and hit most of them, but he wasn't a natural. They'd want a real tenor voice, somebody high and lonesome and smooth as syrup. Also, he'd feel like a hypocrite. He knew a lot of gospel groups who were in it more or less for the money and the music, which was just fine. But these guys were in it for the gospel. That was clear enough already. In the long run it simply wouldn't work out. This was the sort of group that plays a few songs, and when it's time to tune or change instruments, a member of the band fills in the gaps with a personal testimony, how it was before he found Christ, how it is now that he has seen the light. Billy respected that and in many ways envied it. But it wouldn't work out.

And besides, he couldn't very well interview for a job until his eye cleared up. It was turning now from a sick yellow to a deep purple. He tried to avoid mirrors but wasn't always successful, and every time he passed a mirror and caught a glimpse of his face, he thought about the General. He was sure to be missing a couple of teeth, a high price to pay for one drunken gesture. And Billy kept thinking that he was probably a fairly decent guy, a guy who'd just gotten a little too drunk on the beer and the banjo. No, that's stupid. He was probably a jerk, he was probably the scum Jack said he was and he deserved what he got. Billy wondered also about the big guy in the black jacket. What sort of shape had Jack left him in? He kept wanting to thank that guy for not picking up a bottle, for not following his own lead. And what did that say about the guy? Nothing, absolutely nothing. Maybe there wasn't a bottle close.

For a while he worried that they might file charges of some sort, then he decided that they weren't the type for that sort of thing. If they wanted to get even, they wouldn't do it through the courts, and that thought didn't offer him much relief.

Twice already Billy thought he'd seen the big guy. The first time he was sitting at the traffic light where Tennessee crosses Call Street. He looked diagonally through the light and saw him sitting in a red Mustang. He revved the motor the whole time they sat there, the engine growling, the hood rearing up and down. And it seemed to Billy like they sat there facing each other for fifteen minutes, the Mustang growling, Billy trying to hide behind the sun visor.

Then once pulling into the parking lot of The Record Bar, he glanced through the side window and saw him standing just inside the door, a huge black jacket hovering over the cutout rock section. Something like all the sickness in the world settled in his stomach, and he zipped on through the parking lot and back out onto Tennessee.

The phone startled him for a second, then he relaxed, ate the last spoonful of his cereal, and got up to answer it. It was Marilyn McKinley phoning for Jean. The strangest thing. Why suddenly did she seem like an old friend? Sure, he told her. He'd have Jean call.

As he walked into the dark of The Under Thing, he heard the bottle come down on the bar. He walked straight for it, going mostly on ritual and sound, his eyes still trying to adjust to the dark. He propped his guitar cases against the bar and sat down on a stool, then he picked up the glass of Jameson and took a slow sip.

Leon leaned over the bar and took a look at his eye. "Doesn't look too bad. A couple of stitches is nothing."

"Maybe not, but it felt like he was sewing up my whole face."

165

Leon laughed at him. "You're a pussy, that's all."

"I never claimed to be anything else. What about that guy I hit? Did you see him?"

"Ah, he wasn't hurt bad. Always looks worse than it is. Cut his lip and broke a tooth. I think the big guy got hurt worse."

"Yeah?"

"Your buddy Jack put his lights out. Just like something out of the movies. I never seen anything like it."

"So what'd he do?"

"I ain't sure. It was over too quick. About all I saw was the two guys on the floor and Jack dragging you off. That big guy was out for a solid minute. It scared me. I was ready to call an ambulance. Would've had to call the cops then. But he came around."

Billy took a sip of his Irish. "I don't know. I guess the whole thing spooked me a little. I never had anything like that happen before."

"Forget it," Leon said. "Hazard of the trade. Hank Williams used to carry a blackjack in his pocket. That kind of thing happens all the time."

"I don't blow up like that. It's not like me."

"Maybe you never had a good enough reason."

"You think those guys'll come back?"

"I doubt it. They might. So what if they do?"

Billy gave him a look, then took a sip of the whiskey.

"Listen," Leon said. "Let me tell you something about bar fights."

"You've seen some bar fights, huh?"

"I've seen all I want to. But I'll tell you this. They always end with the last punch of the night."

"What does that mean?"

"I mean I never seen anybody hold a grudge over a bar fight. You know who fights in bars? Drunks. And drunks sober up, or most of them do, and then they figure out what kind of asshole they've been and it's all over."

"You think so?"

"I seen it happen too many times. I even knew a guy once in

Commerce, Texas, that punched out a fellow then sent him flowers. Guy was a florist. Beat the shit out of this little red-headed bastard, then when he sobered up the next day he called the bartender, got the guy's name and sent him a dozen roses."

"I ain't expecting any flowers."

"No," Leon said. "I wouldn't hold my breath."

"I got to get out of this business," Billy said.

Leon reached under the bar, came up with a frosted glass, and poured himself a beer from the Stroh tap. "You got it soft. You just don't know it."

"I'm not complaining about this place. I'm talking about the business. I mean, look at me. Where am I getting? I can't play this place for the rest of my life."

Leon poured the head off the beer and filled it to the top. "Probably not. But I ain't thinking of changing the program anytime soon."

"Hell, I even went down to talk with Harold Wright about a job."

"Who?"

"Harold Wright, owns Tallahassee Music."

"So what did he say?"

"Said he needed somebody to teach guitar. Somebody who could read music."

"You don't want to work in a music store."

"Why not?"

"Too many jerks wander into music stores."

"And they don't wander into bars?"

Leon took a long swallow of the beer, then held the glass back under the tap and filled it again to the top. "Sometimes they do. But not as much as music stores. And when they wander into bars all they want to do is drink. They don't expect you to tell 'em how they're likely to be the next Kenny Rogers or Eric Clapton or whatever."

"Well, I don't have to worry about it now anyway." He finished the Irish and sat the glass on the bar.

"You want another one?" Leon said.

"Not right now." Billy turned on the stool and took in the room. It was about half full. A lot more college kids than usual. "I saw something pretty interesting in the want ads this morning."

"So you're checking out the wants ads, huh?"

"Gospel group looking for a tenor."

"Well, you'd look good in a white suit. Get your hair permed up. Grow yourself one of them little pencil moustaches."

"Believe it or not, it doesn't sound all that bad to me."

"You don't want to be on the road. Hell, that's why you're here. What you need is to buy into a place."

He turned around and gave Leon a look. "I need to what?"

"Buy into a club. Go down to the bank, get yourself a loan, and buy into a place. Then you can play if you want to, and you don't have to if you don't want to."

"You make it sound awful damn easy."

"How hard can it be?"

Billy shifted on his stool and looked back over the crowd. "I don't know. I don't know anything about things like that."

"There ain't all that much to know."

He remembered Jerry Lamberti sitting on the porch at Jack's cabin. He remembered how crazy all his talk had sounded. "Jerry said something once about trying to open a place. He's a good man, but I'm not sure he knows enough about it either. The business end, I mean."

"Well, it ain't all that complicated. I been doing it for years."

"Maybe. But then I can't see trying to start something from scratch. Not two guys who don't know shit about it. And then, too, you don't see the want ads full of club owners looking for partners."

"What's wrong with this place?"

Billy looked over his shoulder at Leon. "You're not looking for a partner."

"Not really," he said. "But if you had a mind to do something like that I'd just as soon you do it here. There's plenty enough competition around here as it is."

"You telling me you'd let me buy into this place?"

"I'd think about it. I had a partner once, it was okay. And there's sure enough work for two guys."

Billy didn't say anything for a second. He picked up the Jameson bottle and poured himself another drink. "What you figure it would take? How much?"

"Shit, I don't know about that. I'd have to do some thinking. But you know what I'd like to do? I'd like to buy out that guy upstairs. Run two stages on the weekends, expand this place into a first class club."

"You're talking major money now."

"Banks got major money. All you got to do is ask them for it, sign a few papers. It's the American way."

"Waltz Across Texas," "Mom and Dad's Waltz," "Crazy Arms," Billy didn't feel much like anything but slow songs. Two sets of them before he broke down and played "Wabash Cannonball" for a table of frat boys. But he couldn't get into it, he kept looking at the door. Everytime it opened he took a deep breath. And it seemed hotter than usual, even with the fans going, and the lights made the sweat break out on his face and neck. But he played the song anyway, all four verses, then Jerry Lamberti came in and sat down at the bar, and Billy went back to the slow songs, "Together Again," "Sing Me Back Home." But he couldn't really get into them either. He kept thinking of what Leon said about buying into the place. He started thinking about Jerry Lamberti. Could Jerry come up with the money to do something like that? What did you have to have to get a bank loan? Was Leon just talking or was he serious? And if he was serious, how much money was he talking about? And what would Jean say?

He wanted to ask her, and he sat in front of the television for an hour and a half, waiting. He'd knocked off the last set early and come straight home. And he was home by twelve-thirty, but where was she?

When Star Trek signed off, he pulled himself out of his chair and went into the kitchen for a beer. Something rustled on the deck and he walked over to the kitchen door and pushed open the screen. Over the top of the house, the gray dart of an underwing, huge, maybe an owl, and he walked out onto the deck. It was a warm night and perfectly clear, no moon, and the stars flaring over the pines. The pond was as smooth as a plate of black glass, all across it stars shining up from another heaven. He reached back through the door and switched off the kitchen light, and the stars in the sky and the stars on the water flared a little brighter. He walked down the deck stairs and into the yard.

The edge of the pond was weedy and littered with the debris of teenage fishermen. A worm box, a crushed Coke can, a sandwich bag. The jon boat floated in the shallows, anchored to the bank with a concrete block. Billy picked up the rope and pulled the bow onto the bank. A piece of rough paddle lay wedged between the seats. He picked up his anchor and sat it carefully in the bow. Then he stepped into the boat, picked up the paddle, and shoved off.

The pond was as still as he had ever seen it, and the softest stroke eased the boat over the water. He paddled as quietly as he could and glided out over the floating stars, then he stopped paddling and the boat drifted to a dead stop and the water and the stars settled around him. He laid the paddle across the seat and lay back in the boat. Occasionally a small breeze made the water roll under him, turned the jon boat slightly in the middle of the pond.

He drifted for almost an hour before her headlights cut into the drive. He kept on drifting.

15

When Billy woke up he thought he was still in the boat, something in the residue of his dream turning slightly like the jon boat drifting in the middle of the pond. And there was the smallest sound, like the rustle of leaves on a far off bank. But the night was absolutely dark, no stars, no moon, and what felt like the wind in his hair wasn't the wind. It was the tips of Jean's fingers. He reached up to pull them away and she whispered something to him, or he thought she did, and the fingers stayed where they were, as though that were the natural place for them to be, and the rustling of the leaves grew louder as her face came closer to his. She rolled on top of him, and he thought about pushing her away, but the weight of her body was comfortable, and the shift of that weight made it seem like they were drifting so he closed his eyes and let them drift.

When he woke again, it was almost eleven. Jean had left the curtain open and the sun threw a hot screen of light across the side of the room. Billy shook the sleep out of his head and sat up. Strangely enough, he felt good. Through the window the sky was a bright blue capping the tops of the pines. He swung his feet to the floor and slipped on his jeans, then he went into the kitchen and took a can of Pepsi from the fridge.

The paper, with the want ads folded neatly into Section C, lay waiting for him at the edge of the yard, but he wasn't going out for it. He felt too good for that. He just popped the top on the Pepsi Cola, sat down at the kitchen table, and looked out across the lake. He kept thinking about Leon leaning over the bar and saying to him, What's wrong with this place? And what made him feel so good was the gradual understanding that there was absolutely nothing wrong with that place. Sure enough, there was nothing wrong with it at all, and he felt like someone who had dropped his pick on the stage and couldn't find it until he moved his foot. He'd been right there on top of it all the time.

He stared out the window. The jon boat floating on the shallows was a good memory. Then the wind came up over the pines and drew a long field of ripples across the pond. It rocked the boat at the end of the blue line and ruffled the backs of the ducks huddled on the near bank. Out of the sky above the trees blew a gray and white line of eight Canada geese that spiraled down and landed in the middle of the west cove. Big gray and white birds, absolutely beautiful, wild birds coming from somewhere and going somewhere, and Billy sat for a long time at the table, admiring them.

When Jean came home for lunch, Billy was out on the porch with his guitars. She called as she came through the front door, and he ran a last string into tune, propped the Martin against the table, and walked through the dining room and into the kitchen.

"So what happened to you last night?" he said.

She was fishing in the fridge, bringing out a head of lettuce, a bell pepper, and a bag of sliced carrots. "I had rehearsal, Baby. What else?"

"I mean why were you so late?"

"Sorry about that. Things weren't going very well. Nolan kept us over."

"Way over, I'd say." He pulled out a chair, turned it around and sat down.

"I tried to call twice. You must've been on the pond." She took a cereal bowl from the cabinet and started peeling the lettuce into it.

"You could've called the club."

"I don't like to do that. You know that. Besides, it's hard to get to a phone over there. It breaks everything up. I have to be there on the set all the damn time."

"I worried."

"It's that idiot Betty Freeman. She can't remember her own name. You want a salad?"

"Who's she?"

"Tall dark woman. She's playing Estelle. You met her once at a party. You want a salad? Or I can fix you a sandwich?"

"I had a sandwich already."

"I don't think's she's going to pull it off. Nolan spent most of the night screaming at her. She won't learn her goddamn lines and she's a damn bitch on top of that."

"So why'd he let her have the part?"

"She's an attractive, seductive bitch. It's called type casting." She sat the head of lettuce on a paper towel on the cabinet, took a paring knife from a drawer, and started slicing the pepper.

"So tell her to kiss off and get somebody else."

"You don't exactly do that this far into rehearsals. Even if it's not much of a part. It upsets things."

"So don't you all have understudies, or whatever you call them?"

"I'm supposed to be the understudy. And I'm not setting one foot on that stage." She went back into the fridge, brought out a block of cheese, and sliced a few pieces into the bowl.

"Yellow, huh."

"I'm not yellow. It's just been too long, and I haven't prepared for the part. I've been too busy coaching everybody else."

"You're the understudy though."

"Change the subject," she said. "What have you done today?"

173

"Worked on the guitars. Not much else."

"Anybody call?"

"Not a soul."

"You haven't been on the pond? I thought Marilyn might call."

"She called yesterday. I forgot to tell you."

"Thanks a lot."

"Sorry, I just forgot. Give her a call this afternoon."

"She's on her way to Orlando to see her mother. I suppose she'll call again if she gets close." She took a pitcher of tea from the fridge and a glass from the cupboard. "So, you get into any fights last night?"

"Not a one. Dull night."

"Well, that's not exactly the sort of excitement one really needs." She poured the glass three-quarters full and set the pitcher on the cabinet.

Billy turned slightly in his chair and looked out the window. "Well, something kind of interesting happened last night. I guess you could call it interesting."

"Yeah, what's that?"

"Leon asked me if I wanted to be a partner. He's thinking about buying out the guy upstairs."

"A partner?" She jabbed her fork into the salad and turned around to look at him.

"He said he'd let me buy into the place."

"Buy into The Under Thing? Now what would be the advantage of that? You're already down there three nights a week."

"I'd be part owner. I'd be working for myself, and I wouldn't have to play all the time. I could just play when I wanted to."

"So where does he expect you to get enough money to buy into a bar?"

"The bank, I guess. Take out a business loan."

"Baby, you've got to have collateral to get a loan. And for that kind of money you'd need a lot of it."

"I've got this house and a good job."

"Baby, this house is in my name. All you've got is that truck, and I don't think any bank's going to loan you very much against a Toyota truck."

"So you could co-sign the loan. We'd both be partners."

She crunched a carrot stick between her teeth. "Billy, I don't think I'm really very much up for owning a bar. I mean, I just don't think I'm ready to wrap up what little security I have in something like that."

"Well, I'm thinking about it seriously," he said. "And I might see if Jerry wants to go in on it with me."

"Jerry Lamberti? Give me a break. He doesn't have any money."

"How do you know?"

"How could he? He lives in that rooming house, he doesn't own a thing."

"You never know."

She smiled and shook her head, then she took another bite of the carrot. "So how much money is Leon talking about?"

"He didn't say. He just said he'd think about it."

"My God," she said. "You don't even know how much you need. You really amaze me, you know that?"

"He said it probably wouldn't be that much."

"So what does it matter. It might as well be a million dollars."

Then why didn't Billy feel more discouraged? And when he walked into The Under Thing that night, why did he look at the place in a whole new way? When he walked up on the stage with the D28 in his hand, why did the crowd seem especially enthusiastic? And when he sang one song after another to the real applause, why did those songs seem less tired, less tasteless, less boring? Weren't they still the same old tunes?

All afternoon he'd thought about what Jean had said, and he decided that she actually hadn't reacted as badly as she might have. Jean would come around to anything reasonable, he was certain of that. The question was exactly what Leon called reasonable. He had no idea, and Jean was right about one thing. It was too early to get excited about all of this. First find out exactly how much Leon wants, then find out how to get it and what it's going to cost. In fact, he regretted having mentioned it to Jean. It seemed too early for that too.

The thing to do now was simply to wait on Leon, not to push him. Leon was a good heart and he'd think things through, maybe talk to his accountant, then come up with a fair price. And what would that be? It scared Billy to think about it. But the point was not to think about it. Not yet, anyway. The point was not to worry, to lay back and wait, give Leon a chance. Anything else was just wasting time fretting over things he couldn't control. If it was too much, then that was that. Or was it? What about Jerry Lamberti. Or was Jean right about Jerry not being able to come up with the money? But forget that right now. First find out what Leon wants, and see if you can come up with it. Maybe talk to Turner Kay. Turner's connected all over, he might have some good advice. And wasn't his brother president of North Florida Federal? Or was it his cousin? But first, give Leon a chance, lay back and give him a chance. One good thing about Leon, whatever price he comes up with, it'll be fair. You don't have to worry about Leon trying to cheat you.

But Leon never mentioned it once all night, and by the time Jerry Lamberti and his girlfriend came in to catch the last set, Billy was hurting to talk. Finally, during his break, he walked over to the bar and sat down. Leon slid him a glass and a bottle.

Billy poured himself a drink. "So," he said. "You thought any more about what we talked about?"

"Haven't had much of a chance. But I'll think about it. You in some kind of a big hurry?"

Billy got home late. The front porch light was on, but the house was dark and Jean's car wasn't in the driveway. He thought she might have put it in the garage and gone to bed, so he let himself in easy, switched on the hall lights and checked the bedroom. It was empty, and so was the rest of the house. Rehearsal was over, Jerry Lamberti's girl was out well over an hour ago. There was no reason for Jean to be this late.

He picked up his keys, locked the front door behind him, and walked back out to his truck. It was the tension again, the anger, the little knot tightening behind his eyes. And it frightened him some. Now that he knew what happened when the light snapped, it frightened him, and he didn't want to let it get out of hand again.

He backed out of the drive, the truck making a high whine in reverse, and shifted hard into first. So Billy, when you get to the theater, what then? A scene? Do you grab Jean by the arm and pull her home? Do you make accusations? Plead concern? He'd never stopped to think about that before. He didn't want to think about it now, whatever happened just happened. Maybe he'd just show up and that would be enough. Maybe he'd give Nolan Hughes what he'd given the biker. No, that wouldn't happen. He'd head that off. Maybe he wouldn't even go in.

Ten minutes later he pulled off Tennessee Street onto the FSU campus, climbed the long hill, and turned into the parking lot of the theater. It was all but empty, two cars—Jean's Fiat parked under an oak in the corner of the lot and an MG Midget parked in front of the walkway of the theater. Two women were sitting in the MG. Billy parked the truck a few spaces beyond them and felt them watching him in slight amazement as he closed the door and stood for a minute outside the cab. The building was completely dark, but he walked down the sidewalk anyway and tried the door. When it didn't budge, he stood there for a second thinking, feeling the glares of the women in the MG. It was the tension again. It made him jerk at the handle of the doors, three or four times hard, then again. And when they didn't give, it was the glare of the women. He thought for a minute about giving them a finger, he knew they were thinking the same thing about him. But he didn't, and they only reached into the cooler propped on the luggage rack and came out with two more beers.

He walked back to the truck, backed up, cut on his lights, and eased out of the parking lot. When he got to Tennessee Street, he turned right and headed toward town. People were still wandering up and down Tennessee, a near crowd gathered on the sidewalk outside the Seminole Room, a few frat boys on the benches outside The Thing. He thought he saw Turner Kay walking down the street toward The Brew and Cue, but he didn't stop. He drove all the way down Tennessee and turned left on Monroe, and then he just drove, the bar lights giving way to street lights, and the street lights giving way to house lights giving way to pines opening into dark fields of pasture and scrub farm.

When he crossed the Gar Creek Bridge, Billy slowed, turned left onto Weston Drive and eased into Weston Woods. The road curved uphill, and when it straightened, the woods broke into a suburb of dark houses and shadowy lawns. He took the first right and drove to the end of the street. There were two cars in Nolan Hughes' driveway, a Chevy van and a Mustang, but no lights were on in the house. Or did he see a faint light through the living room window? A faint light like the flicker of a movie projector.

He drove past the house and parked in the shadow of the trees clustering the corner of the next yard. There were no street lights and the moon was already down, so the yard was dark. He crossed it in the open and walked up to the front door. But he changed his mind, edged along the side of the house and looked through the living room window. Nothing, then through a doorway a faint green light filtering from the back of the house. He thought for a second, walked easy across the driveway, squeezing between the bumper of the van and the garage door, careful of his boots on the concrete, then around the side of the garage.

When he reached the back of the house, he stopped and eased his head around the corner. The backyard lay entirely in shadows, and the pool was dark, only one light in the far wing of the house. He stepped around the corner and walked easy along the wall, but no matter how easy he tried to step, the soles of his boots scraped like sandpaper on the concrete patio. He thought for a second about taking them off, then he heard a voice, or thought he did, and stopped in his tracks and listened. Nothing, then the far off grinding of a car on the highway. Then a strange thought. Couldn't he get arrested for this? And what was this exactly? Trespassing? A wind rustled the oak branches at the edge of the patio, and he stopped breathing altogether until the sound died out over the yard. And what if he found her in there? What if she really was in there with Nolan Hughes, and what if, with his own eyes, he saw them locked in some absurd postion of adulterous love? What then? What would he do then? He hadn't the slightest. What would Jack do? Walk back to his Jeep for a pistol and blow them both away? Or what about Jerry, what would he do? He just wanted to know if she was in there. And he almost hoped she was so he'd know something for sure.

He edged on along the side of the house and stopped beside the sliding glass doors that opened onto the pool. The curtains behind them were pulled and the room was dark. He was totally in the shadows, and he looked at his feet and at the path he wanted them to take across the patio. He didn't want to trip on anything, to knock anything over. He looked again at the window in the wing of the house. The light flickered twice and turned from a pale yellow to a pale green. A car revved far back behind him, then cruised down the street. He waited until the sound of the engine disappeared into the suburb, then walked on toward the green light flickering in the window.

Twenty feet from it he stopped. Already he could see in the pale light something of the room, half of a bookcase filled with pictures, half of a buck's rack hung with hats. He sat down on the patio and pulled off his boots, then he crawled on all fours toward the window. There were voices, soft, and muffled laughter. He stopped under the window and leaned close to the wall. There was music too, strings and a keyboard, but he couldn't make it out, then laughter again. He took a deep breath and raised his head toward the window. First only the green smoky light, then the buck's head, the bookcase filled with framed photos, a roll top desk, a poker table, and beyond the table, the back of a sofa. They were sitting on the sofa, watching television. Billy held onto the windowsill for balance and crouched there watching the backs of their heads. Something like panic was building in him and his heart started rushing in his chest. But he held onto the sill, took deep breaths, and watched as they leaned into each other, Nolan's hand brushing through her hair. Then the hand paused on the back of her neck, held for a second, and pulled her head toward his lap. She laughed and jerked back, then the hand pulled again and her head disappeared behind the back of the sofa. He said something, and she laughed again, pushed away from him, and stood up. And when she turned in the light of the television, Billy saw that it wasn't Jean. Something strange washed through him and made him shake, but it wasn't relief. Because the man stood up too. It was the General he'd hit with the bottle.

Billy sat down under the window and let his nerves steady, and when some of the fear drained out of him, a sickness started wallowing in his gut. Then the sickness turned into an anger, anger that he hadn't found what he'd come to find. Just because she wasn't in that room didn't mean she wasn't somewhere else in the house. It was a big house full of dark rooms. And he sat there for a minute taking deep breaths and thinking about that. Then again, this all might just be a terrific mistake. Maybe there was an explanation. Maybe Jean was home right now wondering why he was late.

Either way, there was nothing else to do here, so he crawled across the patio and picked up his boots. He crawled a few more yards and stood up in the shadow of the house. Sure, there might be any number of explanations. They'd all sound like lies, but sometimes the truth came off that way. He thought for a second about putting on the boots, but decided against it, then he started walking easy in his sock feet along the side of the house. Something shattered behind him, a sound like a glass hitting the floor, and the woman shouted something. Billy stood where he was, frozen, listening, but her voice died out and there was silence again, and he edged on toward the corner of the house.

As he turned that corner, something hit him hard in the stomach and a deeper sickness rose in his chest and took away his breath. He doubled over and dropped the boots, and something hit him again hard across the jaw. He went straight to the ground, folded up, hands on his stomach, knees under his chin. He tried to talk, but he couldn't catch his breath.

"I think we got a prowler here," one voice said.

"Looks dangerous to me."

Billy felt the toe of a boot kick him hard in the back. He was breathing again, but he couldn't talk. The nausea made him too weak, he felt like he might pass out.

"Naw, he don't look too dangerous to me."

"You can't take no chances these days."

And Billy felt the boot again, hard in his back. He rolled over and looked up into the faces above him. One of them he'd never seen before, a blond man with a thin beard, the other was the big guy from the bar.

"Hey," the big General said. "This is the guitar man. The guy that likes to swing bottles."

His buddy looked at him, "Is that right?" He bent down over Billy. "Listen here, guitar man, just what the fuck do you think you're doing back here?"

Billy struggled to talk. "Looking for Nolan. Knocked on the front door. Nobody answered."

"I didn't hear nobody knock on no door. Maybe you should've rung the bell." He turned to the big guy. "You hear anybody knock on the door?"

"I didn't hear nothing like a knock. Just some asshole creeping around out here."

"I told you I was looking for Nolan," Billy said.

"Well, Nolan ain't here right now. But we'll tell him you called."

The big guy leaned down toward him. "Hey, guitar man, you come calling a lot with your boots off?"

"Maybe his feet hurt," the other guy said. He kicked his boot heel into the top of Billy's foot.

"I don't much think he's looking for Nolan," the big guy said. "I think he's crawling around back here peeping at pussy."

"Pussy? Now why would a pervert like this be peeping at pussy? Hey, asshole, get up on your goddamn feet so I can see you." He reached down, grabbed Billy by the shoulders, and pulled him up.

Billy stood there for a second, the sickness still making his stomach quiver. The big guy hit him hard again in the stomach, and he doubled over, went down on his knees.

"Shit," the buddy said. "This asshole can't even stand up."

"I don't know, he might be peeping for pussy. He might just be peeping for some of that actress pussy."

"Some of what?"

"Some of that actress pussy Nolan hangs out with. Is that right, bottle-swinger? You peeping around for that actress pussy? Maybe that dark-haired actress pussy that Nolan brags on so much."

The buddy laughed and looked at the big General. "You mean Miss Deep Throat Tallahassee?"

"Mrs. Deep Throat," he said. He looked at his friend. "Hey, what you think that makes him?"

"I don't know," he said. "Why don't we ask him?" He wasn't looking at the big General. He was looking down at Billy.

"Hey, bottle-swinger, what does that make you?"

Billy didn't say anything, only held his stomach and tried to breathe away the sickness. Then somebody kicked him again, hard in the back. It sent a pain all the way into his chest, and he rolled over onto the wet grass. A muscle cramped, his whole back tightening with the pain, and it was all he could do to breathe.

The big guy nudged him with his boot. "You know what, friend? If I was you I'd get up from there and get the fuck on home.

Everybody in this neighborhood ain't as friendly as we are."

Billy didn't say anything, only lay on his side, breathing hard, his eyes closed, his face resting in the wet grass.

"You hear me, bottle-swinger?" the big guy said again. "I'd get on up from there and get the fuck home."

"Get up, asshole," the buddy said.

Billy tried to get up, but the cramp tightened and froze him. He breathed hard for a few seconds, and when the pain died, he pushed himself onto his hands and knees and started looking around for his boots. They were on the ground about a yard away, and he reached over for them.

"I didn't say take no fucking boots," and the buddy kicked down hard on Billy's hand.

The jolt stung all the way into his arm, and he jerked the arm back, grabbed the fingers tight with his other hand. He tried to make a fist, but the pain was too much, the hand would only close halfway.

"Let him have his fucking boots," the big guy said. He picked them up and threw them into Billy's lap. "Now get the fuck on out of here."

Billy didn't say anything, only grabbed the boots with his good hand, then stood up, backing away, keeping his eyes on both of them. It hurt to stand up straight, a sharp pain in his left side, but he stood up and kept backing toward the street. When he was halfway across the yard and saw that they weren't going to follow him, he turned and staggered back to his truck.

16

When Billy pulled into his driveway there were two cars parked in front of the garage, Jean's green Fiat and a silver BMW. He didn't know anyone with a BMW, but the car was only slightly mysterious. It was brand new, and the cardboard tag that hung in place of a license plate read Buckhead Imports.

He parked behind the Fiat and cut the engine, switched on the cab light and looked at his face in the mirror. Not much damage, only a little red welt under his left eye, and the cut above the eye hadn't reopened. But his hand hadn't faired as well. The first finger had started to stiffen, and everytime time he tried to move it, a pain shot down to his wrist. He held it up to the roof of the cab and turned it in the light. It hadn't swelled badly, but it looked puffy and red.

Billy switched off the light, got out of the truck, and brushed off his clothes. There were grass stains on the knees of his jeans, and the back of his shirt was still wet from the dew. He ran his comb through his hair, and when he was satisfied that he looked as presentable as he could, he marched up the sidewalk and into the house.

Jean and Marilyn were sitting at the dining room table, a few magazines and a newspaper spread out on the table between them. Marilyn was drinking a glass of wine, Jean a Pepsi. They looked up when he opened the door, and he stood there for a second and looked back and forth between them.

"Jesus," Jean said. "Where have you been? I finally broke down and called Leon."

He closed the door and locked it. "I been out looking for you. Where have you been?"

"Marilyn came by the theater about eleven-thirty and a few of us went out for a pizza. I called the club just after twelve and you'd already left, then I called here and nobody answered."

He walked to the edge of the hall and leaned against the staircase banister. "I got home and you weren't here, so I got a little worried. I drove over to the theater."

"You knew I was at rehearsal," she said. "There wasn't any need for that."

"Jerry Lamberti's girlfriend came into the club, so I figured rehearsal was over. I thought you might have had some trouble. Car trouble or something."

"Well, it wasn't necessary." She took a cigarette from the pack on the table and lit it with her Zippo.

Billy didn't say anything. He decided to let it drop.

"So, hello," said Marilyn.

"So, hello." He tried his best to smile. He didn't feel like anything else. "You down here for a stay or passing through?"

"On my way south. Jean said you all could put up with me for one night." She reached across the table and took a cigarette from Jean's pack.

"I suppose so," he said.

"Wait a minute," Jean said. "It took you an hour and a half to drive to the theater?"

"I went by the Brew and Cue and had a beer with Turner Kay."

"Sounds like worry, all right. Did you make any contributions to the Turner Kay retirement fund?"

"No, I only drank a couple of beers."

"Is Turner a pool shark?" Marilyn said.

"Not exactly." Then to Jean, "I saw your car in the parking lot, so I figured you were messing around somewhere."

"There's some pizza in the fridge," she said. "You want me to warm it up for you?"

"I'm not hungry, maybe later."

Jean leaned up in her chair and looked at Billy's face. "Look at me," she said. "Have you bumped into something?"

"Where?"

"Your cheek looks a little puffy."

"I fell down in the parking lot."

"You what?"

"In the parking lot at the theater. I fell down. It was dark, I tripped over one of those goddamn crossties they got in front of the theater."

"How in the world did you do that?"

"Who knows? I tripped."

"Are you all right?" she said.

"I think so. My right hand hurts a little. I fell on it."

Marilyn tilted her head to the side and looked at Billy's eye. "Lord, Billy, what happened to your eye?"

Jean gave her a look. "He got into a bar fight, got punched by a heckler." She looked back at Billy. "It's not broken, is it? The hand? Can you move it?"

"Yeah, I can move it, but it hurts a little."

She took a drag on her cigarette. "This hasn't been much of a week for you, Baby. A fight at The Under Thing and a fall in the parking lot at the theater. Your life's getting to be a fairly dangerous activity."

"You might want to put some ice on that," Marilyn said. "It might keep it from swelling."

"That's a good idea." Jean slid her chair back from the table. "I'll wrap a few cubes in a towel."

When she walked into the kitchen, Billy sat down, crossed his legs, and held the hand in his lap. "Looks like you bought a new car."

"You saw it?"

"The back of it. Too dark to see much else."

"Well, the front looks even better."

"What happened to the Mercedes?"

"It was getting a little age, and I thought I needed a change. And it started making funny noises."

"Noises?"

"Less purring, more growling. I'll give you a ride tomorrow. The BMW drives just as well as the Benz ever did. Parks a lot easier too."

Jean came back in with a beer and a towel full of ice cubes. She handed Billy the beer, folded the towel over the cubes, and laid it on the table. "Hold your hand over that for a while."

"Will it do any good?" He lifted the arm and eased the back of his hand down on the towel. It stung cold and he picked it up for a second, then eased it back down.

"You really ought to try to wrap the whole hand," Marilyn said. "I don't think that'll be much help."

"So where did you learn so much about medicine?" Billy said.

"Roy was always spraining things. A failed jock. In the summers he was a walking ice pack."

"I'll make another one." Jean crushed her cigarette in the ashtray and walked back into the kitchen. When she came back out, she had a dish towel and a bowl full of ice. She tied the ends of the towel together, filled it full of cubes, and eased it down on top of Billy's hand. "How's that?"

"Cold." He took a swallow of the beer.

"If that swells up," Marilyn said. "You really ought to show it to a doctor. You might have a fracture."

Billy raised his eyebrows and took another swallow of his beer. He didn't want to think about that.

"Aren't you having those stitches out tomorrow?" Jean said.

188

"He said about a week."

"Well, you should show him that hand. You don't want to take any chances with that. What if you couldn't play?"

"It'll be all right." He didn't want to talk about it. He turned to Marilyn. "So where you headed in that new car?"

"Down to see the infamous Mrs. McKinley." She finished the last of her wine and sat the glass on top of a magazine.

"So, how is she?"

"Going through her second adolescence. About to marry some geriatic Don Juan in Orlando. I swear, it's worse than going through it myself. She's about to drive me off the edge."

"Geriatic Don Juan?" Billy tried to make a fist, and the pain ached through the numbing cold.

"Some retired attorney. He has a condo in the same building. She bought that condo three months ago, and now she thinks she's going to put it on the market and marry this man."

"And she's not?" Jean said.

"When I'm dead and in my grave."

"Well," Billy said, "you ought to be able to tell her something about attorneys."

"Believe me, I've told her plenty. She just doesn't listen very well. She's intent on making a fool of herself. And everyone else. It's actually self-destructive. I believe it's actually self-destructive."

"So how old is this guy?"

"He's seventy-one, she's sixty-nine. Can you believe that? And she hasn't lived with a man in fifteen years."

"Well," Billy said, "they're both old enough to know better."

Jean tapped the can of Pepsi on the table. "Or old enough to know what they're doing."

Marilyn looked across the table at her. "That's easy to say when it's not your mother. Try trading places."

"If my mother wanted to remarry, I'd think it was great. I don't like the notion of her living alone. Nobody wants to be alone."

"All right, what if she were marrying a man who'd been married

189

three times already? What if she'd known him for a total of three whole months? And what if she was ready to sell the condo you'd made the down payment on to supplement their so-called nest egg?"

"I don't know," Jean said. "I just think being alone is the most horrible thing I can think of."

"Thanks a lot," Marilyn said.

"No," she said. "I didn't mean it like that. You're just fine. You know that. I just mean that some people don't do that well. Some people don't need to be alone."

"Well, it's inevitable, you know. For most of us, anyway. So we may as well learn how to live with it."

"That seems like a funny way to look at it," Jean said. "Why not have more if you can have it?"

"I suppose it depends on your point of view." Marilyn put her cigarette out in the ashtray, then she turned to Billy. "Jean says you're thinking about going into business for yourself."

"Jean says that?"

"She says you're thinking about buying into the club. I think that's a great idea."

"I don't know," Billy said. "I don't know if I can swing everything that needs to be swung."

"Well, it's a great idea. The place has been doing well for a long time. And if you get the opportunity to buy in, you should take it. There's some security there, a future. Not that you don't have a future with your music. But you know what I mean."

A pain shot through his finger and made him grimace. He relaxed his hand and waited till the ache died away. "I'm not the one you have to convince," he said. "Jean's the doubting Thomas."

"Oh, I don't know," Marilyn said. "She's a bright woman. She's knows how to take advantage of an opportunity."

Jean gave her an odd look, but didn't say anything. She only reached for the pack of cigarettes lying beside Marilyn's glass. Billy tried to make another fist, but the pain stopped him. "So what do you two have planned for tomorrow?"

"I'm up early and off," Marilyn said. "I've got to put a kink in this ridiculous love affair."

Billy gave her a slight smile. "That might be easier said than done." He grimaced again as he tried to close his hand.

"You know," Jean said, "you ought to go in tomorrow and let that doctor take a look at your hand. Have him take the stitches out of your eye and let him look at that hand. You don't want to take any chances with that."

"You might be right," he said.

17

The Under Thing was almost empty, only a couple of guys sitting at a table near the stage. There was never much of a crowd in the afternoon, but today the place was dead. No jukebox, no radio, only the hum of a fan and a low muffled conversation coming from the television in the office. Billy walked over to the bar, sat down on a stool, and rapped the bar with his fist. When he rapped again, Leon came through the office door. He took a bottle off the shelf and set it down in front of Billy, then he reached under the bar and came up with a shot glass. In the office there was a quiet burst of laughter.

"So what's that smell?" Billy said.

"Water, the essence of life." Leon looked ragged, greasy hair, sweatshirt streaked with dirt.

Billy poured himself a drink and took a sip. "Smells rank. Smells like the end of the world."

"That was last night."

"So what happened last night?"

"What didn't?" He pulled up a glass from below the bar and filled it from the Stroh tap, then he looked over at Billy. "All right,"

193

he said. "I'm closing out the cash drawer and getting ready to go home, everybody else is already gone, and this boom goes off over my head and a sheet of water starts running down the wall of the office."

"You bust a pipe?"

"Some jerk blew up one of the toilets upstairs. How's that for laughs? Ruined a whole wall in the office. It was three inches deep in there before those assholes could shut the water off. Took me all night to get it cleaned out."

"Could've been worse."

"Anything could've been worse."

"So what's it going to cost you?"

"It already cost me a night's sleep. After that it ain't costing me nothing. They're paying for every dime of it."

"Count on that."

"No, I ain't kidding. If I have to I'll call a lawyer."

"You got insurance, don't you?"

"I got all kinds of insurance," he said. "But that ain't the point. It was their toilet and their water and their jerk." He took a long swallow of the beer, then held the glass back under the tap and filled it till the head ran over the top.

Billy smiled and took a sip of the Jameson. "I hate to bring you more bad news." He lifted his hand out of his lap and laid it on the bar. "But I don't think I can play tonight."

Leon stood quiet for a moment, staring at the splint and the taped fingers. "What the fuck happened to you?"

"Tripped and fell."

"Yeah, what'd you trip over, a cliff?"

"A General. The big one that was in here the other night."

"That pisses me off. You okay?"

"Oh, yeah. I think so. It could've been a lot worse."

"Where'd it happen?"

"On my way over to Nolan Hughes's house."

"That's the last time those assholes come in here. If I have to I'll shoot the bastards at the door." He took a long swallow of the beer, then he looked down at Billy's hand. "So what am I supposed to do for music tonight?"

"I'll find somebody for you."

"Why don't you call that Reed guy, the banjo player? See if he can find a guitar player somewhere."

"I was thinking I might ask Jerry Lamberti. It might do him some good to get back on a stage."

Leon didn't look very excited. "Jerry, huh."

"Why not? The last time I heard him play, he was great. And it might do him some good."

"That's just about all I need."

"You like Jerry. You've told me that a hundred times."

"I love Jerry. Fine man and a fine musician. I just don't feel like going broke over the weekend. Not on top of everything else."

"You ain't going broke. Hell, I don't even know if I can get in touch with him. If I can't, I'll call Russell."

Leon shrugged, looked down at the hand again and started shaking his head from side to side. "So when are you going to be back in playing shape?"

"A few weeks. Wasn't much of a break, hairline on the first finger. Good excuse to take a vacation." He took a sip of the Jameson, held it in his mouth for a second, then swallowed. "So I'm thinking about going fishing for a few days next week, but if I do I'll line you up some pickers before I leave."

"Where you going?"

"I don't know, somewhere in south Florida."

"Saltwater?"

"Fresh. Some river Jack Giddens knows down around Sarasota. I think he knows somebody down there with a cabin."

"I fished a little bit around Florida. If you're looking for good bass fishing, you ought to go down around Homosassa. Lots of good fishing all around there."

"I don't even know if I'm going. But if I do I'll just be tagging along."

Leon chugged the rest of his beer and sat the glass down on the bar. He kept staring at the white tape on Billy's fingers. "I tell you what. When you get back we'll sit down and talk about this partner business. I'll try to have things figured out by then, and we'll see if we can work it out."

"All right."

Leon picked up the Jameson bottle and topped off Billy's drink. "And see if you can get me some country pickers, maybe bluegrass. If I don't have to, I don't want to pay for a whole band."

When Billy got home, Jean was sitting on the porch, rocking in the chair behind her wall of plants. She shouted hello and he shouted back. Then he went into the kitchen and took a can of Pepsi from the fridge.

When he walked out onto the porch, she pushed back the hanging plants and turned her chair around. "Shit," she said. "He wrapped up your whole hand."

"Just two fingers. And only the first one's busted."

"It's broken?"

"Just a fracture, a hairline."

She folded down the page of her book and laid it on the floor. "So how long do you have to keep that tape on?"

"A few weeks." He walked over and sat down in the wicker chair and propped his feet on the plexiglass table.

"I suppose it's stupid to ask if you can play?"

"Can't hold a pick."

She wrinkled her eyebrows and rocked back in the chair. "And you can't strum it with your thumb?"

He stared at her for a second. "Not on stage, I can't." Then he looked down at the hand. "At least it wasn't the left one."

"Whatever," she said. "We'll get by. Lots of pork and beans in the cupboard."

Billy took a swallow of Pepsi and looked out over the lake. It was a nice day, a few clouds. Not a lot of action on the pond though, only a few kids fishing on the far bank, and five or six ducks paddling along the shallows of the west cove. He felt good, considering everything. "So when did Marilyn take off?"

"She was gone when I got home from school. I think she left in something of a huff."

"At you?"

"No, I don't think so. More of a universal huff. She really is upset with her mother. That's crazy, really. She'll only make things worse. She should leave the poor woman alone."

"Well, it's her business, isn't it. So it's probably best to let her handle it."

Jean leaned up in her chair and took a cigarette from the pack on the table. "You know, I've been thinking about what Marilyn said. About the club, I mean."

Billy gave her a glance.

"I suppose it would mean a lot more security, and in the long run more money coming in. And the place has been doing well for a long time. It's not like starting something from scratch."

"What brought all of this on?"

"Nothing. Well, Marilyn said it wouldn't be a bad investment. She generally knows about such things."

"She's right," he said. "The thing is, Leon wants to expand. He's thinking about trying to buy out the guy upstairs."

"Has he said anything else about it?"

"Not really. He said he'd let me know something next week."

"Well," she said, "I'm not saying it's something to get overly excited about yet. But I don't think it'll hurt to think about it." She took the lighter from the corner of the table and lit her cigarette. "I'm thinking about skipping rehearsal tonight. Maybe we could have a sandwich out and a movie. Last fling for a while."

"You skipping rehearsal?"

"I think I need a break," she said. "It's all getting to be a little wearing. We'll have a last fling. Just you and me, a little celebration."

"I don't think a busted finger is a lot to celebrate."

"Well, me either. But there's something else, you know. A little good news in the middle of the tragedy. I'm pregnant. Isn't that great?"

Billy didn't say anything. Something uneasy turned in his gut. Not exactly the tension and the anger he remembered from the lantern floating off the island, and not exactly the sickness he felt under Nolan Hughes's window. It was something less disturbing, less frightening, a queasiness that's only slightly unsettling, like a hangover you have day after day and gradually learn to live with. He only stared at her, then out across the yard to the pond and the kids fishing on the bank, then to the ducks circling in the west cove.

"Isn't that great, Billy?" she said.

"So when did you find that out?"

"Yesterday. I went to the doctor yesterday morning, but I couldn't very well tell you with Marilyn here. It didn't seem right."

He looked across the table at her. There was an odd expression on her face. She was noticeably anxious.

"I thought you might be a little more excited," she said. "Isn't this what we've been waiting for?"

"I don't know," he said. "Is it?"

"Of course, it is. You've wanted this as much as me. I know that." And there was something in her voice, not really a quiver yet, but something bordering on it. "I know you've wanted this just as much as me, Billy. I know you have."

"I suppose you're through with Nolan now."

She took a deep breath and rocked back in the chair. "I'm thinking about dropping out of the play, if that's what you mean. It's really too much of a strain."

"Well," he said, "that's almost what I meant."

"I'd been thinking of it anyway, you know. It's gotten to be so much. I'm not a quitter, you know that. But under the circumstances. I mean, since we're going to have a child."

He didn't say anything, only looked out across the cove at the ducks paddling easily in the shallows.

"Well," she said. "What do you expect me to say?"

He looked at her then. Her lips were pressed together, and her jaw set hard. Something about her eyes looked almost fragile.

"No, you're not a quitter," he said. "You don't exactly practice a holiday religion."

"What's that supposed to mean?"

"It means you don't miss a Sunday service or a prayer meeting either."

"If you're going to slander me," she said, "do it in English. I don't speak primitive tongues."

"Forget it," he said, and pushed himself out of the chair.

"You don't have to be this way, you know." She turned away from him and stared out across the pond.

"How did you expect me to act?"

"Quite differently, actually."

"You really did?"

She didn't say anything, only took a drag off her cigarette and flipped the ashes into the ashtray beside her foot. "I'm going to Atlanta for a little while. Marilyn's picking me up on her way home. She's arranging an appointment with a doctor. I want to have a good going over, and I just don't trust anybody down here."

Billy wasn't looking at her either. He was looking at the jon boat floating in the shallows of the pond. The wind made it rock a little at the end of the blue rope.

"You heard me, didn't you? I'm going to Atlanta for a while. A week maybe, or ten days."

"I'm taking a trip myself," he said.

"Really? Where to?"

"Fishing. Jack and I are going to south Florida for a few days. I deserve a vacation."

"Yes," she said, and turned back toward him. "I suppose you do. When is all of this happening?"

"Next week sometime. I'm not really sure."

"Well, I'm leaving Sunday. If we don't get this talked out by then, that'll give us a chance to let our heads clear. It'll all work out, you'll see."

He looked at her, but didn't say anything.

"You'll see," she said. "Everything'll fall right into place. Especially now that we may buy into the club. Everything'll be fine. No, wonderful. Absolutely wonderful." She took another drag off her cigarette and looked back out over the pond.

"You should stop smoking," he said.

"Yes," she said. "I suppose I should."

Part Three

18

Jack unfolded the map, folded it again into quarters, and laid it out flat on his kitchen table. The section he pointed toward was light green streaked with thin fingers of blue. There were two red circles drawn on the blue line that was the river, and his finger came down on the south circle.

"Here's the fishing camp," he said. His finger moved north. "Three miles upstream the river forks, east branch, west branch." He moved up the west branch and pointed to the other circle. "The river house is here, about a mile and a half up." He wrinkled his eyebrows and turned to Nolan. "And you say the house sits on the east bank."

"Right." Nolan pointed to the thin black line running between the two forks of the river. "And the only access is this little road. Big enough for one car."

"Dirt, right?"

"Dirt, sand, sometimes gravel. Runs about six miles to Highway 64, from there it's another six or seven miles to Ona."

Billy leaned against the refrigerator, watching them, but mostly watching Nolan, his gestures, his confident little grins, trying to figure out why he could stand being in the same room with him, trying to figure out why he didn't want to pick up a beer bottle and smash it into his teeth. And trying at the same time to figure out how he'd let this whole business go this far.

"All right," Jack said. "The basic idea is simple enough." His finger traced the route again. "We motor upstream, take the east fork of the river, put in about two miles up, conceal the boats, cross what looks to be just over a mile of sandy pine, and cut the road off."

"So, why don't we just drive in?" Billy said. "Looks like it would be a lot simpler."

Jack smiled. "That'd be just fine with me. I don't like all of this boat business. Limits your exit. And it's slow."

"The road might be watched," Nolan said. "And I'm not sure if anybody'll be in that house. I doubt it, but you can't be too careful. The river's made to order, a quiet way in the back door."

"So," Jack said. "When we hit the road, we'll need to do a quick recon. Nolan'll take the woods to the house and check it out, see if anything's moving, and also if they've got any boats up there. And if they do, he's responsible for putting them out of commission." He looked over at Billy. "And you'll hike up the road a good thousand meters or so and set up an observation post. Find a spot that gives you a good look down the road, in a curve if you can find one. Climb a tree, or build yourself a hide in the brush."

Billy nodded.

"Then you just sit there and wait. Nolan'll be watching the other end of the road. Meanwhile, Cathey and I'll rig the ambush."

Billy nodded again. "So how are you planning on stopping this car?"

"No problem there. We'll find a couple of nice pines, pretty thick ones, eighteen or twenty inches maybe. Pack 'em with a nice wad of C-4. When the vehicle approaches, you call us on your walkie-talkie and we blow down a tree in front of it and a tree behind it."

"C-4?"

"Military plastic explosive. More efficient than dynamite. Mold it to the shape you need, tape it to the side of the tree in the direction you want it to fall."

Nolan pulled a chair from under the table and sat down. "How much of that stuff do you have to use?"

"Six or seven pounds, I'd guess. Cathey'll want to overkill it. We'll let him worry about that."

"Another thing," Nolan said. "How long will it take that tree to fall? I mean, if you blow it too soon, what's to keep these assholes from hearing it, stopping, and turning around?"

"That's why you don't blow it too soon. We'll lead them fifty meters or so, depending on how fast they're moving. On a road like that they can't be going over thirty or forty, right? And the tree'll come right down. Believe me, Cathey knows what he's doing."

"I'd still rather bring that first tree down with a chainsaw, bring it down behind a curve and just have the thing waiting on them. We can blow the second tree behind them."

"Well, if nobody's in the river house and we can find a good curve and you can be sure the Generals don't come down that road before the buyers, then we might do that."

"So," Billy said. "What if I do spot the Generals first? What then?"

"You let us know, and we let them blow on by."

"And how am I supposed to know if it's the Generals or the other guys? They're not likely to be on motorcycles, are they?"

"If they're not on bikes," Nolan said, "they'll be in a brown Chevy van. If they're not, you'll just have to get the best look you can get and make that decision."

Billy shook his head and gave Jack a look. "And what if the buyers and the Generals all come down that road at the same time?"

"Well, that's not very likely. Not coming from long distances and different directions."

"But what if they do?"

"Then we've got two choices. We confront them all, or we let them pass and catch the Generals with the money on the way out."

"And what if they come out together too?"

Nolan rocked back in the chair and pointed his finger at the ceiling. "Then Cathey calls in an air strike."

Jack smiled and looked over at at Billy. "Nobody said there wouldn't be some risk. I only said the risk would be minimal. And I consider that an extremely remote possibility."

"Probably," he said. "I just like to have everything covered. And that plastic stuff, how do you set if off?"

"Electric caps. Touch'em off with a flashlight battery."

Billy looked a little puzzled. "Won't an explosion like that make a lot of noise?"

"It'll make a hell of a noise. But it won't matter. Even if somebody is in that house and they hear it, by the time they can get down the road, we'll be gone. That's the point, get in and get out."

"So when you blow these trees, what's to keep these guys from driving right over them? I mean, eighteen inches ain't a real big tree."

Jack smiled. "Well, trees have branches. Besides we'll set the charge four or five feet off the ground. If it's done right the tree'll hang to the trunk and drop at an angle across the road. Makes a nice obstruction."

Nolan pointed to the black line on the map. "So what kind of ambush are we running?"

"Three of us at the ambush. I figure an L position. Two men in the front of the car, one in the woods on the east side of the road, one in the woods on the west, then a man about five meters down on the west side of the road. Gives us maximum firing power in the kill zone."

Billy felt a little strange. Until now it hadn't seemed very real. Kill zone? He shook his head. "And then these guys are just going to get out of the car and give us the money?"

Jack glanced at Nolan, took a deep breath, and turned to Billy. "Well, we hope so, don't we?" He pointed across the room. "Look at what's on the sofa over there. Now, if you were in that car and that thing was pointed at you, wouldn't you be reasonable?"

Billy turned and saw the rifle lying on the sofa. It was an assault rifle, an ugly thing with a plastic stock and a pistol grip behind the trigger. He stepped across the room for a closer look.

"That's a Colt AR-15. We've got four of them. Not a bad rifle. You modify it with a M16 bolt, bolt carrier, fire selector switch, and auto sear, and you've got a fully automatic M16."

"It's ugly enough," Billy said.

"That's not the magazine we'll carry in it. Cathey's bringing down some forty-round Sterlings. They're awkward to carry as spares, but they're damn good to have on initial contact."

"So why didn't he just round up some M16s?"

"These are legal. You pull the auto sear and you've got a completely legal weapon. One less thing to worry about. Why carry around a felony?"

Billy raised his eyebrows. Initial contact? Felony? Something odd turned in his chest and wallowed out a hollow feeling. He walked back over to the fireplace and sat down in the rocker.

"After we eat, I'll take you down to the range and go over it with you. Let you shoot a few rounds."

"So," Nolan said. "What else did you put together?"

"Well, we each get a little *didi mau* bag. Walkie-talkie, field glasses, five extra thirty-round clips, first aid kit, LRP rations, fifty feet of shroud line, lifeboat matches, a couple of canteens, flex-X cuffs, and a tube of Crazy Glue. And Cathey'll pack a reduced M5 med kit." Jack looked over at Billy. "You got a pocket knife?"

"Sure."

"Don't forget it. I've got a sheath knife for you. But bring a pocket knife too. What size shoes do you wear?"

Billy wrinkled his brows. "Nine and a half."

"Go down to Panhandle Surplus tomorrow and buy yourself a pair of jungle boots. Tell 'em you want G.I. issue. Don't let 'em hand you any Korean shit. Oh, and while you're there, get yourself a pair of camouflage pants and a T-shirt. And get four camouflage masks. I think I've got one, but get four anyway. Tell'em you're going turkey hunting."

Nolan picked up the map and folded it. "So what kind of radios did you get?"

"TRCs. I forget the model. They're in the back of the Jeep."

"TRCs? Radio Shack?"

"They're pretty good walkie-talkies. Three watts."

Nolan didn't looked convinced.

"They're solid," Jack said. "Three mile range, three channels."

"You liked them?"

"I liked them."

"Okay, what about the trolling motors?"

"On the porch," Jack said. "Billy picked them up today. Two Johnsons and two twelve volts."

"Set us back three hundred bucks," Billy said.

"Apiece?"

"No. We got a deal. And I got extra plugs for the outboards and a couple of five-gallon gas cans."

Nolan shook his head and looked at Billy. "You really think we need two trolling motors?"

"I don't, but Jack does."

Jack gave Nolan a firm look. "Better to have the things and not need them. And if we have to move around anybody in the dark, you'll be glad we spent the bucks."

"I suppose."

"You got a fishing license?" Jack said. "We wouldn't want to get arrested for anything stupid."

Nolan smiled. "I got all kinds of licenses. What about handguns? What are you taking?"

"Carry what you want to. I figure the Colts are the obvious choice. You can't do any better than that."

Nolan tossed the map on the table and pushed out of the chair. "You got any Coke?"

"Check the bottom cabinet. I think I emptied all the ice into the cooler."

He took out a liter bottle and poured himself a glass. "Did you do anything about those sound suppressors?"

"Cathey's putting them together."

"So when's he getting in?"

"Any time now, I suppose."

Billy looked at Jack. "Suppressors? Those for the rifles?"

"Suppresses the noise of the shot. All you'll be able to hear is the sonic crack. Hardly anything, like snapping your fingers." Then he smiled. "And that's how easy this is going to be. Take my word for it. Just like snapping your fingers."

Billy sat at the picnic table and watched the shadows of the tall trees streak the clearing. It was still hot, even though the wind off the water had started to cool things some. Out on the lake Nolan paddled the canoe toward the bright patch of yellow where the water held the sun in a circle at the end of the dock. Billy watched him through Jack's binoculars as he cut a perfect, straight line through the water. The way he sat up so straight in the bow, the wind in his hair, the sun going down in a patch of pink over his shoulder, the still water, the yellow canoe, all of it reminded Billy of a beer commercial. Nolan Hughes paddling back to camp with a fresh case of cold Stroh's.

Nolan Hughes. For two days he had thought about him, about Jean, about the whole situation, and what amazed him most was the fact that he couldn't hate Nolan. For days he'd puzzled that over in his head. He'd gone step by step over the events of the last few months and knew that by all rights he should hate him like sin, should want to kill him. But he didn't feel that way at all. Mostly what he felt was a sad brand of indifference, or if he hated anything, he hated the way Nolan could be so cool about everything, could look at him and act like nothing at all had ever passed between them. The actor's trade, the craft of the game. Billy hated that, but he couldn't hate Nolan Hughes, and because he couldn't, he felt that something was missing inside him, something that other people had and he didn't.

But the worst part wasn't that nagging sense of guilt, and it wasn't Nolan's attitude about it all. The worst part was Jean. He was trying to get it straight. Billy, isn't this the way it goes? If you can't hate Nolan, how could you possibly love Jean? And the other way around. If you really loved Jean, wouldn't you have to hate Nolan? Or would you? Billy, that's a tough question. Think about it. If you can't hate Nolan, how could you possibly love Jean? Then why have you been so sick about her?

When Jack came back out of the cabin, he had a bag of charcoal over one shoulder and the AR-15 over the other. He laid the rifle across the table, then set the charcoal on the corner of the bench, ripped open the end of the bag, and poured a tall mound into the grill. "Hand me that lighter fluid, will you?"

Billy lowered the glasses, reached across the table, and handed Jack the can of fluid.

"You been nervous all day. What's up?"

"I'm always nervous," Billy said.

Jack popped the cap on the can and soaked the charcoal. "You'll feel better when we get on the river."

"You think so?"

"Absolutely. You've just got pre-game jitters, that's all. You'll come around. How does that hand feel?"

"There's still some pain in it, but I think I'll live."

"How long before you'll be a hundred percent?"

"A few weeks. It wasn't much of a break."

Jack propped his foot on the corner of the bench and looked out across the clearing. "So what's Leon doing for entertainment?"

"I'm getting something together for him."

"You didn't tell him where we were going, did you?"

"I think I told him we might be going fishing. I didn't say where. Hell, I didn't even know where."

"Leon's all right, but it's not a good idea to let anybody know where we are. In fact, we need to sit down and get a story straight. What did you tell Jean?"

"Jean's in Atlanta. I just told her we were going fishing."

"Atlanta, huh?"

"Visiting her friend Marilyn. She'll be up there a while." Billy lifted his right arm and studied the splint.

"So how's that grip?" Jack said.

"Not much."

"Don't worry about it. You'll be all right. A little of this cow blood'll fix you up."

Billy lifted the glasses again and watched Nolan ease the canoe against the side of the dock. He threw a rope over a post and pulled the canoe in tight. "I'd feel better if I didn't have to worry about that Cathey guy. You think he's going to make it?"

"Not a question in my mind." Jack struck a match and lit the edge of the coals. They caught and spread a small even flame. "He's the last thing you need to worry about."

"What did he say happened?"

"He didn't, but don't worry about it. He'll meet us down there with time to spare." Then he took the can of lighter fluid from the edge of the table and shot another quick stream onto the coals. The fire leaped and pushed him back. "Pyromania," he said. "I like to see it burn."

When Nolan climbed out of the canoe and started up the hill, Billy cut the glasses between the trunks of the tall pines and onto the water and the bank of the far cove. It was a beautiful day, and he wished he felt better. If he did, he might take the jon boat out around the island and fish for some specks. Or he might just ride out into the middle of the lake, cut the motor and drift on into the night. At night on Lake Talquin the drift was great. All that water was almost like being on the ocean, and under him the jon boat felt like a giant feather. Out there in the middle of all that water, alone with the stars, with the sounds floating out of the distant woods, out there he could really drift into some serious clarity.

"So where's the fish?" Billy said.

Nolan walked into the clearing and leaned his rod against the hood of Billy's truck. "I didn't even throw out a line. Just paddled once around the island." He turned to Jack. "That place is full of squirrels, you know that? We ought to make some stew this fall."

"Cathey called. While you were out on the water."

Nolan stepped over to the cooler and took out a beer. Nolan Hughes for Stroh beer. Stroh, with the firebrewed flavor. "Oh yeah, he on his way?"

"Said he couldn't make it. He got held up on post."

"Well, shit. He say what happened?"

"Nope. I don't think he could talk. He'll meet us at the river."

"When did he say he'd get down there?" Nolan twisted the cap off and took a swallow.

"He didn't," Jack said. "He said he'd call back late tonight or early in the morning."

"That's cute."

"Doesn't matter. I've been over this with Cathey, the whole business. He'll be there when the time comes. And he'll know what to do, and he'll do it damn well."

"I never said he wouldn't." Nolan's smile was more of a grimace. He tilted his head a little to one side. "I just said it was cute."

Billy leaned up and propped his elbows on the table. He was trying to judge the expression on Nolan's face. "So nobody's said what this Cathey guy's like."

"He's a little crazy," Nolan said.

"Listen," Jack said. "He's as solid as they come."

"Anybody who fishes with DuPont lures is at least a little crazy." Nolan smiled again at Jack. "But then he's career army. Shit, what do you expect?"

Billy gave him a look. "DuPont lures?"

"Hand grenades," he said. "It's the truth. One time we're down on the Ocmulgee River, first time I ever met the guy, and we're backed up in this bend, me and Jack and Cathey, nobody catching shit, then all of a sudden this Cathey guy chunks something over the side. I thought it was a beer can. Hell, I was about to jump on him for littering up the river. Then whomp and the wake just about turns the boat over. About thirty fucking catfish float belly up, and Cathey just paddles from one to the next, pulling them up in the boat."

"He's as solid as a rock," Jack said. "I'd trust him with my life any day of the week, any situation you can imagine."

Billy rocked back. "You've known this guy a long time?"

Jack nodded a short confident nod. "Fifteen years. Best CRP leader I ever saw. Smart, responsible, cautious. Excellent medic and a damn sight better combat soldier."

"CRP?" Billy said.

"Combat Recon Platoon. Nobody took better care of his men."

The fire was still burning hard. Jack punched at the coals with a stick and spread them out across the bottom of the grill.

"What'd you do?" Nolan said. "Pour on the whole can?"

Billy raised his eyebrows and took a deep breath. "Like I said, I guess I'm still a little weird about all of this."

"You'll loosen up," Nolan said. He sat down on the edge of the table. "Jack's right about his guy Cathey. He's good. Hell, if he wasn't I wouldn't be here. I'm not about to get myself hurt." He paused for a second and looked down toward the water. "Not that I'm a coward, I just got my fans to think about."

Jack gave him a look. "You talking about ceiling fans or window fans?"

"I'm talking about neither, friend. I'm talking about the millions of moviegoers all over this country who would grieve like hell if anything tragic happened to me."

Jack winked at Billy, then he shot Nolan another glance. "Well, luckily, they've got nothing to worry about. Nobody's going to get hurt. This thing'll be as easy as cashing a check."

"I just hope those other guys know that," Billy said. "Some of those Generals seem a little prone to violence."

Nolan frowned a little and edged back on the table. He propped his feet on the bench and turned toward Billy. "That's only when they come on people by themselves. I'll bet it's a slightly different thing when the odds were more even."

Billy didn't say anything, only watched the expression harden on Nolan's face.

"I really wouldn't mind blowing a couple of the assholes away. I've eaten about all their shit I can stomach."

"Well," Billy said, "I don't want any trouble out of any of them. I just want to get the money and get out."

"No," Nolan said. "We won't even see any Generals. If we do, we'll just kill every one of the bastards."

The hollow feeling washed back strong and took Billy's breath. He shifted a little on the bench. "I know that's just talk, but that's the sort of talk that tends to spook me."

"Nobody's killing anybody." Jack cut a glance at Nolan, and their eyes caught hard for a second. Billy had an odd feeling, a feeling that something private had passed between them. "Still," Jack said, "we can't let anybody make us. That's priority one. We talked about it already. So remember, when we face these guys down nobody but Cathey says anything. I mean, we don't even cough."

Nolan looked over at Billy. "So who were the ones that jumped you?"

A mild shock blew through him, and Billy sat there for a second, trying not to show his surprise. What the hell was Nolan trying to pull? He might just as well have asked why you were creeping around his house? And if he knew enough to ask, he sure as hell knew the answer. So why bring that business up now?

Then again, maybe they didn't tell him. Maybe those Generals didn't say anything about it. Was that possible?

"They didn't tell you all about it?"

"Not a word. Jack told me."

Billy gave him a hard look. Of course they did, you asshole. Of

214

course they told you. It happened in your goddamn backyard.

"I don't know," Billy said. "One of them was the big guy that slugged me at the club. Then some other jerk."

"William Cox. He's a pig." Nolan pulled the Walther from his back pocket and popped the clip. "I'd like to put one of these right in his fat gut." He laid the pistol on the table. "So where did they jump you?"

Amazing the way he could be so cool about it all. Billy really hated how cool he could be. Like it was nothing, like it was something that happened all the time, like it was a goddamn game. He gave him a long look. There was nothing in Nolan's face to give him away. "On the road somewhere," Billy said. "They pulled me over."

"Where at? On the way home? They follow you home from the club?"

"Somewhere," Billy said. "I don't really remember. Somewhere between the club and the house, somewhere on the side of goddamn road."

They stared at each other for a second.

"Well," Nolan said, "if you run into that asshole again, you won't be by yourself. And I wouldn't mind much if we did run into him." He looked over at Jack. "He's the bastard that stole my tape deck. Did I tell you that? I found it in the back of his fucking van."

"So what did you do?"

"What could I do? I let it slide. Just like I let everything else slide. Hell, they even started breaking into my house. I come home from rehearsal and these fucking creeps are watching skin flicks on my video player and drinking my booze."

Jack smiled. "So I suppose we all owe you a great debt for these enormous sacrifices?"

"Something like that." He picked up a rag off the table and started wiping down the Walther. "One thing's for sure. If it wasn't for this deal, I'd have cut it off quick."

The fire flickered out and Jack set the grill over the coals. "Well, you won't have to worry about it much longer."

"Maybe not."

Billy looked at Nolan. "Tell me something," he said.

"What's that?"

"Why the hell are you wrapped up in all this shit?"

Nolan grinned. "Well, what do you think? What do you think I make directing a couple of plays a year?"

"I don't have the slightest. I just wondered, that's all."

"Besides, excluding some pretty good ass at FSU, Tallahassee's not exactly what you'd call Adventure Land." He tilted his head slightly and smiled. "Now is it?"

Billy looked at him for a few seconds, hard, then looked off toward the dock and the water. He wasn't going to study what Nolan meant. "So I guess this guy Cathey knows how to get to the river?"

"He's got maps."

"I wish you'd put those steaks on," Nolan said. "All I've had today is a pickle loaf sandwich."

Jack reached into the cooler for a beer. "I'll take care of that right now. What you want on it?"

"Whatever," Nolan said.

"Salt and pepper. How's that?"

"Don't get too exotic."

"Salt then."

"So Cathey didn't say when he'd get in?"

"Nope. But probably Friday night. For sure by Saturday afternoon." Jack twisted the top off the Coors and dropped it into the cooler.

Nolan sat up straight and took a deep breath. "Saturday's cutting it a little close. Don't you think?"

"Not really." Jack took a long swallow of the beer. "Not if you're right about the time of the buy."

"Oh, I'm right. Three o'clock Sunday. I'm not worried about that, but I'd like to have time to go over the whole thing with everybody there. And it wouldn't hurt to check out all the equipment again either."

"I think all that's on the agenda."

Nolan slid off the table and stretched his legs. "I tell you what," he said. "I'll handle the steaks. If you want to go over that rifle with Billy, you better get down there and do it. It's getting dark."

Jack looked at Billy. "You going to have any trouble firing this thing with that hand."

"I don't think so. I got a good finger or two."

19

No more Nolan, no more Jack, no more mysterious Master Sergeant Cathey. Billy opens another beer and retreats into the sanctuary of his room, then into the deeper sanctuary of music, the stereo almost wide open and Billy lying on the floor between the speakers. Troublesome waters much blacker than night, hiding my view of harbor's bright lights. And Lester's voice rich and full, playing around the rhythm, the backup perfect, the guitar perfect, Earl's fingerpicking smooth as a wave. Tossed in the turmoil of life's stormy sea, I cried to my Savior have mercy on me.

And Lester's voice honest enough to heal it all, honest enough to put everything right. So Lester, how do the roots chord? The click beetle, the cricket, the cicada, the toad? Lester, what songs do they sing in the high grass? And that place where all the songs promise to take us. What's it really like? Then gently I'm feeling the touch of His hand, guiding my boat in safely to land. And Lester, that boat? How can you sing about boats with all that dirt around you? Those songs, Lester. Are all those songs telling us the truth?

Hush, Billy, hush and listen.

And Billy closes his eyes and the room starts to drift. Only a little drift, like the jon boat turning easy in the middle of the pond, but he goes with the drift and the music drifting around him. He goes with the deep mellow voice of Lester Flatt. Lester singing from the black box of the speaker cabinet, Lester singing from the black box under the ground, from the Great Beyond, from the land beyond the river. Lester Flatt telling Billy Parker how God gave Noah the rainbow sign, no more water but the fire next time. And Billy Parker going with Lester Flatt, drifting, going wherever Lester's voice cares to take him. How long, Billy? How long is the long drift on the gospel, the music floating away like a little boat? And Billy, what do you think Lester is trying to tell you, that voice crossing the longest water?

Oft I sing for my friends when death's cold hand I see, but when I reach my journey's end, who will sing one song for me? and Billy drifts halfway into that song and into a memory of Jean. Her footsteps climbing the stairs, the door of the room flying open, and the look on her face, the painful accusing look. Then Jean turning off the stereo, and the deep emptiness, the why of it. And he remembers the letter. Where is it now? On the stereo? On the desk? He opens his eyes, he sits up, he reaches again for the tiny blue envelope. He opens it.

Tuesday afternoon

Dear Billy,

I suppose you aren't answering any calls, or you haven't been home. I've worried a bit and thought of calling Leon or Jack, but decided that wasn't fair. If you don't want to hear, you don't want to hear. But I have news, and it is all good. I am in fine shape, or so says an expensive doctor at Emory, and there is, he assures me, no reason for fearing anything. I feel so very good now. After that, you know. And Marilyn and I have been hitting the shops. You can't imagine the places we've been. Yes, well, I suppose you can. I've spent too much, especially now that you'll not be playing for a while, but it's been great fun, and most everything was actually quite a bargain. A wonderful little sun dress — But enough of this, I'll show you all of it later.

Billy, how could we have ever left Atlanta? God, it's grown so in these last two years. Buckhead is crazy. Buildings going up all over, and there's absolutely no room for anything else. Why in God's name am I telling you about Buckhead? Really, who cares?

I do think this little vacation will be very good for us. Everything is suddenly becoming so clear. Billy, I'm not crazy am I? I feel so happy suddenly. I think Marilyn believes I'm upset. She keeps babying me so. Nothing I say makes any difference, she's gotten so motherly. Yesterday we spent the afternoon in Piedmont Park. We had a bottle of wine, I only had a little, and she kept calling me Baby, Baby this and Baby that, the way I talk to you sometimes I suppose. As though she were trying for some reason to comfort me. I tell her I'm fine, but she seems to think that we've come to something unalterable, as though one of us had jumped off a bridge or something. That's really ridiculous, isn't it? Who could love each other more that we do? I won't be here very long, I promise.

Actually it wasn't yesterday that we went to the park, we're in the park now. And I've had a little more of the wine than I should. Why would I lie about that? Marilyn is walking around the pond. She's left me to my mood, as she calls it. I'm sure she knows who I'm writing. And she knows I'll feel better when I've finished. Actually I've had rather too much wine, so I'm not getting out exactly what I want to say. But when did either of us ever do that? It's the truth, you know. It is so very hard, isn't it?

It's a beautiful day here, the sky a bright blue, the pond clear and still, a few ducks waddling around the bank, trying to pinch a cracker or two from a couple on a picnic. I wish I had some bread to feed them. We only brought the wine. You'd like the pond, though I doubt there's very many fish in it. And too,

221

there's all sorts of no fishing signs. God, they're everywhere. You'd think this was the best fishing hole in the state. And I doubt the thing is three feet deep. But it is pretty, and you'd like the wooden bridge.

Yes, I suppose I'm paddling around the issue, so to speak. But isn't that the way it always was? You're the same way, and I don't really mind. Some things don't really need to be said, do they? I'll come home soon, I promise. Did I say that already? Next week, I think. Marilyn offered to drive me down, or maybe you could drive up. We could do something fun. Tomorrow we're going to the High Museum. The new building's supposed to be quite something to see, better than anything in it, I hear. And it's not the High Museum anymore, it's the Woodruff Memorial, or something like that.

How's your finger? I do hope it doesn't hurt too much. How awful for something like that to happen. Listen, if you need any money, cash a check. Don't use the Master Card, we've almost reached our limit. Well, I'm running out of paper. Call me.

20

Twilight. Billy rocks on the screened porch. The rain comes down on the trees and the river, the clouds wallowing in so low sometimes he thinks he might just reach up and grab one. The river is dreary, the rusted screen making the whole world dirty and the steady rain coming down trying to wash it clean and only making it dirtier. And the cabin? Dreary, one big dirty room with four cots the woman at the office called beds, cots with mattresses an inch thick, with springs that groan like the crippled and dying, and a bathroom you couldn't turn around in, no tub, no shower, and a kitchen without a stove or a refrigerator, a porch covered with ashes from the charcoal grill. And the whole thing standing out over the river and shifting a little on its crutches every time the wind gusts or somebody gets up and walks across the room.

Billy sits in a sagging wicker rocker, his feet propped on a cooler of beer not nearly as full as it once was, and he witnesses the rain coming down in one steady shower on the river and the trees, and he thinks how incredible that any one given place in the world could be this sad.

The radio blasts again, Jack listening for the weather. Below Cuba a tropical disturbance is wallowing north. Twelve miles an hour, moving straight for Guantanamo. The dial rolls through the static. Anytime it could become a hurricane, the weather service is thinking of names. Billy rocks and thinks. He's a little disturbed himself. Move off, you bastard, Jack is saying. It might just glance off the tip of Cuba, miss Florida entirely. Or it might wallow up some real anger and come straight north. Wallow up, Billy is saying out here on the porch. Wallow up some real steam and move in. Who wants to really go anywhere tomorrow? Not Billy, he's sober enough to know that. Or drunk enough. Move on in here and bring all hell down, move on in here quick and bring it down on the river and the trees, bring it down on the highways, wash out all the sandy little back roads winding through the woods, wash out all the sandy woods, wash it all away, the whole damn business, wash it all right down into the Atlantic.

Calm down, Billy, have another beer. Rain can be a soothing thing, a beautiful thing. Look at the way it makes the needles sag on the pine branches, the way they droop down toward the river. Why does that look so much like a prayer? So much like the true meaning of reverence? And the boats turned bottom-up along the bank, the way the rain speckles their hulls and plays them like drums. Billy, listen to the little steel drums of the boats. Hear that, that tiny tropical beat? And the river itself, speckled with rain, the river washing off into the trees. Remember the pond, the way the rain comes down on the pond? The way the wind swirls on the water and the rain tilts back and forth and the big waves run all the way cross the pond, under the fence, and into the cove? Remember Jean standing in the rain at the edge of the yard? How she would hold out her arms to the clouds, how she would hold herself absolutely still, and if you sat at the kitchen table and stared at her long enough, how your eyes would blur and she would turn into a tree? And remember the willows at the edge of the water, their limbs drooping toward the water like the needles of the pines? And the ducks paddling around the pond, their heads bobbing in and out of the shallows? Just calm down for a minute and remember. Calm down and have another beer.

Hey, Cathey, how about some cards?

Turn off that goddamn radio. Or find some music.

Last night Billy lay awake on the cot for hours, awake and listening to the river moving under him. Sometimes the cabin swayed on the water like the jon boat turning in the wind, a rock and a shift, and the water slapping under him. And Billy, doesn't the river make funny noises? Different from the pond, odd rushing noises, noises full of slow urgency. And all the things down there, Billy, all the things moving around in their own lives, in their own dark world. Like the things in the pond. No, but almost. Big things. Remember what the lady in the office said about the monster gar, big fish of the long toothy snout? Think about that, a hundred and five pounds of ugly prehistory, primitive as any dream. How many men to bring it out of the river? And the sixty-five pound catfish, the two men who struggled for half an hour with the trotline. Billy, what was that weird story about catfish, the way they talk to themselves, the way they sing to each other like dolphins and whales, high little voices like seabirds? Like the voices of seabirds? Who told you that?

Listen, would you cut off that damn radio? It's not likely to change anything.

Billy, you want to play some cards?

Leave him alone. He's in a rough mood.

Listen, I don't care if he's in a mood. He's always in a mood. I want to play some damn cards.

Play some fucking solitaire.

Fish singing to each other. Imagine that, and voices like the voices of seabirds. And Billy, you can listen for them so hard that you actually start to believe you hear them, a little ringing in your ears, then you listen harder and it starts to grow, and you notice that if you turn your head toward the water it rings a little louder, and if you turn your head away it fades. You turn back toward the river and listen

hard, then you start thinking about getting a little closer, just a little
bit closer. And you slide your chair all the way to the edge of the
porch, and you listen harder. You hear that, Billy? So you lean up a
little in the chair, and now you're right on the edge of the rocker and
you're thinking about getting up. You're thinking about getting up
out of the rocker and walking down to the edge of the water. Sure,
they're out there all right, way out there at the end of the river, out
there just beyond the bend where the river snakes into the trees, little voices like the voices of seabirds rising in a chorus, little waves of
voices almost becoming the phrases of a song. And pretty soon
you're thinking about a boat. And sure enough the bank is littered
with boats. But, Billy, you don't fall for that. You know you're not
going anywhere you have to get to in a boat.

Billy, let's play some cards.

I'm getting hungry. Anybody else getting hungry?

You're always hungry. You been hungry since we left.

I could eat something too.

But the rain. The rain makes it harder to hear them. The rain
drowns everything, like listening to an old record. All that background noise, all that dust and static. Billy what is that song? That
night at Jack's, didn't Jerry sing it when the lights went out? Roll on,
O river, deep and wide. So many songs about rivers. Roll on, O Jordan, deep and wide. My home is on the other side. The Jordanaires?
All this business about water! The Jordanaires? Now didn't it rain,
children? God's gonna send the waters from Zion. And all that harmony, smooth as a river. And absolutely clean in the highs and lows,
perfect balance. The Jordanaires!

There's a whole bag full of groceries over there.

Cans. I don't feel much like cans.

Run down to that burger joint then. Bring us something back.

In this shit? That joint's ten miles back.

Pick a card then. Low man goes.

What about him?

Leave him alone. He can't drive, anyway.

Is he gonna be all right?

Sure he is. Billy's gonna be all right. He's just gonna lay down for a while. He's just gonna lay down his burdens, down by the riverside. As sung by his grandmother with the seabird voice, the grandmother with the scratchy seabird voice. And her moving through the house with a string of kids trailing behind her. Lay down my burdens, down by the riverside. Any riverside, any green bank, any Jordan River. As we look beyond the river to that blessed promised land, we by faith can see the beauty on the other side. Remember that one, Billy? The Primitive Quartet.

Get me a cheeseburger, no ketchup, large fries.

Same thing, all the way.

What about Billy?

Get him a cheeseburger and some fries. How bout it, Billy? Cheeseburger and fries?

And pick up some more beer.

No, we don't need any more of that. We gotta get straight tomorrow.

I am straight.

You know what I mean.

So where's the fucking flashlights?

So when did it get dark? Billy rocks back and looks at his watch, the little green hands glowing off his wrist. That late? They'd be eating about now too. But not cheeseburgers. You can bet on that. They'd be eating something incredibly French or Italian. And where would they be? The Abbey? The Mansion? The Rue de Paris? Some place intimate and expensive. Maybe some little place tucked away at the end of a Buckhead alley. Very expensive and very private. Sure, a small table and a candle hardly giving off any light at all. But there's enough light to see all they want to see. And Jean runs her finger across the white lace of the table cloth. It reminds her of a wedding gown, intricate and delicate, and she sees it draped across her shoulders, the white lace on the white shoulders, a long train falling behind her. No, she never had a wedding like that. Those are the shoulders of her mother as she walks down the steps of St. Philip's toward the bottom of the gold frame and the cluttered top of the dresser.

Cathey, you got the keys?

Here, take my Jeep. And put some gas it in.

Anything else?

Listen to the radio. Maybe you can pick up something about the weather.

A waiter passes their table and the candle flickers as he passes. The thin shadow of her hand quivers on the lace. This is like watching her nerves leap suddenly out of her body. Jean is fascinated by the shadow of her arm crossing the tablecloth like the shadow of a tree crossing a field of snow. Marilyn reminds Jean of snow. She is that beautiful. And Jean thinks her dress is as black as the sky on the coldest night in winter. The pearls at her throat whiter than stars. Marilyn runs her finger around the rim of the glass. The wine is very dry and very cold. When she brings it to her lips, she leaves a red half moon on the edge of the glass. Tonight that is the only moon, and Jean watches the way the candlelight seems to pull it into the little pool of wine.

Listen, Hughes ain't going to pull any of his Hollywood shit, is he?

Forget it.

Well, we need to make that clear.

It's clear.

Good. The rain's enough to worry about. I don't think it'll let up.

Don't say that.

Hell, look outside. Looks like the fucking monsoons.

So we get a little wet. You've been wet before, right?

Getting wet's not the point. Anybody sees us taking a couple of boats up river in shit like this is likely to have odd thoughts.

Well, there's nobody around here but the old couple in the office. We'll just have to take the chance.

I don't like chances. You know that.

That's not what I call high risk. The office is down river, we're going up.

Maybe, but that's not my big worry. I just hope Hughes has his facts straight. You ever think there might not be anybody coming? You ever think of that? They might just call this whole business off. Or bring it off somewhere else. We're sitting on the edge of a fucking hurricane.

A little rain won't stop anybody. Them or us. And if it does, the worst thing that happens is we get a little wet.

Why they are so quiet is beyond either of them. And the conversation at the other tables is muffled and fragmented, not even conversation, only sounds that belong somewhere inside the dark, the familiar voices of the unknown, the field voices and the water voices and the tree voices, all nameless and going on just beyond the edge of the light, and being at that table, in the faint light of that candle, is like being inside a dream where nothing is spoken and everything is understood.

Jean watches the moon in the wine, then the moon on the glass. She thinks about love as though it were a pool you might fall into and never get out of. She wants to touch the icicle at the tip of Marilyn's ear. She knows it will not melt in her hand. The waiter comes again, a tall man in a black tie. He doesn't look at either of their faces, only at the feather in Marilyn's hat, the black veil shading her eyes. She opens her menu and closes it. They aren't ready to order, and he moves away as quietly as he came. Jean watches the candle turning the edge of the feather purple. What sort of feather? Jean doesn't know birds, but she thinks of a raven. She takes a sip of her wine. It is cold and dry, and she thinks of all the clichés she has heard about love and warmth. How wrong they are.

Marilyn takes a cigarette from the case beside her water glass. She brings it to her lips and leans toward the open flame of the candle. Jean reaches across the table toward the purple edge of the feather, then touches the hole where the tiny gold wire passes through Marilyn's ear.

Hey, has he passed out?
Leave him alone. He'll be all right in the morning.
Look at him. He's out like a cold fish.
So let him sleep.
So I can't figure why you brought him along in the first place.
You can't be responsible for the whole goddamn world. Hey, don't turn on that damn radio.

Sandpaper on sandpaper. Loud, then softer. Then piano notes, scratchy, then clearer. Chopin? A nocturne? But which one? Who knows? Jean would. Billy, isn't it strange the way Jean knows so much?

How's that? That okay?
That's fine. Now see if you can get it a little better.
It's the rain.

Beautiful, and quiet and intricate and simple. Billy breathes deep, and he listens to the fingers coming down on the keys. Only ten fingers coming down on the keys of a piano. Imagine that. No, not hardly. Not just fingers coming down on keys. A lot more than that. Billy knows that it's a whole world more than that, and he wonders what it would sound like on the guitar? Could anybody transcribe it? Maybe somebody like Pepe Romero. God, those hands, the way they touch the guitar, the clarity and tone. But more than that. Something in the music itself, something in the music that changes things. Something that grabs hold of everything and changes it for the better. And you wonder what was behind this music, what was behind it that so badly needed changing. What was it back there that needed so much beauty? A sickness, a death, a woman? And Chopin, a little ragged and sick, leaning over the piano in the half dark of a candle, working it all out with the notes. Chopin leaning over the keyboard, coughing his lungs out, thinking of the sickness, the death, the woman, working it all out in the notes. Whatever it was, the music must have made it all right.

Turn it up a little.
It's up.

All the way.

It's up.

The way Jerry makes it all right when he picks up the silver body of the beautiful National Steel. Jerry, turn that Peavy up all the way. Let those folks hear you. Hunker down into that microphone and let that National Steel sing, let it proclaim the blues. The one about the woman as tough as nails, they'll like that one. Play it hard and gritty, and forget the requests. Find some woman and sing it straight to her. Look for a blonde in red boots, she'll listen. Play her the grittiest ones, the ones where all the women are rotten and no good, mean as dirt, in love with themselves. Play them the mean songs, the tough songs. Yes, yes. But Jerry, listen, we don't really believe that do we? About the women?

Hand me that map case. The green one.

That Harley he's got?

Yeah?

How much you figure it cost?

I don't know. When he gets back, ask him.

No, we couldn't believe that. No, Jerry, we could never really believe that. Listen. What was that? Out there in the bend of the river. Something like a screech. Listen. Hear it? No, we couldn't really believe that. Not about all the women. Could we? Not about Jean.

That's a nice bike. I'd like to have a bike like that.

What would you do with a motorcycle?

I'd ride the goddamn thing. Bikes are good transportation.

Bikes are dangerous. You might get killed.

You telling me motorcycles are dangerous? You're crazy, you know that.

People smash up bikes every day.

People smash up everything every day. You gotta be careful, that's all.

Sure.

I was thinking about taking a couple of weeks vacation. Maybe

231

taking a trip down to the Keys. That'd be a nice bike trip. You ever think about something like that?

Forget it. I like four wheels under me. Come over here a minute and look at this map.

And now their bodies are so white. And the candle is a globed candle on a night table. The dress that was once as black as the sky on the coldest night in winter is now a pool of black ice Marilyn steps across as she moves toward the bed, the feather a whole wing flying across the footboard, across the blue sheet. Its tip touches the lobe of Jean's ear, flutters down her neck, and across her shoulder. Her arms are spread like wings, her fingers light as feathers as they curl off the sheet. But all she feels is the one slow feather writing on her body, and her nipples hardening into small cold stones. She doesn't know what those words are, but she knows what they mean. She thinks this is like the stories she has heard of people who suddenly speak and understand ancient languages. The feather moving down her stomach is moving out of time and into mystery, and she is sure it must be writing the most beautiful words in the world. This is what she thinks, if she thinks at all, as the feather moves into her hair and suddenly moistens.

And now they are so quiet. Quieter than the rain drizzling on the river, the hulls of the boats hardly drumming at all, quieter than the soft three-part snoring, the grate and squeak of cot springs. They are quieter than all of that, and they are quieter than the creak of the cabin floor as the cabin shifts on its stilts, quieter than the wind spitting through the slit in the screen. They are that quiet and quieter. And the room without the candle is as dark as the bottom of the river. If anyone could look all the way into that darkness, what would he see? More than he could understand.

21

Billy woke to the rock and squeak of the cot. He rolled over onto his back, opened his eyes, and saw Jack standing over him, right foot propped on the end of the frame. The room smelled like coffee and cigars, and the sun threw a tunnel of bright light through the opened door. He had a sharp pain inside the back of his skull, something jabbing like an ice pick, and he closed his eyes again and tried to rub it away with his hands.

The cot shook and squeaked. "Roll out, sport."

The pain eased a little, then moved up across the top of his head. He rubbed his eyes, the little dots inside his eyelids going off like a flurry of purple and yellow fireworks.

"Roll out, sport. It's time to get moving."

"What time is it?" He eased his eyes open and looked at the ceiling, the thin strips of dark knotty pine, the gray light fixture filthy with dust and dead insects.

"Ten fifteen. We're leaving at eleven." Jack walked back over to the table and sat down.

Billy propped himself up on his elbow and let his eyes adjust to the light. "I guess I got a little drunk."

"I guess you did. How do you feel?"

"Not too good."

"So how did you expect to feel?"

Billy turned his head slowly from side to side. His neck felt like he'd slept all night with his head hanging off the side of the mattress. He pushed himself up in the bed and took a few deep breaths. "I'm sorry about that."

"What's to be sorry about?"

"Fogging out like that."

"I figured it might loosen you up a little. Did it?"

"I don't know what it did. I can't quite tell yet."

Jack took a sip of his coffee and leaned back in the chair. "Get some food in you and take a couple of Bufferin. You'll live."

"My stomach's rolling like a bad wave."

Jack nodded toward the porch. "We got chili and beans on the grill. And there's bread and crackers."

"We brought some Pepsi, didn't we?"

"In the cooler on the porch."

Billy eased his feet to the floor and sat for a second while the room steadied around him. Goddamn, Billy. How could you do something like that? You could have screwed up everything. He took a deep breath and looked over at Jack. "I didn't piss anybody off, did I?"

"How?"

"Fogging out that way. I just got out on that porch and one thing led to another."

"Don't worry about it. Cathey got a little drunk himself."

"He did?"

"Why not? He's a big boy, so are you."

Billy stood up and stretched his back. The room rocked for a second, then steadied. "So where are they?"

"They took a boat up river to check out the walkie-talkies." Jack took another sip of his coffee.

"What's the weather like out there?"

"Beautiful. Clouds broke about eight this morning. Blue skies, stiff breeze. You couldn't ask for a better day."

Jack was right, it was a beautiful day. Deep blue sky, a few scattered clouds blowing off toward the north, the trees and the brush around the river a plush green. The river wasn't wide, twenty or thirty yards across, but it was deep for a small Florida river, the saw grass only waving up through the water in the shallows along the banks. There was a good deal of driftwood, mostly around the banks, but the water was remarkably clear, especially after such a heavy rain.

Billy sat in the stern with his left hand wrapped around the throttle of the Johnson outboard. They were taking it easy, cruising up river at a smooth unhurried clip. Fifty yards in front of them, Nolan was setting the pace in Jack's boat, Cathey sitting in the bow with his binoculars trained on the pines, their fishing rods dangling over the stern.

When they lost sight of the fishing camp, the river bent to the west and narrowed. Billy saw several brushy holes along the banks, good cover, and it felt incredibly odd not to be shutting down the motor.

Around the second bend he spotted an anhinga perched on a snag in the river. It sat like a stuffed trophy, sunning its wings, still as the dead, and he remembered the first time he and Jean had taken the jon boat down the Wakulla, how fascinated she'd been by them, the way they could stand motionless for so long, their wings spread like crosses, how she'd made him cut the engine and drift slow between the banks.

He pointed toward the snag. "Crucifix bird," he said. "Jean's favorite. Anhingas and ducks."

"Haven't seen any ducks at all." Jack brought the glasses up to his eyes and scanned the bank. "So when's she getting back? We'll need to have a party."

"Hard to say."

He moved the glasses down the bank, then froze for a second on the anghina. "She's a tough girl, isn't she?"

"What do you mean?"

"I mean she's got spunk, guts. And I like that."

Billy throttled up a little, swerved around another snag, then eased off. "What makes you say that?"

"Nothing, it just occurred me." He lowered the glasses. "You're the same way too. You might not know it."

"Yeah? Well, I don't feel real gutsy right now."

"You ain't supposed to, sport. You're just supposed to be able to do what you need to." He turned in the bow and trained the glasses on the bend Nolan was steering his boat into.

Is that what you call it, Billy, doing what you need to? Is that what Jean did? But what if it hurts somebody? Surely she must have thought about that. And what does that say about the intensity of the need?

The river bent back to the east and widened. And as they came through the bend, they saw that Nolan had slowed the boat. Cathey was standing in the bow and pointing to the left bank, to a black tree leaning out over the water, a black tree spotted with tiny pink fruit.

Billy throttled down and kept his distance, and Jack trained in with the glasses.

"See if you can ease in close," he said.

Billy leaned on the tiller and let the boat slide toward the left bank. He'd seen hundreds of them circling fields and woods, gliding for what seemed like hours on one slow wing beat. But he'd never seen so many at one time, shoulder to shoulder, enough to fill a whole tree. And he'd never seen them so close.

He throttled down more, and they eased toward the tree, the black leaves shining now, the pink fruit turning red. Billy looked hard and close, and the raw fleshy faces seemed almost sad, like the faces of old people who have seen over the years too much grief.

"Odd birds," Jack said. He took the binoculars up and down the tree, "Damn odd birds."

Billy edged by a tangle of driftwood and eased the boat back toward the middle of the river. "Spooky."

"I sort of like to think of them as angels," Jack said. He lowered the glasses and looked back over his shoulder. "Dwarfed black angels."

"Not my sort of angel. Too ugly."

"Well, ugly or not, that's my kind of resurrection."

They rounded another small bend, then they had almost a mile of straight river. Sometimes the banks narrowed so much that the trees met each other over the middle of the river, and the light sifting through the leaves made them look like a strange orange canopy. Then another bend to the east and the river widened and split into two branches. Billy followed Nolan up the east branch.

"Almost there," Jack said. "Nervous?"

"What do you think?"

"I think you are. But that's okay. That's makes for caution, and a little of that won't hurt a thing." He pointed to a patch of driftwood lodged against the east bank. "Gator."

Billy looked hard, but all he could see was a knot of dead branches washed up under a bush.

"Here we are," Jack said.

Billy saw Nolan pointing to a low spot on the left bank where the river washed slightly out of the bed and into a patch of grass. Nolan leaned on the tiller, throttled, and ran his bow onto the bank. Then Cathey hopped out and pulled the boat halfway out of the water. Billy steered to the far side of them, throttled, and ran the jon boat right up to Cathey's feet.

Cathey grabbed the bow and pulled them in, then he gave Jack a hand up. "Tarzan country," he said.

"Absolutely."

"Did you see those goddamn buzzards?"

Billy leaned up in the boat and picked up a rifle.

"Just leave all that stuff in there," Jack said. "Lock the prop up on that outboard, we'll drag the boats over here in the trees."

Billy leaned back over the stern and pulled the motor out of the water. He locked it into place and pulled the saw grass off the propellers, then he stood up and Jack gave him a hand out of the boat.

"Let's go," Nolan said. "Let's get this shit in the woods."

Cathey grabbed the bow of Billy's boat and pulled it all the way up on the bank. Jack picked up the stern, and they carried it into the trees.

Nolan had already pulled the other boat onto the bank. "Here," he said. "You get the light end, and be careful with that busted hand."

Billy stepped over and wrapped his left hand around the bow handle, and they picked it up and followed Cathey and Jack.

They dropped it about ten yards into the woods. Cathey was already stripping down, rolling his shirt into his pants and stuffing them into his backpack. It was odd seeing him like that, standing there in the woods, in only his green boxer shorts and his boots, the gray hair curling off his red chest. It sent a strange feeling into Billy, disturbing. Something he couldn't explain.

Jack was slipping out of his shirt. He pointed at Billy's boat and made little circles with his hand. "Turn the bow around so that it faces the water. That way all Billy'll have to do is drag them into the river."

They picked the boat up again, and Billy backed between a couple of pines while Nolan walked around him. They sat it back down behind the other boat, peeled as fast as they could, and slipped into the camouflage pants and T-shirts. All that green and brown made Billy feel like a part of the woods. Odd again, and a little scary. When he saw his arm moving in the corner of his eye, it didn't seem like his arm. It seemed like something else, something that was attached to him but didn't quite belong to him.

Jack winked at him. "You look like a real trooper."

"I don't feel much like one."

"How do you know?" Cathey said. "Maybe you do and just don't know it. You look like you could eat nails."

Jack pointed to the shirt and pants Billy had laid in the bow of his boat. "Take your street clothes with you," he said. "If we get separated for some reason, you can always make your way over to the highway."

He reached into the boat, picked up the rifles, and handed one to Billy. "All right," he said. "Cathey on point, then Nolan, then Billy, then me. Ten yards apart, move quietly and quickly, and watch where you step. We got corals, rattlers, and mocassins."

They slipped on their masks and stood for a second looking at each other. A feeling of dread washed through Billy, and he took a deep breath and tried to shake it off. It was something about the masks, they were all bothered by it. Cathey shouldered his rifle. "Let's go," he said, and turned and walked off into the woods.

They walked then for fifteen minutes, Cathey beating out a path through the brush. It was mostly a pine forest with a scattering of palmetto and dogwood and magnolia, occasionally an oak. The ferns and air plants in the branches of the pines reminded Billy of Jean's corner on the porch, the curtain of plants she liked to rock behind. He wandered what she'd say if she knew what he was doing. My God, Billy, wouldn't this knock her back? He thought again of the letter and of what she might be doing in Atlanta? How long did she say she'd be up there? That letter, what did you do with it? Didn't you put it in your wallet? But don't worry about that now. Forget it, keep up.

When Billy came out of the trees, Cathey was standing at the edge of the road, shaking his head. "So why would anybody pull off a drug deal way out here?" he said. "Look at this place, it's made to order."

Jack lifted his eyebrows and looked off down the road. "Maybe that's why. Somebody could be setting something up."

"Maybe."

Nolan slipped off his backpack. "This place belongs to one of the guys buying the dope."

"Oh, yeah?"

"Well, he's in real estate. It belongs to his company. A couple of the Generals have been down here before. They were talking once about buying it, using it for a place to party, hide out for a while when they needed to."

"Well," Cathey said. "Nobody'd find them down here. That's for sure."

Jack lifted the muzzle of his rifle and pointed to a pine tree. "That's our tree right there, Cathey."

"One of them."

Jack turned to Nolan. "Whose idea was it to meet down here, anyway? You know that?"

"I think it was Cox's."

"The Generals?" he said.

"I think so. I might be wrong."

Cathey smiled and looked at Jack. "Smells bad, don't it? Smells like somebody's due to get fucked."

"Could be," Nolan said. "It wouldn't surprise me." He reached into the backpack and took out his radio. "I'll let you know as soon as I've checked out the house."

"Okay," Jack said. "Be careful. There might just be somebody down there. Give the whole place a good look from all angles before you go in close."

Nolan slipped the backpack over his shoulders, picked up his rifle, and headed into the woods. He wasn't fifteen yards into the trees before he disappeared. There was only the occasional sound of a footstep, and then, far off, a movement in the branches of the scrub pine.

Jack turned to Billy. "Okay, sport," he said. "Keep inside the tree line, find your best concealment, and when you establish your post, get on that radio and check in. And keep that thing on you all the time."

And Billy, watching the eyes behind the camouflage, thought he knew then what bothered him about the masks. It was a facelessness that turned Jacks's eyes into the eyes of any other animal in the woods. It was more than the anonymity, it was an anonymity that was frightening and primitive. It projected a violence that made his heart race.

He took a deep breath and nodded at Jack, then turned and walked back into the woods. When he was out of sight, he stopped and let himself calm. Billy, you're not really a part of this, you're only a point man, you're only a lookout. This helped some, and when he was steady he leaned his rifle against a tree, slipped off the backpack and took out the little green radio, the thing that looked like a toy, a little piece of Japanese science fiction, and wedged it under his belt. He swung the backpack over his shoulders again and picked up the rifle. The road was about fifteen yards through the trees. He decided to keep it there and stay in the woods until he got where he wanted to be.

What Jack had said about snakes was true, especially after a downpour, so he walked slowly and watched every step, the muzzle of the rifle out in front of him like a blind man's cane, his feet coming down easy on sand and needles. And he started off counting those steps. Hadn't Jack said a thousand meters? Wouldn't that be about a thousand steps? But after a while he lost count. Billy, how many football fields have you crossed? Seven, maybe. Eight? And yards to meters? Close. Then he looked off to his left and the road wasn't there.

A little jolt of fear shook him, that hollowness in the chest. Stupid, Billy. How do you lose a goddamn road? Watch what you're doing, you'll get somebody hurt. Double back, find the place where it curved. That ought to be the spot you want.

He hadn't walked fifty steps back when he saw it on his right, twenty yards or so through the trees, not a sharp curve, but a decent enough curve for such flat ground. He stopped just inside the tree line and took a good look at the area. The road was sand and wide enough for only one car, though it seemed to widen a little into the curve. Billy looked at the road closer, it was dry as a chip. After all that rain, and the sand looked completely dry. Interesting facts, Billy. What a stupid little dream about the storm washing all the roads away.

On the other side there was a rise covered with thin sand pine, not really a hill, just sightly higher ground. And there were a few big rocks clustered in front of the curve at the foot of the rise. Billy studied them and decided they wouldn't make much cover. The best cover seemed to be right where he was, in the trees at the mouth of the curve. From here he could look straight up the road for a hundred yards or so before the sand disappeared again into the trees.

He took off his backpack and laid it at the foot of a pine. He thought for a minute and walked around the curve, still inside the tree line. The road straightened for another hundred yards or so, then veered into the pines and off toward the river house. When he got back to his pack, he took another careful look around. Nothing, so he stepped out into the road and walked up it for thirty yards or so. Then he turned around. He wanted to see exactly what the men in the car would see when they came down that road. He wanted to see exactly where the thickest cover was, so he could make sure he was in it.

There were a few decent spots, but the best place looked to be in the trees, in a pine in the first bend of the curve. The brush, the grass, and the hardwoods provided good enough cover if he wanted to sit ten yards back in the woods, but from the branches of a pine in that first bend he could get a good look straight up the road. From there it would be just like aiming down the barrel of a gun.

He walked quickly back to his pack, picked it up, and carried it to the foot of a big pine with a thick bush of needles. The only problem was getting to the first branch. It was ten or twelve feet off the ground, and the trunk was too thick to shimmy up, especially with a bad hand.

Then Billy remembered the rope, and laid the rifle on a patch of needles, opened the pack, and took out the yellow coil. He reeled off about half, cut it with his sheath knife, and stuffed the coil back into his pack. Then he tied a noose in one end of the rope, stood up and threw the other end over the first branch of the pine, but it didn't fall far enough over, so he jerked it down and threw again. He slid the backpack over his shoulders, picked up the rifle, and slipped the sling over his head and right shoulder. The hand would be a problem, he knew that, but he stepped into the noose anyway, tightened it around his hips, and grabbed the other end of the rope. He leaned back easy and felt his weight.

He was heavier than he thought, and his right hand wouldn't close tight enough around the rope. Billy eased his grip for a second, took a deep breath and tried again. The left was strong and would pull him up, but when the right tried to hold his weight, a sharp pain cut into his hand. He eased off and let the pain die. Then he tried one more time. No, this wasn't going to work, the hand was too weak.

He stepped out of the noose, and jerked the rope off the limb. He looked at it for a second as it lay on the needles at the foot of the pine, then he looked at the splint and the taped fingers. Think about it, Billy. Don't be so stupid. He picked up the straight end of the rope, stretched it out for twelve or fifteen feet across the ground, and began to tie large loops in it, large loops a couple of feet apart until he had seven of them strung up the rope like the rungs of a ladder. He threw the noose end over the branch again, strung the rope through it, and pulled it tight.

Billy held the rope with both hands, tested his weight, and put his left foot into the first loop. When he lifted his right foot, his legs swung out in front of him, startled him and almost made him fall, but he held on and managed to get his right foot into the next loop. Then the left into loop above the right, the rope turning with him now, his feet swinging out in front of his body, until he worked his way up to the branch, threw his arms across it, and pulled himself up.

He was out of breath. He sat still for a minute in the shallow fork where the first branch met the trunk of the pine. From here he had a perfect view up the road, but he could see less in the other direction. But that didn't matter, they wouldn't be coming from the river. He turned slightly on the branch and looked straight up the trunk of the tree. Wouldn't the cover be better a little higher up? A few branches higher the bush of the tree thickened into a solid wall of needles, so he untied the rope, coiled it, reached over his shoulder, and wedged it under the flap of his backpack. He stood up carefully, his good hand on the branch above him, his feet wedged into the fork of the first branch, and started to climb.

One limb up, two limbs. And halfway to the top he sat down in a fork where the trunk split and made two trees for another twenty-five or thirty feet. There was nothing to do now but wait. Hopefully not a long wait, but there was nothing else to do. He pulled the rifle sling over his head and shoulder, unfastened it at the butt, looped it over the limb above him, and fastened it again. Then he slid out of the backpack, looped both straps over another limb, and took out the binoculars.

He popped the lens caps and dropped them into the pack. A green blur. Then a flurry of needles, then the road beyond them. He focused on the spot where the road bent again into the woods. This was a fine lookout. He'd see them easily at a hundred yards or so, plenty of time to radio the others. He moved the glasses slowly down the road, and a rabbit ran across his field of vision and into the brush. He shifted a little and focused on the brown tree line, but he couldn't find the rabbit, so he moved the glasses to the road again and eased down the far side. A couple of sparrows in the weedy sand, then on the rocks at the foot of the rise a lizard stretched out in the bright sun. Billy watched him for a minute, the green head perfectly still, the red throat pulsing. Then he moved the glasses back to the road and eased across it, and there it was, as plain as any roadsign, a long line of footprints snaking into the woods.

Stupid. He let the glasses drop into his lap, looked off into the trees and took a breath. Stupid. Stupid. But what about it? Come on now, would anybody coming down that road in a car notice those footprints? Not likely. He looked back through the pine branches and down at the road. But think about it, Billy. They'll have to slow down coming into that curve, and they might slow down a lot. Okay, but even if they did happen to notice them, would they think anything about it? Probably not. Why should they? But Billy, the real question is this, Can you afford to take the chance?

He brought the glasses back up to his eyes. There they were again, so clear he could see the tread from the soles of his boots, and they were walking straight down the middle of the road, walking straight toward him. Damned stupid.

He put the lens caps back on the glasses and eased them into the pack, then he took out the coil of rope and started back down the tree. Easy, one foot at a time firmly in the forks of the branches. When he reached the bottom branch, he sat in the fork and started to uncoil the rope. Then he changed his mind, dropped the coil, and jumped down after it. The landing jarred a pain into his hand, but it was better than trying to fight the rope.

What he wanted was something bushy, so he looked around for a dead branch, something fairly heavy. A few yards into the woods he saw a small magnolia, several branches hanging close to the ground. He found one with enough weight and leaves, hacked it off with his sheath knife, and carried it to the edge of the road. Stupid, he thought to himself again. Then he walked the line of footprints all the way to the end and started wiping them away with the end of the magnolia. Halfway back to the woods, he heard a noise. He froze, a little startled. A motor? Maybe, but far off. He listened and thought about heading back for cover. But it didn't seem to be getting any closer, then it faded, and he went back to work on the footprints, his heart still beating a little faster than he wanted it to.

When he finished, he stood at the edge of the road and looked at what he'd done. Better. Now it only looked like a great swirl of sand where a trail of footprints had been wiped away. But it was all he could do, and he'd done it, so he dragged the branch back into the woods, found his rope, and struggled again up the tree.

He sat for a few seconds on the first branch and got his breath. Then he untied the rope, coiled it, and climbed back to his perch.

When he stuffed the coil into the backpack, he took out the radio. Hadn't Jack said to use the A channel? How did the band selector get flipped to the C? He switched it back to band A and held down the talk button. "Jack," he said. "Can you hear me?"

He let off the button and listened. Nothing. So he said it again, slightly louder, "Jack, am I coming through?"

He let off the button and listened. Nothing. He sat for second and looked at the thing. Then he shook his head and pulled up the antenna. "Jack, can you hear me?"

A silence, then, "Talk to me, sport."

"I'm up here in a tree. About halfway into a curve."

"How far up the road from us?"

"Six, maybe seven hundred yards."

"Do you have a good view of the road and how far can you see up it?"

"Great view. A good hundred yards or so."

"Good. Be careful and hang loose."

"What about Nolan?"

"No word. Hang loose and stay by the radio."

"Right." He took his finger off the talk button and listened. Nothing else. He turned the volume knob all the way up and laid the radio carefully inside the backpack. Hang loose? How could you hang loose in the top of a pine tree overlooking a road you knew two carloads of drug dealers were going to come down? Come on, Jack. Hang loose?

He took a deep breath, then another. Drop it, Billy. Think about something else. The letter. What did you do with the letter?

He reached into the backpack and took his wallet out of his jeans. He thought he'd folded it behind his money, but it wasn't there. And it wasn't in the pocket under his credit cards either. What was there was an old Polaroid of Jean, a tiny black and white he'd taken before they were married. Jean sitting in a folding chair in front of a tent. In front of a tent? That must have been taken at a festival. Lavonia maybe. No, it couldn't have been Lavonia. They were only there once, and they'd just met. They wouldn't have taken any pictures then. But wasn't that Marilyn's camera? That old white plastic Polaroid? And he didn't remember taking Marilyn to any festivals.

Then it came to him, their first and last camping trip, the trout stream outside Blairsville, and Marilyn's husband Roy with his two hundred dollar Orvis flyrod, his waders, his five boxes of flies. And then the two days of rain, the leaky tent, and the one fish caught all weekend, the eight-inch trout Marilyn caught on yellow corn. Roy Saunders, what a jerk. He didn't talk to anybody all the way back to Atlanta.

"Nolan here, Jack. You there?"

"Go ahead."

Billy reached into the backpack, took out the walkie-talkie, and turned down the volume.

"House vacant. No sign of any recent activity. Two boats in a dock house, disabled. Everything on this end looks good."

"Good job. How close did you get to the house?"

"I'm standing here in the kitchen. There's a beer in the fridge, you want me to bring it?"

"Negative on the beer. Just bring yourself back up here."

"Right. Billy find his spot?"

"That's an affirmative."

Billy laid the radio in his lap, slid the photo back into his wallet, and dropped it into the backpack.

"Jack here, Billy. You want to acknowledge?"

He pressed the talk button. "Yeah."

"You hear that?"

"I heard it."

"Okay. Everything looks smooth. Keep your eyes on the road, and don't fall out of that tree."

"I'll watch it."

"And as soon as that car passes you, get back to the river quick and get those boats in the water."

Billy waits. He watches the empty road and listens to a bird far off in the trees, a mockingbird somewhere, or a jay. He looks at the strange black tube on the end of the rifle. The wind brushes it with the green needles of the pine. He waits. Any time now, Billy. Any time now and that car might come barreling around that curve. He looks at the green radio in his lap. He looks at the rifle hanging from the limb above him, at the backpack hanging to his left. Any time now, Billy, and he notices that the fingers of his right hand are trembling, little worm-like fingers crawling in their white cocoon. He brings the hand up to his lap and rubs it on his pants. A little tingling, a numbness under the tape, so he rubs it easy with his other hand. Billy, your hands are covered with sweat. Calm down, you're nervous as hell.

He checks his watch. An hour and twenty minutes. Where the hell are they? And he thinks for a minute about calling Jack, just to check in, to make sure everything is all right. Forget it, Billy. Everything's all right. Wouldn't you have heard something? Calm down, it's only the waiting. It's got you spooked. He held his hands out in front of him and looked at them. The quivering had stopped, but they didn't look like a pair of hands that might inspire any confidence. That's okay, they're steady enough. Sure, Billy, try to believe that.

Then he remembered what Jack had said about Jean. Guts? What did he mean by that? Was he trying to tell you something? He looked again at his watch. One thing about Jean, though. She finally did find the guts to do something. You can't deny that, Billy. She knew what she wanted and what she had to do to get it. And she did it, and here you are up in this pine tree and shaking like so many needles. Yes, but those are two entirely different things. You can't begin to compare them. Billy, do you really believe that?

Maybe it wasn't so easy for her either. Did you ever think about that?

He saw it come out of the trees at the end of the road. A red car, and moving slow. He pulled the glasses out of the backpack and popped off the caps. A red Blazer or Scout, coming slow, but coming. His heartbeat almost cut off his breath. Calm down, take it easy. And he picked up the radio and pushed in the talk button.

"They're coming. A red Blazer."

Nothing.

"They're coming, goddamnit. A red Blazer." Shit. He took his finger off the button.

"Many? Repeat, how many?"

"Two men in the front for sure. I can't see the back."

"How far are they from you and how fast are they moving?"

"Fifty yards, maybe. Not moving fast."

"Can you see any weapons?"

"No. Wait a minute, they're coming into the curve now. They're right under me. Okay, two men in the back, maybe three."

"Good job. Get down from there, get the boats in the water, and get the motors idling."

Billy took a deep breath, his heart slamming like a fist against his ribs. He put his hands against his chest and pressed hard. That calmed him some, but he felt drained, a little dizzy, everything gone out of him. He took a few more breaths and hurried the lens caps onto the glasses, dropped them into the backpack. And as he reached up and slipped it off the limb, the first blast of the C-4 startled him. A loud sharp crack, then the second blast and a sound like a hundred glasses shattering on a concrete floor. Then something roared at the other end of the road, a Mustang sliding around the curve and into the ditch. His hand jumped for the radio, but hit it with the splint and fumbled. He tried to catch it with his left, but it was already out of his lap, making a small crack against a limb, then a thud at the bottom of the tree. The tail of the Mustang swerved in the loose sand, then the wheels caught and it jumped back onto the road. Billy dropped the backpack and fought with the swivel on the rifle sling. He couldn't unfasten it, it was stuck. He pulled out his sheath knife and cut the sling. The car was sixty yards away, fifty. Then he caught the grill in his sights and jerked the trigger. The gun rocked him, shoved him off balance, but he caught himself with his legs and shot again. The windshield shattered and the Mustang spun sideways and crashed into the rocks at the foot of the rise. Two men with pistols jumped out and ran into the woods on the other side of the road. One of them was the big General.

22

Billy held tight to the stock of the rifle and climbed down the tree, paused for a second on the bottom branch, then jumped to the ground. He stopped for a second to get his breath, to fight the panic, then he listened. Only a faint hissing from the Mustang, and the wind coming down the road, rustling the ends of the branches. The radio and the backpack lay a few feet beyond him on the other side of the tree. He hurried over, picked them up, then crouched low behind the trunk.

The antenna on the radio was bent a little forward. He straightened it, then pressed the talk button. "Jack. Two Generals in a Mustang." He let off the button.

Nothing.

"Jack. Goddamnit, Jack." He let off the button.

Nothing.

He shook the radio and tried it again. His heart was going crazy, he was covered in sweat. Still nothing. What now, Billy? What do you do now? He pushed the antenna down and stuffed the radio into the backpack, then swung the pack over his shoulders. Be quiet, listen. Did something move across the road? He held the rifle out in front of him and eased his head around the tree. Only the brush, the road, and just outside the curve, the Mustang steaming against the rocks. What now, Billy? Where did they go? Over there in the woods. They're over there in those trees. Or are they?

Three shots went off in the trees above the Mustang. They rang in loud waves down the road. He couldn't tell where they hit, but they weren't close. What does that mean, Billy? That they don't know where you are?

The sand jumped in the road at the back of the curve, and another shot rang out. He felt himself start to panic again, a little surge of fear and energy, and he had the sudden urge to turn around and run as fast as he could back to the boat. Damn, Billy, get a hold. You can't do that. Get down that road and tell the others. There are two men up here with guns, they might be headed that way. But Billy, it isn't that easy, is it? Not when you're almost scared to death.

He took a deep breath and looked around for the best path through the trees. Something moved in the woods directly across the road, a crackling of branches, light, almost silent. He froze and listened. It moved again farther down the road, a small rustle. Damn, Billy. Get off your ass, somebody's getting in front of you. He stood up and looked around the other side of the trunk. Then he saw him, thirty-five yards through the brush, the flash of a black T-shirt, the barrel of a shotgun, the big General jumping out of the woods and crossing the road.

What now, Billy? And he moved ten yards through the woods to the cover of a large pine. What now? What's he trying to do? Get behind you, or get down the road to see what that explosion was? And what do you do? Try to work around him and get back to the others? Come up behind him before he comes up behind them? Or do you stay right here and wait on Jack or Cathey or Nolan on the chance they might have heard those shots? Sure, Billy that's the tempting answer. But if you do that, one of them, all of them, might get ambushed.

He eased his head around the trunk of the tree. Only the woods, and ten yards through those woods, the clearing that was the road. He moved off easy, stepping quietly and quickly through the brush, making a very shallow circle to his left.

Something moved near the road and he ducked behind a pine. Or did it? He listened, then stepped back out and walked fifteen or twenty quick yards across the woods. It rustled again, and he froze in his steps. Then it rustled closer, but more to his left. Billy held his breath and listened hard. Wind churned up the needles in the tops of the pines and made a hushing sound, and a few shards of light crawled over the dark needles on the floor of the woods. He took a deep breath and watched one thin scattering of light trickle like a path through the trees. Behind him a noise, the slamming of a car door or a trunk, and he turned back toward the curve. Someone was getting something out of the Mustang. The dope? Another gun? He listened for footsteps coming down the road. Nothing. Then the wind again in the tops of the pines, and he turned to watch the trail of light flickering through the woods. It was moving off toward Jack and the others, but fainter now, as though it might vanish. He took a deep breath and looked around the trunk. Only the trees and the shadows and the dark floor of needles, so he gripped the rifle tight in both hands and ran off down the flickering trail.

Twenty yards, thirty, his feet crunching down on yellow needles, and the wind died and the trail vanished in a small half-clearing of fallen trees. Billy stopped, his heart racing. Over to his left a crackling of brush, and he moved behind a pine. Then the crackling again, closer, and a flash of black running through the woods, and he went rigid, gripping the rifle until his arms ached, and watched, startled, as the big General broke through the brush and fell headlong over the branch of a fallen tree. Billy spun around the trunk of the pine and brought down the muzzle of the rifle. Five yards in front of him the big General was up on his knees, scrambling for the stock of the black shotgun.

Billy jerked the butt of the rifle to his shoulder and caught the

General in his sights, the black T-shirt stretched tight over the broad chest, the General's face pale against the black beard and streaked with dirt and sweat. Then all he could see was the shotgun rising in front of the face, the barrel pointing straight at him, trembling, the muzzle almost close enough to touch. He squeezed the rifle tight with both hands but the barrel shook uncontrollably. He squeezed tighter and tried to pull the trigger, but the barrel shook and his hand cramped hard and refused to move. Something scratched his side, the shotgun jumped, and the blast rang through the woods. Something punched him hard in the arm and jerked him backwards, the blast again, and he fell on his backpack in a thatch of pine needles and lay there, breathing hard, hearing only the ringing in his ears, his head tilted back at a deadly angle, looking straight up through the trees where the sky glimmered like pieces of broken glass.

Billy, somebody has set your arm on fire. He lifted his head and looked down at his hand still holding the grip of the rifle. The arm broke backwards at an odd angle where two white bone splinters punched out of the pink flesh just below his elbow. It was odd and frightening. It made something sick turn in his stomach. It was like suddenly having two elbows, one of them a pink soup of torn muscle and bone fragments, horrible, spurting bright red blood. He grabbed the elbow with his left hand and tried to squeeze off the bleeding, but he couldn't put enough pressure, and the blood kept spurting into a little pool on the brown needles.

He tried to lift his right hand, but the hand wouldn't move. Only the elbow moved, the sharp pain running through it. Suddenly the sickness in his stomach wallowed hard, and he lay his head back on the ground and tried to get his breath, still squeezing with his left hand but rolling a little on his side, trying to get more pressure on the arm.

A dull thud of footsteps ran up the road, the brush crackled, and another blast rang out through the trees. Someone was tearing the woods apart with his feet, then a short crack, crack, crack, like the snapping of fingers. Billy breathed hard and fast, trying to keep up with his heart. A silence, and another crack, crack, crack, and Billy lay watching the tops of the trees, the way the wind in the needles shattered the sky into little shards of blue glass.

More footsteps ran hard along the road. "Billy!"

"Over here."

"Shit."

And Billy raised his head, the brush flying apart, Jack slapping at low branches with the barrel of his rifle, dropping to his knees and throwing off his backpack.

"Two of them with pistols." The muscles in his arm tightened hard against the burning. "They came up in a Mustang."

"Hush, now," Jack said. His left hand pushed Billy's away from the arm and clamped down hard, his right tearing at his belt buckle, jerking the belt through the loops of his pants.

"It hurts, Jack. It hurts something awful."

"Calm down, don't talk. You're going to be fine."

"What about the other guys? The guys in the Blazer?"

"Don't worry about them. They're not a threat." And he wrapped the belt around the arm and pulled it tight.

Not a threat? Billy, what does that mean, not a threat? Through the needles in the tops of the pines the sky looked like a spidered windshield. "I dropped the radio." Then the pain, and the muscles tightening against it. "It busted. Goddamn, Jack. Goddamn, it hurts."

"Okay, sport. Just relax."

And Billy watched the shards of blue light spilling through the needles of the pines. He reached up with his left hand and pulled at the mask, but the hand slipped away. Jack leaned over and eased the mask off his face. Cooler, Billy. And the sky started to spin a little, the way it spins when he's drifting in the jon boat in the middle of the pond. He went with it for a moment, the blue light glittering in the needles, the branches of the pines drifting slightly to one side, back to the other. Then he closed his eyes, felt Jack's hands

255

tightening the belt, tearing the shirt away from his arm.

Someone was running in the woods, then Cathey was standing over Jack's shoulder, the med bag in his hand. "Shit. Goddamn, shit. All right, hold that thing tight. I'll check his side."

"He's in pain. Give him something for the pain."

"You got that tourniquet tight? Is it still bleeding?"

"Oozing some. Where's Nolan?"

"Hold it fucking tight." Cathey pulled out his sheath knife, cut up the side of Billy's T-shirt and pulled it away from the wound. "He looks a little flush. What's his pulse like?"

"I don't know. I just got here."

"Is he breathing all right?"

"Seems to be. Billy, you having any trouble breathing?"

"It hurts, Jack. It hurts bad."

"The side's nothing. It'll wait."

"So where the fuck is Nolan?"

"He hit that other guy, followed him into the woods." Cathey put his hand on Billy's wrist, groping for a pulse. A silence, and Billy stared straight up into the sky. The trees were still and quiet, so quiet Billy could hear his heart. Then the wind rustled, the sky shifted. "Pulse is rapid and thready. We got to get some fluids in him. He's going into shock."

The pain surged hard and Billy tightened his muscles against it, his face hardening around a grimace, his left hand balling into a fist. "Goddamn, Jack."

"Give him something, goddamnit."

Billy, what's happening? That fire in the arm, and the sickness in the gut, the hollow sickness spinning in the gut and in the head. Why won't it let you alone?

"Come on, goddamnit. Give him something."

"Not till he stablizes." And Cathey leaned down and cut the straps on Billy's pack. He eased it away from him, then lifted his feet and wedged the pack under them. "Lay your head back, pal.

Try to relax."

But Billy raised his head slightly and watched Cathey fish a bottle of clear fluid out of his bag. He punctured the black stopper with the end of a tube and handed the bottle to Jack. "Hold it high."

The fluid ran down the tube and through the needle in Cathey's hand, and Billy lay back and watched the needles in the tops of the pines. Something wrapped itself around his left arm, and he felt it tighten. Then something cool swabbed the inside of his elbow, and Cathey started tapping the spot with his fingers.

"What's wrong?" Jack said.

"Veins collapsed. Okay, there's one."

When Billy felt the needle ease into his arm, he leaned up a little and watched the bright red blood seep into the tube. Then it went down again and back into his arm as the clear fluid ran out of the bottle.

"Hold it up a little. We'll run the whole thing in him. You holding that belt tight?"

A minute of silence passed, two minutes, the light trickling through the trees, throwing spots of yellow onto Billy's face and chest as he watched the fluid go down in the bottle.

"Where the fuck is Nolan? Hurry up with that thing, goddamnit, we'll get him over to the hospital in Ona."

Cathey looked at Jack, then he looked down at the arm.

Billy turned his head. He was trying not to look at the arm again. The pain told him all he needed to know. It surged again and he tightened his body against it. "It hurts bad, Jack. Will it be all right?"

"Fine, Billy. Just fine." He brushed the needles out of Billy's hair, then looked hard at Cathey. "Give him something, goddamnit. Can't you see he's in pain?"

"I can't give him anything till I get this fluid in him."

Billy watched the last of the liquid run down the plastic tube, then the sickness wallowed hard in his stomach and he eased his head back and tried to breathe.

Cathey pulled the needle out. He leaned over Billy's chest and looked again at the arm. "Is it still oozing?"

"A little bit, I think."

"We'll let him rest a second, then I'll give him some morphine."

"We don't have time to rest, goddamnit. We got to get him to a fucking hospital."

"Get your head together, all right?"

"My fucking head is together. We got to get this arm put back."

Billy watched the sky and the green needles turning against the sky. Cathey stood up and Billy watched his face. It was gray and blank and looked like it was cut out of cardboard. He was looking for something in the med bag, and when he came out with a hypodermic, Billy turned his eyes back to the trees. They seemed to be moving in circles now, the needles against the sky, and Billy tried to pretend he was in the jon boat, the wind turning him slowly on the pond. A little pain stabbed into his left arm, then a heavy calm passed through him. It swallowed him like a thick cloud, and Billy lay there watching the green needles blurring against the blue sky.

Footsteps far away on the road, footsteps far away but coming on fast and hard, then the brush crackling over the sound of the wind, the brush crackling closer, the woods breaking apart.

You find the other one?

Bled out a mile or so up the road. I dragged him back into the woods. How's Billy?

Not too good. He's lost a lot of blood. We need to get him over to the hospital in Ona.

You know better than that. Get your head together.

My head is together.

The wind in the tops of the trees, and the blue shards glittering through the green needles, the blue shards throwing little patches of warmth over his face and chest.

We're taking him to the hospital to get this goddamn arm stitched back.

Get your head together, man. There's nothing to stitch.

Bullshit, I've seen worse. They can do all sorts of stuff now.

Not if they don't have something to work with. Jack, look at this. The arm's gone. It's hanging by a thread, the bone's blown all over the goddamn woods.

So they can reconstruct it with something.

Come on, Jack, get it together. There's nothing to reconstruct. Even if it was a clean cut, we'd have to pack that arm in ice. You see any ice around here? And it'd still be dead by the time we got to a hospital.

We can give it a shot, can't we? We can give it our best shot.

Listen, we're wasting time. I've got to get a dressing on that arm. You want that thing to get infected?

What do you mean?

I mean the rest of that arm's got to come off now, and I've got to get a dressing on it.

Bullshit.

You know he's right, Jack. I can see it from here.

Bullshit. Nobody's taking that arm off.

Goddamnit, look at it. We're wasting time.

The wind whips up and the limbs sift down a fine powder of yellow light. It glows like rosin on the bark of the pines.

Listen, nobody wants to do this. But, goddamn, there's nothing else to do. We couldn't take him to a hospital anyway. You know that. We're dealing with a gunshot wound.

That's right, Jack. Nobody goes to a hospital. We all knew that. That's why Cathey's here.

Are you sure, goddamnit? I mean about the arm, are you really sure?

It's gone, man. It's already gone. I wouldn't lie to you. You know me better than that.

The wind is shaking the tops of the trees, and Cathey is standing as tall as a tree, his sheath knife sparkling in the sunlight filtering through the needles of the pines.

Nolan, cut down something to make a litter out of. I can handle this now. You go up and check out that Mustang.

What for?

Dope. If they find a carload of dope, it'll look funny. Dealers don't leave that shit lying around.

Nolan can do it. I'll help you here.

You sure?

I can't leave him.

All right, slide over here and dig into that bag. Get me some dressings, that big one, the abdominal pad, and that bottle of Betadine.

A rustle in the woods, the sky turning in slow circles over the green blur of needles, the wind cool, oddly cool. A rustle and a hacking of trees, and the sky turning blue circles over the pine branches, the sky turning blue circles over the deep green blur. Footsteps, and the crushing of brush.

Here, hold onto the end of these things. We'll run 'em between a couple of shirts.

The boat swerves into a bend, and the river narrows and the sun shoots down like rain through the trees and traps itself between the branches and the water so that they seem to be riding through a tunnel of orange light. The outboard growls behind the boat, a loud painful growl. Billy lies back in the bow, his head on a flotation cushion, his legs stretched over the first seat, and he watches Jack hold the tiller in his left hand, guide the boat around snags and driftwood. But Jack is often a blur, and when he isn't his face is blank, his eyes set hard on the river. There is nothing in it for Billy to read. The spray is all around, and the air smells like moist dirt. Billy wonders why the fire in his arm has burned itself out, and he presses easy with with his left hand against the dressing, the belt tied around his arm, and he presses again, trying to feel something besides the grip of the bandage. And there it is, a dull little ache below his fingers. Whose fingers, Billy? So hot and sticky, and he raises his head off the cushion and looks down. His left hand is smeared red, his left hand and half his forearm smeared dark red. The bandage on his right arm is white and red.

Lay back, Billy. Try to relax.

He watches Jack's lips close into a frown and feels with the back of his head the hot cushion draped across the bow seat. Billy, why is everything so hot? And your mouth, Billy, it feels like hot sand. Then the hollow sickness he believes is fear wallows hard again in his chest, and he takes a deep breath, and then another.

The boat roars down the tunnel of light, the trees on the bank touching over the middle of the river, Billy watching the gold roof of leaves shimmer in the wind. The boat swerves and straightens, and the shift of weight rocks a pain in his side and his arm. The sickness rolls again, so hard it almost cuts off his wind. The branches blur into the sky, and he closes his eyes, tries to relax. The dark is frightening, but he keeps them closed until the breath comes back.

Stay with me, sport. That's better. Think about all that cash. Just pretend you're back home spending it somewhere.

Jack throttles down, and the boat swerves again, then he throttles up fast and the pain burns dull, fades. The roof of leaves shivers over the boat, sprinkles the river with little drops of light. Billy breathes slowly. The outboard growls, and the water slaps in waves against the bottom of the boat, a sound like the hollow throb of a heart beat. Billy, why couldn't you just be somewhere else? Why couldn't you just close your eyes and be somewhere else?

But that's not the way it works, is it? You can't just wish yourself anything or anywhere. But what if you could? Just think about it. If you could be somewhere else, where would that be? In the jon boat out on the pond, with the boat turning under you in a slow drift? Or on the floor of your room, the stereo wide open, the whole house filled with the sound of Lester's voice, the whole house drifting off on the gospel ship of Lester Flatt? Or maybe in the dark bedroom, under the gentle wave of Jean's weight? Billy, remember that? The easy rock of the mattress, the gentle wave of Jean's weight?

That dark, Billy, that gentle wave and drift, then that other kind of wait. That hard and constant pain. But Billy, that's all over now. And isn't that all right? It was a very long wait for her, all those specimens and tests, the monthly charts, the waiting rooms of clinics, and now it's over. And Billy, after all of that pain, how can that not be all right? Now it's over, and now there's only the long drift inside the body, such a fragile and frightening drift. But, Billy, the drift that promises everything, the drift that's worth anything. No, how can you blame Jean? What an awful thing to hold that promise, only to lose it in a pool of blood.

But Billy, that's okay now. After a loss, isn't any salvation that much sweeter? And, Billy, maybe Jean knew that all along. Maybe that's what drove her so hard. Maybe she thought you'd figure that out. This is something to think about, something to think about hard, a whole new way of looking at the world. Billy, this may be the only way left of looking at the world. And what will Jean say about that?

Not much longer, sport. Hang on now.

And the boat swerves into a bend, and the roof of trees parts as the river widens, and the sky is suddenly a bright ball of yellow light. Billy shades his eyes with his hand, and Jack's face is grim, his eyes trained on the river, his eyes hard on the river, trying to give nothing away. The boat swerves again to Billy's left, Jack throttles. The river slaps a pulse into the bottom of the boat, and Billy moves his hand away from his eyes and rests it on his chest. The arm grumbles again, then eases. Billy squints at the bright yellow sky and turns his head slightly to the right. The pines streak by, another blur of green, and a white bird flushes out of the trees. The sky it flies into is white hot. But Billy doesn't want to close his eyes.

Another mile, Billy. Stay with me. How you feel?

No, really. Suppose you could just close your eyes and be anywhere you wanted. The pain almost fades, but the sickness strikes hard in his chest. And he is mostly afraid of the sickness. Billy, can

262

someone be afraid of fear? Is that possible? He grimaces and turns his head, the sky is a murderous white. Think yourself away, Billy. Think yourself away, be somewhere else. And relax, let the sickness pass. Billy, isn't your body awfully heavy? You'd think it would sink the boat. But the boat is clipping along, a full roar.

Another motor roars, and he turns his head. The boat pulls along side, Cathey standing up in the bow, holding to the anchor line, the boat bobbing up and down on the water, pulling closer, and Cathey standing in the bow, riding it like a giant ski.

How's he doing?

He's hanging in there.

Hanging in where, Billy? He presses his hand against his chest, and the sickness wallows. Billy, why does your tongue feel so thick? Your mouth so incredibly dry? I'll bet if you tried, you couldn't talk. But then what is there to say? The trees blur over Cathey's shoulder. He sits down in the boat, and the boat pulls off.

Billy rolls his head, the sky is like a white torch, he squints and rolls it back. Billy, what's going on with the sky? And this sickness. Where did this sickness come from? Why won't it leave you alone?

Hang on, sport. We're getting there.

And Billy moves his hand from his chest and hangs onto the side of the boat. The boat jumps a little, then again, and his legs rise heavy off the seat. Billy, this incredible sickness, the green blur leaning over the river and leaning back as the sky opens up over the boat, an odd sky, white hot. And another bird flies out of the woods, white against the sun. An anhinga? He wonders where it's going.